Blacks in the
Abolitionist
Movement

A Wadsworth Series:
Explorations in the Black Experience

General Editors

John H. Bracey, Jr., Northern Illinois University
August Meier, Kent State University
Elliott Rudwick, Kent State University

American Slavery: The Question of Resistance
Free Blacks in America, 1800–1860
Blacks in the Abolitionist Movement
The Rise of the Ghetto
Black Matriarchy: Myth or Reality?
Black Workers and Organized Labor
The Black Sociologists: The First Half Century
Conflict and Competition: Studies in the Recent Black Protest
Movement

The anthologies in this series present significant scholarly work on particular aspects of the black experience in the United States. The volumes are of two types. Some have a "problems" orientation, presenting varying and conflicting interpretations of a controversial subject. Others are purely "thematic," simply presenting representative examples of the best scholarship on a topic. Together they provide guidelines into significant areas of research and writing in the field of Afro-American studies. The complete contents of all the books in the series are listed at the end of this volume.

Blacks in the Abolitionist Movement

Edited by

John H. Bracey, Jr.
Northern Illinois University

August Meier
Kent State University

Elliott Rudwick
Kent State University

Wadsworth Publishing Company, Inc.
Belmont, California

Acknowledgments

The authors wish to express their appreciation to Mrs. Barbara Hostetler, Mrs. Patricia Kufta, and Miss Eileen Petric at Kent State University for helping in the preparation of this manuscript, and to Miss Linda Burroughs and Mrs. Helen Peoples of the Kent State University Library. They are especially indebted to James G. Coke, former Director of the Kent State University Center for Urban Regionalism.

July 1970 JHB
AM
ER

L. C. Cat. Card No.: 70–154813
ISBN–0–534–00020–7
Printed in the United States of America

1 2 3 4 5 6 7 8 9 10—75 74 73 72 71

For
Ben Quarles,
scholar and friend

JHB
AM
ER

Contents

Blacks in the Abolitionist Movement

Introduction

Historians have disagreed on the nature of the participation of American blacks in the abolitionist movement — the militant phase of the antislavery movement that began around 1830. Several questions emerge. To what extent were Negro leaders responsible for the break that William Lloyd Garrison and other important white abolitionist leaders made with the gradualist colonization movement, which had dominated the antislavery cause from its founding in 1816 to the end of the 1820s, and which maintained that emancipation of the slaves could best be brought about if accompanied by expatriation to Africa? How active were blacks in the creation and administration of abolitionist societies — the American Anti-Slavery Society founded in 1833 and the American and Foreign Anti-Slavery Society that resulted from the schisms in abolitionist ranks in 1840? How important were blacks as spokesmen and writers for the antislavery cause and in the operation of the Underground Railroad? And what were the attitudes and policies of the white abolitionist leaders toward their black colleagues? Were the white abolitionists genuinely egalitarian, or did they share to some extent the racial prejudices of the vast majority of white Americans? How did their attitudes affect the blacks' participation in the movement?

Until the middle of the twentieth century, the prevailing view was that the white abolitionists deserved an overwhelming share of the credit for initiating and carrying on the work of the movement. Famous blacks like Harriet Tubman, the noted Underground Railroad worker, and Frederick Douglass, the great orator and newspaper editor, were regarded as exceptions; and even their contributions were usually slighted. Only a few black and white students of Negro history recognized the importance of the black abolitionists. The pioneering research of Charles Wesley and Herbert Aptheker is particularly notable in this connection. Since the late 1940s, historians have shown increasing interest in the subject, and important historical problems have emerged.

The first section of this book contains descriptions of four leading black abolitionists — James Forten, Frederick Douglass, John Mercer Langston, and William Still.

The second section treats the broad historiographical problem: how did blacks function in the abolitionist movement? Charles Wesley's "The Negro in the Organization of Abolition" is a succinct statement of the view traditionally held by black and white scholars in the field of Negro history concerning the active role Negroes played in the anti-slavery societies. Leon Litwack, in his *North of Slavery* (1961), attacked the problem from a different perspective. Stressing evidence of prejudice among white abolitionists, he concluded that they kept black participation to a minimum within the organized societies. We reprint here his later essay, "The Emancipation of the Negro Abolitionist," which further develops this thesis. Soon historians were debating the matter. James McPherson, in *The Struggle for Equality* (1964), saw the abolitionists as essentially egalitarian in their views, far in advance of most American white opinion; but William and Jane Pease argued even more forcefully than Litwack that a racist mentality existed among them. In *From Plantation to Ghetto* (1966; Revised Edition, 1970), Meier and Rudwick attempted to resolve the debate by moving away from an examination of white abolitionist attitudes to an analysis of how blacks actually functioned in the abolitionist movement. Drawing upon their own research and the work of other scholars — especially Larry Gara's important study of the Underground Railroad, *The Liberty Line* (1961) — they concluded that blacks were largely excluded from decision-making positions in the organized antislavery societies but that through their lecturing, writing, and activities in the Underground Railroad, they played a central role in the fight against slavery.

Between 1830 and 1835 Negro leaders had held annual conventions to protest against conditions oppressing the race. Excluded from the inner councils of the antislavery societies, they revived the convention movement during the middle 1840s. Nevertheless, as Howard H. Bell's essay on "National Negro Conventions of the Middle 1840's" demonstrates, the Negro abolitionists shared the ideologies of those in the mainstream of the antislavery movement. When the American Anti-Slavery Society split over philosophical and tactical issues in 1839 and 1840, black members were found on both sides. In addition to analyzing the divergent Negro views on this matter, Bell describes other proposals for racial advancement made at the conventions and introduces the reader to several prominent black protest leaders of the ante-bellum generation.

The third section of this book takes up another problem, that of the role of Negroes in John Brown's raid at Harpers Ferry. The first selection, from W. E. B. Du Bois's biography of Brown, emphasizes the participation of Negroes in the planning stages and the degree to which Brown consulted them. In contrast, David Potter's essay pictures blacks as having given Brown little support. The final selection, from Philip Foner's biography of Frederick Douglass, is a detailed description of Brown's relationship with the leading black abolitionist.

Four Black Abolitionists

1

James Forten: Forgotten Abolitionist

Ray Allen Billington

The most important single incident in the American antislavery crusade was the conversion of William Lloyd Garrison and Theodore Dwight Weld to a belief in racial equality. These two men, and the thousands who flocked to their standards, held that no biological differences distinguished Negroes from whites. As this was the case, they argued, the slaves should be emancipated either immediately or gradually, then educated and equipped to share the responsibilities of society with their fellow citizens. Social and political equality for all Americans was the objective of abolitionists from the day that Garrison proclaimed his intention to be "as harsh as truth and as uncompromising as justice" until the last slave was freed.[1]

The Garrisonian doctrine of equality was completely antagonistic to the generally accepted racial views of both northerners and southerners in the early nineteenth century. Enlightened men on both sides of the Mason-Dixon line had, since the Revolution, detested the institution of slavery, yet few among them were willing to concede that Negroes were physically or intellectually equal to whites. Instead they believed that the blacks were inferior creatures, halfway between animals and humans, who were fit only for the barbarism of Africa or servile life in the United States. The popular attitude was typified in the objectives of the American Colonization Society upon its formation in 1817. Members recognized the evils of slavery but insisted they should be shipped back to the African jungles for which nature had fitted them.

To men who held these views the concepts of Garrisonianism were thoroughly shocking. Between them and the abolitionists there was no compromise. The "colonizers" based their platform on a belief in racial inequality; the "abolitionists" built their program about a belief in racial equality. For the next thirty years northerners debated these two beliefs, as abolitionism slowly gained supporters and strength. Southerners, however, moved in the opposite direction. Driven to greater conservatism by the northern attack on white supremacy, they had by the 1850's ceased to apologize for slavery as a necessary evil, viewing the institution instead as a positive

From Ray Allen Billington, "James Forten: Forgotten Abolitionist," published by the Association for the Study of Negro Life and History in Vol. XIII of *Negro History Bulletin,* pp. 31–36, 45, November 1949. Copyright © 1949 by the Association for the Study of Negro Life and History, Inc. Reprinted by permission of the publisher.

good. When a Republican victory in 1860 warned them that the concept of racial equality was to be enshrined in the White House they deserted the Union.

Viewed in this light the doctrines of abolitionism become important in explaining the course of American history. Where did those views originate? Who first suggested that the races were equal, and that Negroes should be accorded the same legal and social status as whites? Doubtless a handful of forward-looking reformers from the days of antiquity onward had preached equality, but their opinions were of little importance; concepts only deserve recognition when they influence man's behavior. Avowals of racial equality, no matter how sincere, had no impact on American life until they fell on the ears of the humanitarians who launched the abolition crusade. Apparently the doctrine, in usable form, was first suggested to Garrison and his followers by a small group of Negro reformers whose contribution has been largely overlooked by historians of antislavery. Of these none was more important than James Forten, a wealthy free Negro of Philadelphia, whose efforts in behalf of the slaves launched pre-Garrisonian abolitionism in the United States.

Born in Philadelphia on September 2, 1766, James Forten was the son of Negro parents whose ancestors had lived in Pennsylvania as freemen for at least two generations.[2] His education was unusually scant even for that day; after a brief introduction to learning in the school of the famed Quaker philanthropist, Anthony Benezet, the death of his father in 1775 forced him to assume his share of the family's financial burdens.[3] For a few years he worked in a grocery store, but the outbreak of the Revolution turned his thoughts to a more adventurous career. After repeated pleadings broke down his mother's opposition, the fifteen year old Forten in 1781 enlisted as powder boy aboard the *Royal Louis,* a Pennsylvania privateer commanded by Stephen Decatur, Sr.[4]

The next year was crammed with excitement for the young Philadelphian. The *Royal Louis* was a formidable vessel, mounting twenty-two guns and carrying a crew of two hundred men, twenty of whom were colored.[5] Its commander, the father of the naval hero of the War of 1812, was already a seasoned privateer, having commanded the *Comet* and the *Fair American* in successful forays against English shipping.[6] Surely with his stout new ship he could surpass the feats of his last voyage when his *Fair American* brought to bay no less than three British merchantmen, four brigs, and a packet.[7] Little wonder that the youthful Forten looked forward to rollicking adventure and handsome profits as Decatur's ship sailed smoothly down the Chesapeake Bay on a warm July day in 1781.

For a time his bright hopes seemed about to come true. Scarcely had the *Royal Louis* put to sea when a lookout sighted fair game, the English brig-of-war *Active,* which struck its colors after a sharp skirmish.[8] On the next cruise, however, fate was less kind. Once more a sail was sighted; once more Decatur gave chase. This time the expected victim turned out to be a powerful enemy frigate, the *Amphyon.* Undaunted, the crew of the *Royal Louis* prepared to give battle, only to see the sails of two other war vessels, the *Nymph* and the *Pomona,* loom over the horizon. Hopelessly outclassed, Decatur was forced to surrender.[9]

That was a sickening moment for young Forten. Negro prisoners, he knew, were seldom exchanged; instead they were sent in chains to the West Indies to be sold into slavery. That he escaped this grim fate was due to a fortunate circumstance. Aboard the *Amphyon* was the youthful son of its commander, Sir John Beasly, thirsting for the companionship of some one his own age. The two boys, so unlike in background, struck up an immediate friendship. Young Beasly was particularly intrigued by his companion's skill at marbles, and the two spent much time together at the game. According to legend, Sir John was so impressed with Forten's character that he offered to take him to England for an education. This offer, Forten later testified, was haughtily refused. "No, No!" he reported himself as saying, "I am here as a prisoner for the liberties of my country; *I never, never, shall prove a traitor to her interests.* "[10] Thus rebuffed, the British commander transferred the fifteen year old powder boy, with a number of other captives to the prison ship *Jersey,* which was anchored in Wallabout Bay on the lonely shore of Long Island. "Thus," Forten often remarked in later life, "did a game of marbles save me from a life of West Indian servitude."[11]

During the next seven months, however, he probably had occasion to wish that his fingers were less skilled. The *Jersey* was a rotting old hulk, so leaky that pumps ran constantly to keep her afloat and so decayed that snow drifted through the cracks in her hull. A thousand prisoners were crowded into her stinking hold without light, ventilation, or sanitation, there to exist on food condemned as unfit for the English forces; frequently the starving captives had to knock worms from the biscuits or shred mahogany-colored meat that was too hard to cut. Thanks to his youth and stamina, Forten escaped the fate of the ten thousand prisoners who died aboard the ship during the war.[12] So unquenchable was his spirit that on one occasion he even gave up an opportunity to escape in favor of a companion worse off than himself.[13] He was finally released in a general exchange of prisoners, reaching home safely as the Revolution was drawing to a close.[14]

Although still in his teens, Forten was ready to exhibit the freedom-loving spirit that marked his later years. Why, he asked himself, should he stay in a land that proclaimed all men equal yet condemned those with dark skins to second-class citizenship? Why not escape to England where men were judged by character rather than color? These were the motives that sent him overseas for one of the most important twelve-month periods of his career. The slavery question was just beginning to captivate public interest at that time; the Somerset case[15] had already decreed that any slave touching English soil became free but the slave trade still flourished and the first reformers were lifting their voices against the evil. Forten lent an avid ear to their arguments, particularly to the pleas of Granville Sharp, a humanitarian who led the parliamentary assault on bonded servitude.[16] During the year that he listened young Forten became an avowed abolitionist, ready to dedicate his life to the crusade for freedom.

Back in Philadelphia once more he was apprenticed to Robert Bridges, a sailmaker whose loft was a landmark on the south wharves of the city. With a lack of prejudice all too rare in that day, Bridges in 1786 elevated his twenty-year-old helper to a position as foreman; twelve years later, when the owner died, Forten assumed control of the establishment. For the next forty years he conducted the business successfully, employing as many as forty men at times and amassing a comfortable fortune in the process. According to contemporary accounts many of his profits originated in a device to handle sails which he perfected and patented.[17] The popularity of his invention allowed him to provide a comfortable home for his widowed mother, a sister, a wife, and a growing family of eight children.[18]

The passing years not only assured James Forten economic security but gave him an opportunity to shine as a civic leader among Philadelphia's Negroes. On at least four occasions he rescued persons from drowning near his sail loft, a service that was recognized in 1821 when the managers of the Humane Society presented him with an Honorary Certificate "as a testimony of their approbation of his meritorious conduct."[19] During the War of 1812, when British troops pressed close on Philadelphia, he enlisted 2,500 colored patriots to improve the city's defenses. Marching with them from the State House yard to Gray's Ferry, Forten directed earthworks construction for two uninterrupted days.[20] Nor did he neglect the spiritual welfare of his race. When the St. Thomas' African Episcopal Church was incorporated in Philadelphia in 1796 he was among the pioneer members, serving on the first vestry. He remained active in the church from that day until his death.[21]

These activities prepared James Forten for a role in the cause that interested him most — abolitionism. His interest in the problem was awakened in 1800 when two of Philadelphia's most prominent Negroes, the Reverend Richard Allen, pastor of the African Methodist Church, and Absalom Jones, a founder of the St. Thomas' African Episcopal Church, circulated a petition among the city's colored citizens, urging Congress to modify the Fugitive Slave Act of 1793 and to adopt "such measures as shall in due course emancipate the whole of their brethren from their present situation."[22] Forten, as a signer, watched the fate of the petition with interest. To his disgust only one congressman sympathized with the petitioners. Representative George Thatcher of Massachusetts[23] supported their request in language faintly prophetic of that used by abolitionists a generation later; the remainder not only refused to listen but resolved that such petitions had a "tendency to create disquiet and jealousy, and ought therefore to receive no encouragement or countenance from this House." When this resolution was adopted by a thumping vote of eighty-five to one (with Thatcher casting the lone ballot in opposition),[24] James Forten wrote a letter of appreciation to the champion of his cause.[25] From that time on he was resolved to change the attitude of his unsympathetic fellow-countrymen.

His next opportunity came in 1813 when the Pennsylvania legislature considered a bill to bar free Negroes from the state. Forten, in a series of five letters published in pamphlet form, led the attack on the measure. "Has the God who made the white man and the black left any record declaring us a different species?" he asked. "Are we not sustained by the same power, supported by the same food, hurt by the same wounds, wounded by the same wrongs, pleased with the same delights, and propagated by the same means? And should we not then enjoy the same liberty, and be protected by the same laws?" He passionately "hoped that the legislators who have hitherto guarded their fellow creatures, without regard to the colour of their skin, will still stretch forth the wings of protection to that race, whose persons have been the scorn, and whose calamities have been the jest of the world for ages."[26]

The importance of Forten's views on racism cannot be overestimated. Unlike most reformers, even among Negroes, he was convinced that no biological differences distinguished whites and blacks. In this conviction he anticipated the abolitionists of a later day; indeed the basic concept underlying abolitionism was nowhere better expressed before 1820 than in his outspoken letters.

Like most intellectual pioneers, Forten was far ahead of his time. This was demonstrated three years later when the American Colonization Society was formed.[27] This antislavery organization was based on the concept — then generally accepted in North and South alike — that the Negro was fit only for the barbarism of Africa or the servile life of an American slave; its objective was gradual emancipation followed by a wholesale deportation of the freedmen to the land of their ancestors. Despite this, many prominent northerners of both races gave colonization their unqualified support. James Forten, however, refused to be misled. Believing unreservedly in the equality of the races, he hewed to the line later held by William Lloyd Garrison and Theodore Dwight Weld; the slaves, he insisted, should be freed, educated, and fitted to take their rightful place in American society. His views stamp him as one of the first true abolitionists in the United States.

He first made himself heard on the subject in 1817 when supporters of the American Colonization Society, recognizing his influence among the freemen of Philadelphia, asked him to endorse their program. They dangled a tempting bait before him; a man of his prestige, they said, could become the Lord Mansfield of the society's Colony of Liberia if he cast his lot with them. Forten refused to listen. He would, he reputedly told them, "rather remain as James Forten, sailmaker, in Philadelphia, than enjoy the highest offices in the gift of their society."[28]

To a man of such sincere conviction a mere refusal to support colonization was not enough; his fellow countrymen must be warned against a plan that might eventually drive all Negroes from their adopted land. With this in mind Forten sought the support of the Reverend Richard Allen, Absalom Jones, Robert Douglass, and others prominent in Philadelphia's colored population, with them arranging a mass meeting of protest at the Bethel Church in January, 1817. The hall was crowded that night when Forten mounted the rostrum to serve as chairman; speeches were heard and then previously prepared resolutions were adopted by a unanimous vote:[29]

Whereas, our ancestors (not of choice) were the first successful cultivators of the wilds of America, we, their descendants, feel ourselves entitled to participate in the blessing of her luxuriant soil, which their blood and sweat enriched; and that any measure or system of measures, having a tendency to banish us from her bosom, would not only be cruel, but in direct violation of those principles which have been the boast of this republic.

Resolved, That we view with deep abhorrence the unmerited stigma attempted to be cast upon the reputation of the free people of color by the promoters of this measure, "that they are a dangerous and useless part of the community," when, in the state of disfranchisement in which they live, in the hour of danger they ceased to remember their wrongs, and rallied around the standard of their country.

Resolved, That we will never separate ourselves voluntarily from the slave population of this country; they are our brethren by the ties of consanguinity, suffering, and wrong; and we feel that there is more virtue in suffering privations with them, than fancied advantages for a season.

Resolved, That without arts, without science, or a proper knowledge of government, to cast into the wilds of Africa the free people of color, seems to us the circuitous route by which they must return to perpetual bondage.

Resolved, That, having the strongest confidence in the justice of God and the philanthropy of the free states, we cheerfully submit out destinies to the guidance of Him who suffers not a sparrow to fall without His special providence.

Persuasive as these resolutions were, they failed to check a mounting interest in colonization among Philadelphia's citizens. By July 23, 1817, the society's leaders felt confident of enough support to call a preliminary meeting to plan a local branch for the city.[30] This stirred Forten into action once more. The protest meeting that he arranged was held on August 10, 1817, in the school house at Green Court with a crowd of almost three thousand present. Again James Forten was in the chair; again enthusiastic speakers denounced colonization before a lengthy "Address to the humane and benevolent inhabitants of the city and county of Philadelphia" was adopted. This able document argued that colonization would doom free Negroes and ex-slaves alike to the hazards of a life for which they had no training, as well as depriving them of the benefits of religious instruction. Liberia, the writers predicted, would soon be the "abode of every vice, and the home of every misery." Furthermore, they believed that wholesale deportations would raise the price of slaves still in bondage, thus tending to perpetuate the institution. "Let not a purpose be assisted which will stay the cause of the entire abolition of slavery in the United States," the Address concluded, "and which may defeat it altogether; which proffers to those who do not ask for them benefits, but which they consider *injuries,* and which must insure to the multitude, whose prayers can only reach through us, *misery, sufferings, and perpetual slavery.*"[31]

Printed copies of this appeal were spread throughout Philadelphia and sent to Joseph Hopkinson, the Federalist representative serving Pennsylvania in Congress.[32] Despite a favorable reaction among Negroes, the Philadelphia Colonization Society was formed on August 12 as an auxiliary of the American Colonization Society.[33] Undaunted by this defeat, Forten continued the attack with renewed vigor, certain that colonization would collapse when his countrymen learned the true nature of the movement. In November, 1819, he again presided over a large meeting of Philadelphia Negroes which condemned the American Colonization Society's efforts to "perpetuate slavery in the United States:"[34]

> *Resolved,* That the people of color of Philadelphia now enter and proclaim their most solemn protest against the proposition to send their people to Africa, and against every measure which may have a tendency to convey the idea that they give the project a single particle of countenance or encouragement.

A decade later Forten was primarily responsible for a national convention of Negro delegates which assembled at Philadelphia on September 15, 1830, to oppose colonization. Similar conventions were held yearly thereafter, usually in Philadelphia but occasionally in other cities, and in all Forten played a leading role. Due to his influence, as much as any other thing, the free Negroes of the North were arrayed in a solid phalanx against colonizers by the time abolitionism demanded their support.[35]

Nor did the passing years alter his views. In 1833, when nearly seventy years of age, he spoke with all the fire of youth when a companion asked his views on colonization. "My great-grandfather," he said, "was brought to this country a slave from Africa. My grandfather obtained his own freedom. My father never wore the yoke. He rendered valuable service to his country in the war of our Revolution; and I, though then a boy, was a drummer in that war. I was taken prisoner, and was made to suffer not a little on board the Jersey prisonship. I have since lived and labored in a useful employment, have acquired property, and have paid taxes in this city. Here I have dwelt until I am nearly seventy years of age, and have brought up and educated a family, as you see, thus far. Yet some ingenious gentlemen have recently discovered that I am still an African; that a continent, three thousand miles, and more, from the place where I was born is my native country. And I am advised to go home. Well, it may be so. Perhaps if I should only be set on the shore of that distant land, I should recognize all I might see there, and run at once to the old hut where my forefathers lived a hundred years ago."[36]

James Forten's attack on the concept of racial inequality which underlay colonization had important results. In all probability his unwavering belief in the equality of the races helped convince William Lloyd Garrison that colonization was not the answer to the slavery problem, thus laying the basis for the rise of abolitionism.[37] This, in turn, gave Forten the reforming opportunity he had long sought; he threw himself into the Garrisonian crusade with a zeal that belied both his advancing years and his upper class position.

For by the 1830's Forten was a man of substance. His sailmaking shop, where as many as forty white and Negro workmen were employed,[38] had by 1832 rewarded him with a fortune of $100,000, a sizeable sum for that day.[39] This he used "to live in as handsome a style as anyone could wish to live"[40] in a spacious house on Lombard Street in Philadelphia.[41] Under his roof were gathered his ever-growing family: his wife, his eight children and other relatives; at times no less than twenty-two persons gathered about the family board.[42] A man of "commanding mind and well informed," he was highly respected by Negroes and whites alike. Particularly admired were the moral causes to which he dedicated his life. He never drank, and was a steadfast supporter of temperance societies. His liberal contributions gave strength to the movements for universal peace and women's rights.[43] Forten was also the guiding spirit behind the American Moral Reform Society, an agency of colored men dedicated to the "promotion of Education, Temperance, Economy, and Universal Liberty."[44] As a founder and perennial president of that organization he directed its efforts toward bettering the standards of Negroes in Philadelphia and the nation.[45]

All this security and comfort James Forten was willing to sacrifice to aid the slaves. Recognizing that abolitionism was the nation's most unpopular cause; knowing that mobs might damage his property or threaten his aging limbs if he persisted in its support, he still showed no hesitation when the banner was unfurled by William Lloyd Garrison. To him the Boston leader was a "chosen instrument, in the Divine hand, to accomplish the great work of the abolition of American slavery,"[46] and must be aided without regard to cost. Even before the first issue of *The Liberator* appeared, Forten solicited subscriptions among Philadelphia Negroes; on December 31, 1830, he could send Garrison money from twenty-seven subscribers and a pledge of continued support. "I hope your efforts may not be in vain," he wrote "and that 'The Liberator' be the means of exposing more and more the odious system of Slavery, and of raising up friends to the oppressed and degraded People of Colour, throughout the Union. Whilst so much is doing in the world, to ameliorate the condition of mankind, and the spirit of Freedom is marching with rapid strides, and causing tyrants to tremble; may America awake from the apathy in which she has long slumbered. She must sooner or later fall in with the irresistible current. Great efforts are now making in the cause of Liberty; the people are becoming more interested and determined on the subject."[47]

Forten did not relax his efforts after the launching of *The Liberator* on January 1, 1831. A month later he sent Garrison twenty additional subscriptions;[48] on March 1 he arranged a mass meeting of Philadelphia Negroes where the paper's purposes were explained and unanimously endorsed.[49] From that time on he was a regular contributor to *The Liberator* and to abolition societies; with the exception of the wealthy New York merchants, Arthur and Lewis Tappan, Forten was probably the most generous supporter of the radical antislavery cause.[50] His only reward was the mounting strength of Garrisonianism. "It has," he wrote Garrison jubilantly during the spring of 1831, "roused up a spirit in our Young People, that has been slumbering for years, and we shall produce writers able to vindicate our cause."[51] Garrison, in turn, developed a warm affection for "the greatly esteemed and venerable sailmaker of Philadelphia," as he called Forten.[52] Seldom did he pass through Philadelphia without visiting the spacious house on Lombard Street, to dine with the family, spend the night, or simply engage in an hour's conversation on abolitionism. Such visits, wrote the elderly Forten after one of them, "are cheering, they are as green spots in the journey of life."[53]

His early contacts with Garrison allowed Forten to play a significant role when the American Anti-Slavery Society was formed. Many of the reformers who gathered in Philadelphia for the organizational meeting in December, 1833, made the Forten home their headquarters; about the family table plans were discussed and strategy mapped.[54] Until forced to retire from active labors by advancing age, he served frequently on the society's Board of Managers,[55] as well as collecting subscriptions for *The Liberator*[56] and lending the paper needed financial support.[57] Little wonder that members of the American Anti-Slavery Society, while recognizing the contributions of leading members during the 1840 meeting, lauded Forten with:

> James Forten, right well
> I love to hear tell,
> Of thy aid in our much boasted war;
> And mark with what scorn
> Does thy noble heart spurn
> The friends of Liberia's shore
> James Forten!
> The friends of Liberia's shore.[58]

Nor did national acclaim blind Forten to the local aspects of abolitionism during his declining years. In 1832 he circulated a petition among Philadelphia Negroes, praying that the Pennsylvania legislature take steps to prevent the return of escaped slaves.[59] A year later he presided over a large meeting of colored people where resolutions were adopted expressing sympathy for education, antislavery, and anticolonialization.[60] In 1836 he prepared a memorial to the legislature urging the members to condemn slavery and wipe out distinctions against men of color in the state. "Let our motto be," he pleaded, "the Law Knows No Distinction."[61] During the following year he served as one of two delegates from Philadelphia to a convention at Harrisburg which urged the end of slavery and colonization.[62] Undeterred by criticism or advancing age, James Forten gave unstintingly to the day's most unpopular cause. Few men, either white or colored, could boast such an outstanding record.

Only with death could his followers show the full measure of their appreciation. Ill health beset him increasingly in his declining years; by the fall of 1841 he was forced to write to Garrison that he could exert himself in the cause of abolition no longer, but that his interest was as firm and ardent as ever.[63] A year later he died at the ripe age of seventy-six. His funeral, held on February 24, 1842, was one of the largest in the history of Philadelphia; several hundred whites and several thousand Negroes marched in the procession that followed his body to the grave.[64] At a public meeting to honor his memory a large group of friends, without distinction of color, paid him tribute in the eulogies common to that day.[65]

James Forten passed from the scene with the cause that he sponsored still in its infancy. Yet even on his deathbed he could take solace in the fact that his children were equipped to carry on the crusade with a zeal matching his own.[66] To them, if not to their father, came the privilege of seeing his fondest dreams fulfilled when Abraham Lincoln's Emancipation Proclamation completed the reform to which he had devoted his life.

Notes

[1] *The Liberator*, January 1, 1831.

[2] A close friend of Forten's, Lydia Maria Child, is authority for the statement that so far as he could recollect, no member of his family had been slaves. *The Freedmen's Book* (Boston, 1865), 100. Another friend, however, later quoted Forten as saying that his great-grandfather had been brought from Africa as a slave, and that his grandfather had obtained his freedom. Samuel J. May, *Some Recollections of the Antislavery Conflict* (Boston, 1869), 287.

[3] For accounts of Forten's boyhood see Child, *Freedmen's Book*, 101–102; William C. Nell, *Colored Patriots of the American Revolution* (Boston, 1855), 166–167; and Robert Purvis, *Remarks on the Life and Character of James Forten, Delivered at Bethel Church, March 30, 1842* (Philadelphia, 1842), 4. A brief sketch of Forten's career is in the *Dictionary of American Biography* (New York, 1928–1937), VI, 536–537.

[4] All contemporary biographers of Forten place the date of his enlistment in 1780 and state that he was fourteen years old. Nell, *Colored Patriots*, 166; Child, *Freedmen's Book*, 101; Purvis, *Remarks on the Life and Character of James Forten*, 4. Actually the *Royal Louis* was not commissioned until July 23, 1781, and sailed from Philadelphia at once. *Naval Records of the American Revolution* (Washington, 1906), 449. Apparently his early biographers based their accounts on Forten's memory, which was faulty. He was also responsible for the statement that the ship mounted twenty-six guns rather than twenty-two. William C. Nell, *Services of Colored Americans in the Wars of 1776 and 1812* (Boston, 1851), 16.

[5] Forten is responsible for the latter statement, as no list of the crew has been located. Nell, *Services of Colored Americans*, 16.

[6] Information about Stephen Decatur will be found in Alexander S. Mackenzie, *Life of Stephen Decatur* (Boston, 1846), 9–10; William Decatur Parsons, *The Decatur Genealogy* (New York, 1921), 10; and the *Dictionary of American Biography*, V, 186–187.

[7] A record of Decatur's previous conquests is in the *Naval Records of the American Revolution*, 445; and more fully in J. Thomas Scharf and Thomas Wescott, *History of Philadelphia* (Philadelphia, 1884), I, 423.

[8] *Pennsylvania Archives, Second Series* (Harrisburg, 1874), I, 373.

[9] Scharf and Wescott, *History of Philadelphia*, 423; Nell, *Colored Patriots*, 168.

[10] Child, *Freedmen's Book*, 101–102; Nell, *Colored Patriots*, 168. These two accounts, which agree in substance, were apparently based on Forten's reminiscences.

[11] Nell, *Colored Patriots*, 169.

[12] Descriptions of the *Jersey* are in Gardner W. Allen, *A Naval History of the American Revolution* (Boston, 1913), II, 631–637; Edgar A. Maclay, *A History of the United States Navy* (New York, 1904), I, 138–139; and John R. Spears, *The History of Our Navy* (New York, 1899), I, 223–224. The reminiscences of several prisoners confined to the ship while Forten was aboard fail to mention him, but add colorful details of life aboard. These include Thomas Andros, *On Board the Old Jersey Prison Ship* (Boston, 1833), 1–80; Captain Thomas Dring, *Recollections of the Jersey Prison-Ship* (Providence, 1829); and Ebenezer Fox, *The Revolutionary Adventures of Ebenezer Fox* (Boston, 1839), 93–228.

[13] The youth who escaped was Daniel Brewton who was carried from the ship in a sea

chest in which Forten had planned to escape. Later steward of the *Lazaretto* in Philadelphia, Brewton showed both William Nell and Robert Purvis a certificate testifying that he had been aboard the *Jersey* with Forten, and described the rescue. Nell, *Colored Patriots*, 170–172; Purvis, *Remarks on the Life and Character of James Forten*, 7–8.

[14] Forten was released after seven months on the *Jersey*. His mother had given him up for dead when he finally reached Philadelphia.

[15] The Somerset case arose in 1771 when a slave, James Somerset, was taken by his master from Virginia to England. Refusing to serve his owner there, he obtained a writ of habeas corpus which allowed him to carry his case before the British courts. They eventually held that slavery was contrary to the laws of England and that Somerset was a free man. John W. Cromwell, *The Negro in American History* (Washington, 1914), 245.

[16] Purvis, *Remarks on the Life and Character of James Forten*, 8–9.

[17] Henry E. Baker, "The Negro in the Field of Invention," *Journal of Negro History*, II (January, 1917), 25. A search of patent lists for the period, however, fails to reveal any patent issued either to Forten or to his employer, Robert Bridges. Apparently the invention was never patented, but was still immensely profitable. See *A Digest of Patents, Issued by the United States from 1790 to January 1, 1839* (Washington, 1840); *A Classified Index of Subjects of Inventions* (Washington, 1872); *A List of Patents Granted by the United States for the Encouragement of Arts and Sciences, alphabetically arranged, from 1790 to 1820; Continued by Supplements to April, 1823* (Washington, 1823); *List of Patents and Inventions and Designs issued by the United States from 1790 to 1847* (Washington, 1847); *Subject-Matter Index of Patents for Inventions issued by the United States Patent Office from 1790 to 1873, Inclusive* (Washington, 1874).

[18] Nell, *Colored Patriots*, 172–174; Child, *Freedmen's Book*, 102–103.

[19] The certificate, which was dated May 9, 1821, is printed in Nell, *Colored Patriots*, 174–175. Nell states that Forten rescued seven persons during his lifetime; Mrs. Child sets the number at twelve. Child, *Freedmen's Book*, 103.

[20] Scharf and Wescott, *History of Philadelphia*, I, 573–574; Nell, *Colored Patriots*, 191.

[21] William Douglass, *Annals of the First African Church in the United States of America, now styled the African Episcopal Church of St. Thomas* (Philadelphia, 1862), 107. When, in 1804, a school was established by the church, Forten was chosen one of the Board of Trustees. *Ibid.*, 110.

[22] The petition from the "free blacks" of Philadelphia was laid before Congress on January 2, 1800, by Robert Waln, a representative from Pennsylvania. *Annals of Congress*, 6th Cong., 1st Sess., 232.

[23] George Thatcher, a Federalist, represented Massachusetts in Congress between March 4, 1789, and March 3, 1801. *Biographical Directory of the American Congress* (Washington, 1928).

[24] The petition was debated on January 2 and January 3. *Annals of Congress*, 6th Cong., 1st Sess., 239–246.

[25] Nell, *Colored Patriots*, 176. The letter is printed in Purvis, *Remarks on the Life and Character of James Forten*, 12–14.

[26] James Forten, *Letters from a Man of Colour, on a Late Bill before the Senate of Pennsylvania* (Philadelphia [1813]), 3–4, 7. One of the letters is reprinted in Carter G. Woodson, *Negro Orators and Their Orations* (Washington, 1925), 42–51.

[27] For an account of this organization see Early L. Fox, *The American Colonization Society, 1817–1840* (Baltimore, 1919).

[28] Nell, *Colored Patriots*, 177.

[29] A full account of the meeting, together with the text of the resolutions adopted, is in G. B. Stebbins, *Facts and Opinions Touching the Real Origin, Character, and Influence of the American Colonization Society* (Boston, 1853), 194–196. For briefer accounts of the meeting see: Nell, *Colored Patriots*, 177–178; William Lloyd Garrison, *Thoughts on African Colonization* (Boston, 1832), Pt. II, 9–10; Lewis Tappan, *Life of Arthur Tappan* (New York, 1870),

135–136; Booker T. Washington, *The Story of the Negro* (New York, 1909), I, 290; Cromwell, *Negro in American History*, 28; and Louis R. Mehlinger, "The Attitude of the Free Negro toward African Colonization," *Journal of Negro History*, I (June, 1916), 276–301.

[30] Scharf and Wescott, *History of Philadelphia*, I, 590.

[31] The meeting is described in Garrison, *Thoughts on African Colonization*, Pt. II, 10–13. The Address is printed in Mehlinger, "Attitude of the Free Negro toward African Colonization," *loc. cit.*, 278–279, and in Woodson, *Negro Orators*, 52–55. See also Herbert Aptheker, *The Negro in the Abolitionist Movement* (New York, 1941), 3–32.

[32] A search of the *Annals of Congress*, 14th Cong., 2nd Sess., and 15th Cong., 1st Sess., failed to reveal any mention of the petition.

[33] Scharf and Wescott, *History of Philadelphia*, I, 591.

[34] *Niles Register*, XVII (November 27, 1819), 201–202.

[35] Carter G. Woodson, *The Negro in Our History* (Washington, 1941 edn.), 271–273.

[36] May, *Some Recollections of the Antislavery Conflict*, 287.

[37] Archibald H. Grimké, *William Lloyd Garrison* (New York, 1891), 144, holds that Garrison's conversations with Forten helped convince him that colonization was an evil, thus laying the basis for the beginnings of abolitionism. This is also the thesis of Clarice A. Richardson, The Anti-Slavery Activities of Negroes in Pennsylvania (unpublished master's thesis, Howard University, 1937), 10–11.

[38] May, *Some Recollections of the Antislavery Conflict*, 286.

[39] Carter G. Woodson, *The Works of Francis J. Grimké* (Washington, 1942), IV, 96 n.

[40] *Some Recollections of the Antislavery Conflict*, 286.

[41] Forten occupied a house at 92 Lombard Street through most of his life. *Philadelphia Directory for 1813* (Philadelphia, 1813); *Philadelphia Directory for 1842* (Philadelphia, 1842), 88.

[42] According to the Census of 1830. Carter G. Woodson, *Free Negro Heads of Families in the United States in 1830* (Washington, 1925).

[43] Child, *Freedmen's Book*, 103; Purvis, *Remarks on the Life and Character of James Forten*, 17.

[44] The objectives of the society are described in its monthly publication, the *National Reformer*, I (February, 1839), 81.

[45] Nell, *Colored Patriots*, 181; Cromwell, *The Negro in American History*, 35.

[46] Nell, *Colored Patriots*, 178.

[47] James Forten to William Lloyd Garrison, December 31, 1830. Dorothy B. Porter, ed., "Early Manuscript Letters Written by Negroes," *Journal of Negro History*, XXIV (April, 1939), 199–200.

[48] James Forten to William Lloyd Garrison, February 2, 1831. *Ibid.*, 200–201.

[49] The meeting was held on March 1, 1831. *The Liberator*, March 12, 1831. See also Herbert Aptheker, "The Negro in the Abolitionist Movement," *Science and Society*, V (Spring, 1941), 162.

[50] Woodson, *Works of Francis J. Grimké*, IV, 96 n.

[51] James Forten to William Lloyd Garrison, March 21, 1831. Porter, "Early Manuscript Letters Written by Negroes," *loc. cit.*, 201–202.

[52] Washington, *The Story of the Negro*, 290.

[53] James Forten to William Lloyd Garrison, July 28, 1832. "Early Manuscript Letters Written by Negroes," *loc. cit.*, 204–205. For an account of one of Garrison's visits to the Forten home see Anna D. Hallowell, ed., *James and Lucretia Mott. Life and Letters* (Boston, 1884), 119.

[54] May, *Some Recollections of the Antislavery Conflict*, 286. May reported that he and several other convention delegates dined at Forten's home and "were entertained with as much ease and elegance as I could desire to see."

[55] His name appears in the *Second Annual Report of the American Anti-Slavery Society, May 12, 1835* (New York, 1835), 12; *Fifth Annual Report of the Executive Committee of the American Anti-Slavery Society, May, 1839* (New York, 1839), 13.

[56] *The Liberator,* September 17, 1841, contained a letter from Forten stating that he was sending additional subscriptions.

[57] Woodson, *Works of Francis J. Grimké,* IV, 96 n.

[58] *The Liberator,* May 22, 1840.

[59] *Ibid.,* April 14, 1832.

[60] The meeting was held on April 1, 1833. *Ibid.,* April 13, 1833.

[61] *Human Rights,* II (September 4, 1836).

[62] Forten and Robert Purvis, his son-in-law, were the two delegates from Philadelphia. *Proceedings of the Pennsylvania Convention at Harrisburg* (Philadelphia, 1837).

[63] *The Liberator,* September 17, 1841.

[64] Accounts of the funeral are in *ibid.,* March 18, 1842, and in the *National Anti-Slavery Standard,* March 24, 1842. Briefer descriptions by those who attended are in Child, *Freedmen's Book,* 103; and Hallowell, *James and Lucretia Mott,* 232.

[65] *National Anti-Slavery Standard,* March 24, 1842.

[66] Among Forten's children who were active in abolitionism were Margaretta, who served as secretary of the Philadelphia Female Anti-Slavery Society, James, who spoke and sang in the cause of freedom, Robert, who refused to live in a United States that condoned slavery, Harriet, who was married to the well-known reformer, Robert Purvis, who was one of the organizers of an antislavery convention that met in New York in 1837.

Abolition's Different Drummer: Frederick Douglass

Benjamin Quarles

The time and place — August 11, 1852, at the Masonic Hall in Pittsburgh. The occasion — the national convention of the Free Soil party, a political group that four years previously had been formed to combat the extension of slavery into the territories. The afternoon meeting had been in progress for more than an hour when a Negro, wearing a white linen coat and dark blue trousers, entered the hall. Before he could find a seat someone shouted his name, and others spontaneously took up the cry. The presiding officer, his voice drowned out, resorted to sign language to welcome the visitor and invite him to speak. Amid cheers, the newcomer proceeded down the aisle.

Facing the audience, he showed no sign of nervousness — he had a talent for talking fluently. For the space of a few moments, however, he said nothing, as if to satisfy those among the two thousand spectators who might wish to size him up as a physical specimen. Broad-shouldered, six feet tall and in the prime of manhood, he could bear scrutiny. His skin was bronze-colored and his mass of black hair was neatly parted on the left. His eyes were deep-set and steady. But at the moment they were less expressive than his well-formed nose that now, as he prepared to say his first words, inhaled deeply, almost critically, as though the air might offer to nonwhites an inferior oxygen, if vigilance were relaxed.

"Gentlemen, I take it that you are in earnest, and therefore I will address you," he began in low but carrying tones that searched the recesses of the auditorium, hinting of a readiness to defy faulty acoustics. But there was no answering challenge to this voice that had tested itself in damp groves, in tents and on ship decks. "I have come here, not so much of a free soiler as others have come," he continued. "I am, of course, for circumscribing and damaging slavery in every way I can. But my motto is extermination — not only in New Mexico, but in New Orleans, not

From Benjamin Quarles, "Abolition's Different Drummer: Frederick Douglass," in *The Antislavery Vanguard: New Essays on the Abolitionists,* ed. Martin Duberman, pp. 123–134. Copyright © 1965 by Princeton University Press, Princeton Paperback, 1968. pp. 123–134. Reprinted by permission of Princeton University Press.

only in California but in South Carolina." The theme was a familiar one with the speaker, but he saw no need of talking about new wrongs as long as the old ones still existed.

He proceeded to criticize the Fugitive Slave Law. Because an alleged runaway might be carried away without trial by jury, "the colored man's rights are less than those of a jackass," since the latter could not be seized and taken away without submitting the matter to twelve men. He had a solution, said the speaker: "The only way to make the Fugitive Slave Law a dead letter is to make half a dozen or more dead kidnappers. The man who takes the office of a bloodhound ought to be treated as a bloodhound." The crowd applauded, many of them knowing that the speaker's strong language resulted in part from his twenty-year experience as a slave.

When the noise died down, the speaker continued along a different line — denunciation was but one of his weapons. The Constitution, he contended, was against slavery inasmuch as "human government is for the protection of rights and not for the destruction of rights." But even if the Founding Fathers had expressly said that one man had the right to possess another man, such a stipulation would lack the binding quality of rationality: "Suppose you and I made a deed to give away two or three acres of blue sky; would the sky fall, and would anybody be able to plough it?" The speaker's sentences had now gained momentum. Those who were listening to him for the first time became aware of a voice that employed every degree of light and shade, a rich baritone giving emotional vitality to every word.

He resumed in a conversational manner — he had all the gifts requisite to an orator — "You are about to have a party, but I want to be independent and not hurried to and fro into the ranks of Whigs and Democrats." Possibly some in the audience may have reflected that it was this desire for independence that had led him to break with his slave past and to strike out on his own.

Now that he was at the point of bringing his remarks to a close, he had a parting bit of advice. "It has been said that we ought to take the position of the greatest number of voters. That is wrong. Numbers should not be looked to so much as right. The man who is right is a majority. If he does not represent what we are, he represents what we ought to be."

The crowd cheered again and again as the speaker concluded in this high strain. He had difficulty making his way down the aisle, past those who wished to shake his hand.[1] The clapping and shouting, however, were not primarily an approval of what the speaker had said. Rather they were a personal tribute to a man who had devoted his talents to the building of a better America.

For to Frederick Douglass this address differed from his others only in externals. All his public appearances grew out of a career that had sought the storms in a period that was itself shaped by stress and passion. By the time he delivered this impromptu speech his career had been inexorably charted, Douglass having become a reformer of the first water.

Douglass acquired prominence in his day because of his qualities of mind and spirit and the fact that he was a Negro. These two outstanding causative factors may be examined in turn.

Douglass had become a professional reformer by having come to the attention in August 1841 of the Massachusetts school of abolitionists, headed by William Lloyd Garrison and Wendell Phillips. Persuaded to join the cause as a paid lecturer, Douglass cut loose from his odd-jobs work in New Bedford to become a careerist in reform. To say that Douglass became an abolitionist solely as an alternative to sawing wood, sweeping chimneys, and blowing bellows is to venture beyond the record. Outward circumstance may have been reinforced by inner calling. But whatever the motivation, Douglass had no difficulty in internalizing his role, becoming a typical reformer in outlook and style.

As one who was single-mindedly bent on wiping out institutions he regarded as outworn, Douglass viewed things with an almost theological purity. He was given to absolutes of feeling, making him tend to overstate his case. To him the slave system was "a grand aggregation of human horrors." For the master class he had no charity: "Every slaveholder is the legalized keeper of a house of ill-fame, no matter how high he may stand in Church or State. He may be a Bishop Meade or a Henry Clay — a reputed saint or an open sinner — he is still the legalized head of a den of infamy."[2]

But if Douglass tended to overreact, it was due to the failure of the great majority to react at all. Charged with irritating the American people, Douglass replied that this was what they deserved: "The conscience of the American public needs this irritation. And I would blister it all over, from center to circumference, until it gives signs of a purer and better life than it is now manifesting to the world."[3]

Douglass was not a gradualist, prepared to await for abuses to be corrected "in the fulness of time." At one of the reformist gatherings Henry Ward Beecher stated that rather than see slavery abolished as a result of mercenary motives, he would prefer to wait seventy-five years to have the evil struck down by the power of Christian faith. Douglass, who followed Beecher on the program, immediately replied that "if the reverend gentleman had worked on plantations where I have been, he would have met overseers who would have whipped him in five minutes out of his willingness to wait for liberty."[4]

Douglass' whole philosophy of reform was one of no quarter. He had little patience with well-intentioned men like the influential Unitarian pastor, William Ellery Channing, who deplored harsh language, seeking instead to win over the slaveholder by a policy of sweet reasonableness. Douglass, in a West India Emancipation celebration speech in August 1857, pointed out that "those who profess to favor freedom and yet deprecate agitation are men who want rain without thunder and lightning. Power concedes nothing without a demand. It never did and it never will."[5]

Douglass brought more to the reform movement than a "hard line" against the opposition. He had the gift of words. His sentences, although sonorous as befit the style of his day, arrested the attention. One example may suffice. Speaking in Rochester in 1852 on "The Meaning of July Fourth to the Negro," he posed a long rhetorical question concerning the "equal manhood of the Negro race":

Is it not astonishing that, while we are ploughing, planting, and reaping, using all kinds of mechanical tools, erecting houses, constructing bridges, building ships, working in metals of brass, iron, copper, silver and gold; that, while we are reading, writing and ciphering, acting as clerks, merchants and secretaries, having among us lawyers, doctors, ministers, poets, authors, editors, orators and teachers; that, while we are engaged in all manner of enterprises common to other men, digging gold in California, capturing the whale in the Pacific, feeding sheep and cattle on the hill-side, living, moving, acting, thinking, planning, living in families as husbands, wives and children, and, above all, confessing and worshipping the Christian's God, and looking hopefully for life and immortality beyond the grave, we are called upon to prove that we are men![6]

Douglass tinged his eloquence with humor. When Stephen A. Douglas was debating with Abraham Lincoln in 1858, Douglass had this to say of the Illinois Senator: "Once I thought he was about to make the name respectable, but now I despair of him, and must do the best I can for it myself."[7] In mockery Douglass was devastating, as evidenced in an address at Faneuil Hall on a June day in 1849: "I want to say a word about the Colonization Society of which Henry Clay is President. He is President of nothing else."[8] Cheers and applause greeted this quip at Clay's long-held White House ambitions. A clever mimic, Douglass was often called upon to deliver his "slaveholder's sermon" — a white clergyman's address to the bondmen.[9]

A typical example of Douglass' raillery was his account of the plight of Bishop James O. Andrew, whose family holdings in slaves precipitated the shattering sectional split in Methodism at the General Conference in New York in 1844:

A slaveholding bishop, Bishop Andrew of South Carolina, married a slaveholding wife and became the possessor of fifteen slaves. At this time the Methodist Church in the North was of the opinion that bishops could not hold slaves. They remonstrated with the Conference to induce Bishop Andrew to emancipate his slaves. The Conference did it in this way. A resolution was brought in, when the Bishop was present, to the following effect: "Whereas Bishop Andrew has connected himself with slavery, and has thereby injured his itinerancy as a bishop . . ." It was not, "Whereas Bishop Andrew has connected himself with slavery, and has thereby become guilty, or has done a great wrong," but "has thereby injured his itinerancy as a bishop, we therefore resolve that Bishop Andrew be, and he hereby is," — what? — "requested to suspend his labors as a bishop until he can get rid of" — what? — slavery? — "his impediment." (Laughter.) This was the name given to slavery. One might have inferred from the preamble that it was to get rid of his wife. (Laughter and loud cheers.)[10]

Douglass' considerable abilities as an abolitionist lecturer were heightened by the fact that he was a Negro. Here was no stammering fugitive from the South; here was no shiftless former slave unable to cope with the responsibilities of freedom. Here was a different breed of Negro, a different brand of abolitionist — a symbolic figure in race relations and in reform.

Douglass' accomplishments were trumpeted by abolitionists as an example of Negro improvability. As no other colored man or woman, Douglass was a challenge to the widespread belief that the Negro was innately inferior in character, intelligence, and ability. To those who held that the rightness or wrongness of slavery pivoted on the capacity of the colored man, Douglass was a figure who could not be overlooked.

This image of Douglass as an able Negro had owed much to the publication of his autobiography, *Narrative of the Life of Frederick Douglass*, in 1845. Slave narratives were effective weapons in the abolitionist crusade. "It is often said that the evils of slavery are exaggerated. This is said by the masters," wrote Theodore Parker in 1847, after reading a number of slave narratives.[11] Douglass' book was by far the most effective of the lot, in part because he had written every line.[12] If its prose was simple and unadorned, the Douglass autobiography was forceful and vivid, a tribute to a man who less than seven years previously had been a slave calker in a Baltimore shipyard. Aside from what it said in the text, the *Narrative* spoke volumes for the capacity of the Negro. Indeed, Douglass always recognized that whatever he said or wrote had a meaning beyond the letter. When he launched his own weekly in Rochester in 1848, he appended his initials to his editorials in order to demonstrate that a former slave could write good English.[13]

If others saw him as a Negro before all else, the maturing Douglass never sought to escape such an identification. If some Negroes affected a studied indifference to race problems, he did not. He had no trace of the self-hate that leaves its mark on many members of an oppressed minority. "Whatever character or capacity you ascribe to us, I am not ashamed to be numbered with this race," he said in an address to the American and Foreign Anti-Slavery Society in May 1853.[14] "I shall bring the Negro with me," he once wrote in response to an invitation to lecture. " 'I am black, but comely,' is as true now as it was in the days of Solomon," he wrote in April 1849 in reviewing Wilson Armistead's lengthy Book, *A Tribute for the Negro*.[15]

Douglass' sense of identification with his Negro fellows expressed itself in his concern over their plight. In the August 10, 1849 issue of his newspaper, *The North Star*, he proposed that an organization be formed exclusively of Negroes, for the purpose of opposing slavery and improving their own condition. The society would bear the title "The National League," with the motto "The union of the oppressed for the sake of freedom." After more than two months the suggestion had met with almost no response in Negro circles, much to the mortification of its sponsor. "We have among us our little Popes and Bishops," Douglass wrote in an acid editorial on October 26, 1849.[16]

Although Douglass had proposed an all-colored improvement society, he never thought of the Negro as apart from the mainstream of American life. As he put it, it was better to be a part of the whole than the whole of a part. "We are Americans, and as Americans we would speak to Americans," ran a sentence in a statement which the Colored Convention of 1853, meeting in Rochester, addressed to "the People of the United States." This lengthy address, composed in the main by Douglass, was entitled, "The Claims of Our Common Cause," and its insistent theme was the Americanism of the Negro.[17]

To Douglass one of the best ways that the Negro could exercise his full rights as an American citizen was to make contacts across the color line. Setting an example himself, he made it a point to defy Jim Crow practices in restaurants and on common carriers. To be "roughed up" for seeking service in places open to the public was no novelty to Douglass. Prominent Negroes who accepted segregation drew his fire. He wrote a bitter editorial chastising Elizabeth Taylor Greenfield (the Black Swan") for giving a concert at Metropolitan Hall in New York in April 1853, ₜo which whites only were admitted.[18]

Douglass was a protagonist for "integrated" schools. When his nine-year-old daughter was put in a room and taught separately at Seward Seminary in Rochester, his protest could be heard throughout the city. But his indignation did not spring solely from the protective sympathies of a parent. "If this were a private affair, only affecting myself and family, I should possibly allow it to pass without attracting public attention to it; but such is not the case," he wrote to the editor of the *Rochester Courier* on March 30, 1849. "It is a deliberate attempt to downgrade and injure a large class of persons, whose rights and feelings have been the common sport . . . for ages."[19]

Because he mixed with whites as a matter of principle, the Douglass of the abolitionist crusade felt no uneasiness in their presence. Within a few years after his flight from his master, his slavery-days dislike of whites had evaporated. His close association with them as fellow reformers left him permanently shorn of racist thinking. He viewed whites individually, not lumping them together.

By the time he had reached his prime as a man and as a reformer, Douglass had placed himself "upon grounds vastly higher and broader than any founded upon race or color," to use his own language. His own freedom from preconceptions enabled him to view things in the round. To him the abolitionist crusade had become less a separate movement than a national impulse; to him the struggle of the Negro was more of a human struggle than one of race. Paradoxically, it would seem, his belonging to a despised group had given him a deeper, more inclusive sense of human brotherhood. This broad concern led him to take an active role in reforms that were not Negro-centered, among them the woman's rights movement.[20]

In the closing years of the abolitionist crusade, Douglass was one of its chief ornaments. He carried himself with the assurance of one who had risen above obscure birth, color prejudice and all the Pandora's box of human besettings. Of the many assessments made of him by contemporaries, the words of Albion W.

Tourgée would not seem wide of the mark: "Three classes of the American people are under special obligations to him: the colored bondman whom he helped to free from the chains which he himself had worn; the free persons of color whom he had helped make citizens; the white people of the United States whom he sought to free from bondage of caste and relieve from the odium of slavery."[21]

Douglass' chief claim to enduring recollection has been voiced by a present-day poet, Robert E. Hayden, akin to Douglass by color if not by century. When freedom, writes Hayden, is finally won:

> this man, this Douglass, this former slave, this Negro
> beaten to his knees, exiled, visioning a world
> where none is lonely, none hunted, alien,
> this man, superb in love and logic, this man shall be remembered . . .[22]

Notes

---

[1] Quotations from this speech are from the New York *Herald,* August 12, 1852.

[2] Philip S. Foner, *The Life and Writings of Frederick Douglass* (4 vols., New York, 1950–55), II, 142.

[3] Speech before the American Anti-Slavery Society, May 11, 1847, "The Right to Criticize American Institutions," Foner, *Life and Writings,* I, 237.

[4] *Annual Report of the American Anti-Slavery Society for 1853* (New York, 1853), pp 51, 55.

[5] Foner, *Life and Writings,* II, 437.

[6] *Ibid.,* p. 191.

[7] New Orleans *Daily Delta,* September 19, 1858.

[8] Foner, *Life and Writings,* I, 390.

[9] An excerpt from this sermon is reproduced in Benjamin Quarles, *Frederick Douglass* (Washington, 1948), p. 363.

[10] *Report of a Public Meeting Held at Finsbury Chapel, Moorfields, to receive Frederick Douglass, An American Slave on Friday, May 22, 1846* (London, 1846), p. 16.

[11] "Letter to the People of the United States Touching the Matter of Slavery," December 22, 1847, in James K. Hosmer, ed. *The Slave Power,* by Theodore Parker (Boston, American Unitarian Association, n.d.), p. 55.

[12] Benjamin Quarles, ed. *Narrative of the Life of Frederick Douglass* (Cambridge, Mass., 1960), pp. xvi and following.

[13] *Frederick Douglass' Paper* (Rochester, New York), June 26, 1851.

[14] Foner, *Life and Writings,* II, 246.

[15] *Ibid.,* I, 380.

[16] *The North Star* (Rochester, New York), August 10, October 26, 1849.

[17] *Proceedings of the Colored National Convention held in Rochester, July 6th, 7th and 8th,* Rochester, 1853.

[18] *Frederick Douglass' Paper,* April 8, 1853.

[19] Foner, *Life and Writings,* I, 373. For a brief account of this episode, see Quarles, *Frederick Douglass,* p. 108.

[20] At the convention at Geneva Falls, New York in July 1848, which formally inaugurated the women's rights movement in the United States, Douglass was the only male to play a prominent role. "We bid the women engaged in this movement our humble Godspeed," he wrote in an editorial in *The North Star*, July 28, 1848. The August 11, 1848, issue of this weekly carried a complete report of the proceedings of this historic meeting.

[21] *A Memorial of Frederick Douglass from the City of Boston* (Boston, 1896), p. 29.

[22] Langston Hughes and Arna Bontemps, eds. *The Poetry of the Negro, 1746–1949* (New York, 1949), p. 171.

John Mercer Langston: Black Protest Leader and Abolitionist

William F. Cheek

Prejudice, priority, and principle have dictated a white historical past. Together they help to account for our greatest handicap in reconstructing the black heritage: the scarcity of source materials. Humiliating though it may be for the historian to admit, diligent research, combined with imaginative use of interdisciplinary skills, can restore all too little of the preciousness, the particularities, the usefulness of the lives of previous Negro Americans.

Still, we have barely begun to tap the records that are available or to consider subjects that merit investigation. One largely unexplored field is the role of the black abolitionist, who more often than not combined his antislavery labors with agitation for civil rights. Major works on the antislavery movement and even general histories of the Negro do little more than list the names of some black participants, with only brief factual comment on their areas of involvement.[1] Of the twenty or so men and women who achieved some celebrity as black activists in antebellum America, only the preeminent Frederick Douglass has received more than limited attention from scholars.

One measure of our ignorance in their regard is the almost total neglect of a versatile and articulate Negro leader, John Mercer Langston. What little has been written about him falls in the period after 1861, when admittedly he achieved his greatest prominence, as recruiter of Negro soldiers, educational inspector for the Freedmen's Bureau, Republican party orator, law dean and later acting president of Howard University, member of the Board of Health of Washington, D.C., minister to Haiti, president of a Negro college in Virginia, and, climactically, congressman from Virginia's fourth district.

Nowhere recognized are his pre-war contributions as an Ohio protest leader and abolitionist.[2] Fortunately, since a partial record of his early career survives, it

From William F. Cheek, "John Mercer Langston: Black Protest Leader and Abolitionist." *Civil War History*, Vol. 16, No. 2, June 1970, pp. 101–120. Reprinted by permission of the publisher.

is possible to reconstruct some of his activities, as well as to speculate both on his motivations and attitudes. Most celebrated as an orator, he emerges also as a writer, agitator and organizer. Working at times with white abolitionists but more often with the black convention movement in Ohio which, partially because of his efforts, was the most militant and sustained of the black state movements in the 1850's, Langston advocated freedom for the slave and full legal and social equality for the northern black man. Though he and his co-workers were powerless to effect those changes in the Negro's condition they so strongly desired, Langston demonstrated by the variety and scope of his involvement a persistent refusal to accept the contemporary realities of slavery and racism.

Born in Louisa County, Virginia, in 1829, Langston was the third son of a white plantation owner and his part-Indian, part-Negro freedwoman. Both parents died when the boy was quite young, but he was left with a generous inheritance that not only paid for an excellent education, with consequent social and professional advantages, but also underwrote his reform efforts. Moreover, in contrast to many half-white Negroes, who hated or were ashamed of their fathers, Langston drew strength from the image of his father as a prosperous and kindly planter who believed in educating his slaves and then freeing them; who, despite ostracism by neighbors, loved his light-skinned mistress and lived with her for more than twenty years.[3]

After the deaths of his parents the boy, at the age of four, was taken to Ohio, where over the following decade he lived with five different families, two white and three black. Judging from his later impassioned relations, his relationship with his first foster family, the William Gooches, who were old friends of his father, provided him with the most happiness and, when broken abruptly after six years, provoked the most grief. During these years he was raised as a member of the white family and, indeed, apparently believed himself to be white.[4]

Afterwards, while moving from rural Chillicothe to urban Cincinnati, boarding with families whose ways of life varied considerably, working as a farmhand and then as a bootblack, young Langston had to try to deal with each shifting circumstance and, at the same time, to understand the fact of his race and what it meant to be Negro in Ohio in the 1840's. While able to live in relatively comfortable homes and to attend school, advantages not available to most Negroes, he was nonetheless like them subject to indifference, insult, and even physical danger. During the harrowing riots in Cincinnati in 1841, for example, he had to run and hide from the white mob that terrorized the Negro section of town.[5] Of necessity, during these years of his childhood, he learned to rely on himself and to value his independence. At the same time, perhaps, he began to have a feeling of kinship with others of his race and a sense of the wrong done them all.

At a number of points his life was touched by abolitionists, both white and black, as well as by Negroes interested in reform. Among the latter were his older brother Charles (a teacher and dentist who became very active in the state black convention movement), and two black Oberlin College students, George B. Vashon and William Cuthbert Whitehorn, who were his tutors.[6] With their help, it seems probable that Langston, while still quite young, not only had an emotional apprehension but also at least the beginnings of an intellectual understanding of the problems of his race.

Having done well in his early studies, the slight, fair-skinned boy, at the age of fourteen, was enrolled in Oberlin College, one of only four schools in the country that accepted Negroes. Over the course of the next nine years, he finished preparatory school and earned A.B., M.A., and theological degrees, the first Negro to take the theological degree in the United States. In the process he acquired a classical education strongly laced with ethics and evangelism. Under the tutelage of President Asa Mahan, a moral philosopher and antislavery activist, and revivalist extraordinary Charles Grandison Finney, Langston encountered fervently held beliefs about the vast improvability of man and one's personal responsibility to work toward betterment.[7]

The community itself, with its love-thy-neighbor philosophy and its willingness to experiment in reforms ranging from plain living to abolitionism to women's rights, could scarcely fail to impress him by its tolerance of men and ideas. Its racial attitude, while less than ideal, as Langston himself pointed out, was predicated on the notion of equality to a degree not paralleled by many American towns. If some Oberliners still believed the black man to be inferior, there were others dedicated to disproving that notion. This latter group, in particular, had a stake in Langston's success, and sometimes helped him toward it. These people could refute the "nigger" stereotype with his example: here was a black man who was hard-working, not lazy; educated, not ignorant; responsible and respectable, not shiftless and immoral. On public occasions in Oberlin, nearly always when the topic was antislavery but sometimes on such "non-Negro" events as the coming of the railroad, above the bunting on the speaker's platform and among the prominent citizens, there would be a chair for the town's distinguished Negro orator, and much applause when he was through.[8]

Against a setting of antislavery sentiment in Ohio's Western Reserve, Langston moved on to professional and political successes. After reading law in the office of Philemon Bliss, a white newspaper editor (later, antislavery congressman), from nearby Elyria, Langston stood an examination in 1854 before a panel of district court judges. Apparently impressed by his performance, the court decided to take advantage of his light skin color and, drawing on an earlier Ohio decision that "a colored man who is nearer white than mulatto or half breed" was entitled to the rights of a white man, pronounced Langston fit to practice law in the courts of Ohio. Only a year later, in 1855, with his election as clerk of a township close by Oberlin, the first Negro to be admitted to the legal profession in the West became the first Negro to be elected to public office in the United States.[9]

Political events and the moral climate around them, coinciding with Langston's coming to maturity, helped to determine the nature of his involvement in protest and abolitionist activities. By the late 1840's the Negro question had been reintroduced into national and state politics. The annexation of Texas and the territory picked up in the war with Mexico forced a hitherto complacent nation to face the likelihood of slavery expansion. Abruptly, northerners brought up to believe in a philosophy of progress, who had been expecting the simple passage of years to eliminate slavery, were disabused of their comforting illusion. Recognizing the possibilities in this newly aroused concern, the abolitionists stepped up their crusade to gain active support for the termination of slavery. Following the passage of the Fugitive Slave Act in 1850, they drew heightened attention to their cause by stressing even more strongly than in the past the theme that slavery endangered the civil liberties of all Americans. Further, their shift from moral to political suasion, begun in the previous decade, continued as they steadily filed into the ranks of the Liberty and Free Soil parties.

In like manner, black abolitionists, assisted to some extent by white abolitionists (most of whom were interested primarily in the slavery issue), as well as by a small number of antislavery politicians, sought by various persuasions, as they had for many years, to broaden northern concern to include the free Negro. An organized black convention movement had existed on the local and state level as early as 1817 and on the national scene since 1830. Convening off and on over the years the assemblies, using petitions and addresses to the public, assailed slavery and also advocated, in a number of instances actively working toward, the improvement of the free Negro's condition.[10]

The Negro population was shackled by legislation and custom in every northern state. In Ohio, the so-called "Black Laws" required freedom papers and the posting of a five hundred dollar bond of its Negro inhabitants. Negroes were denied the right to vote, and forbidden to sit on juries or to testify in any case involving a white man. Further, they were excluded from the militia, prohibited from entering asylums for the deaf, dumb and blind, and barred from the public schools. Segregation of public and most private facilities, then extending to cemetaries in Cincinnati, was the accepted rule.[11]

In Ohio by the mid-1830's white abolitionists, most notable among them the American Anti-Slavery Society agent Augustus Wattles, were at work among the free Negroes, setting up schools and supplying teachers, establishing temperance societies, and lecturing on thrift and moral rectitude. Black abolitionists cooperated with their white supporters, and operated several schools themselves. On their own, they petitioned the state legislature to repeal the oppressive Black Laws.[12] Change was indicated in Ohio in 1848 when the state legislature passed its first public school education bill for Negroes. The following year the Free Soil and Whig parties joined forces in the legislature to abrogate a portion of the Black Laws.[13]

The heightening protests against slavery extension in the country, together with the modestly encouraging portents in Ohio, coincided with and unquestionably stimulated an upsurge in militancy among Ohio's black leadership. The new mood was reflected primarily in the revival and subsequent aggressiveness of the convention movement. Meeting on eleven different occasions from 1849 to the Civil War, Ohio Negroes put together the most continuous, energetic and aggressive of the various state convention movements of the fifties. Embracing the doctrine of self help and appealing to the philosophy of higher law, the leaders of the movement, some drawing on long experience and others on youthful vigor, utilized a wide variety of means to attack slavery and to expose the "wretched" condition of the "half-free" black man in Ohio.[14]

Newly turned nineteen years of age and a senior at Oberlin at the time of his first convention in 1849, J. Mercer Langston, as he signed himself in those years, thus found a ready channel for his rather prodigious energies. Alongside other activists in the convention movement, often himself taking the lead, he plunged into black protest and reform efforts in Ohio.

Langston himself defined the reformer's role as demanding "all his attention and his energies" — "his pen and purse, and tongue and talents." "In public and in private, in society and in solitude," he continued, "this [the reform effort] must be the all-absorbing subject of his thoughts."[15] With some allowance for rhetoric and human limitations, the statement mirrors Langston's conception of his own role, and he seems to have attempted at least to live up to it. During the first part of the fifties, while in graduate studies or reading for the law, Langston devoted months at a time, including the better part of 1850 when he did not attend school, to lecture tours or other work on behalf of antislavery and reform. Later professional demands, both of his moderately successful law practice and more especially of his duties as town clerk of Oberlin and the surrounding township, an office he held from 1857 to 1859, forced him to give his time in smaller measures.[16] Still, few months went by during the decade without some kind of active involvement on his part.

Because of his financial position (in addition to his earnings, he increased his inherited funds through a number of real estate ventures), he was relatively free to engage in reform activities, sometimes even making charitable contributions. In one known instance, he paid the way of a young Negro to Oberlin College. Not surprisingly, the state convention movement, which generally relied on dues of fifty cents a person and infrequent contributions, often was unable to finance its projects, but Langston at times offered emergency support. As for his speaking tours of the state, he was generally unpaid, sometimes, indeed, taking his expenses out of pocket.[17]

Langston's most notable work for the convention movement was as an orator, both in the assemblies themselves and, especially, on his travels throughout the Ohio countryside. On the speaker's stand, neatly attired in black frock coat and doeskin pants, satin vest and cravat, a less conservative dress, to be sure, than that worn by some of his fellow orators, he created an initial impression of self composure and serious purpose. In the only description of him during this period, the Negro writer and reformer William Wells Brown singled out his "high and well formed forehead," "full but not particularly striking eyes," and "mild and amiable countenance."[18] His bearing was that of the gentleman, a "talented, educated and eloquent gentleman," as the Oberlin community, abolitionist conventions, and his own colleagues commonly referred to him.

Unlike those antislavery orators who felt compelled to overstate the case that they might be heard, Langston strove to reach his audiences by weighty factual evidence, clarity and reason. Classical and Biblical references, along with an occasional snippet of poetry, were sometimes included, rather modestly according to the rhetorical standards of the time. In contrast to Frederick Douglass's imaginative outpourings of words and felicity of phrase, Langston's speeches were carefully constructed, composed of sentences both logical and balanced if only rarely remarkable for poetic effect. His language was more often bold than bitter, and more often firm than harsh. Still, he was capable of the barbed phrase and cutting word. In 1854, after the state legislature refused to let him present a petition before it, he acerbly attributed its action to "eyes blinded by prejudice and Negro hatred."[19] He resorted infrequently, however, to the sarcasm and stinging wit characteristic of the oratory of black co-workers like Douglass and Charles Lenox Remond, and, indeed, of many of the abolitionists. Douglass's use of mimicry and Brown's skill at imitations were effective means of exciting any audience, but for Langston such devices were unnatural. Douglass was an inspirational "character" speaker; Langston a gentleman orator.

"He is not fragmentary in his speeches," wrote Brown in the early fifties, "but, as a deep, majestic stream, he moves steadily onward, pouring forth his rich and harmonious sentences in strains of impassioned eloquence."[20] His voice was described as "striking in its range." Another black abolitionist, William C. Nell, who accompanied Langston on a lecture tour of Ohio in 1856, looked on admiringly as a white farmer, obviously emotionally unstrung by Langston's remarks, threw up his hands and shouted, "My God! Can these things be true?"[21]

As a peripatetic agitator for Negro rights, speaking in hostile camps as well as friendly, Langston became skilled at handling crowds. He is reported to have been in difficulty on only one occasion, during a speaking trip through Ohio with Douglass in 1850, when the two men were said to have been mobbed but, fortunately, not injured. Family legend has it that Langston always kept one hand in his pocket whenever he was speaking, seeking to give the impression he had a gun.[22] It seems more likely that he relied on tactics similar to the one he employed one afternoon in Lorain county in northern Ohio, when he and several white men, all representing the Liberty party, were on the platform. One of the white speakers was interrupted by a voice from the audience: "Are you in favor of nigger social equality?" Taking up the cue the crowd began clapping, and the speaker was forced to retreat. Langston was then introduced. His position, he explained, was that freedom was the birthright of all men and that social equality was a matter involving individual choice. Only those opposing human rights would take it upon themselves to inject such a topic into the discussion. A heckler objected: "You learned that at Oberlin. You learned another thing, to walk with the white women there." To the crowd's delight, Langston responded tartly, "If you have in your family any good-looking, intelligent, refined sisters, you would do your family a special service by introducing me to them at once."[23]

In contrast to those Negro abolitionists whose speeches were touched up by whites, Langston wrote his own, and exercised his pen on numerous other occasions as well. The Negro convention movement, from time to time, called on him to draft petitions to the state legislature, write addresses to the public, and edit the proceedings of the conventions for publication. Asked to contribute an article to Julia Griffith's *Autographs for Freedom,* a giftbook hawked at abolitionist fairs and bazaars, he wrote on the withering of human capacities by the "poisonous touch" of slavery. He also composed a spirited article on the Oberlin-Wellington rescue case, the heroic saving of a fugitive slave in which his brother Charles figured prominently, for the first issue of *Anglo-African Magazine.*[24]

Within the black convention movement in Ohio, as one of its principal organizers, Langston displayed ability and tenacity. The group of less than a dozen men who led the movement called themselves the State Central Committee, and on this he consistently served. Convening several times a year, the committee issued calls for conventions, carried out, where possible, the dictates of the conventions and, when it was deemed essential, devised and implemented policies of its own.[25]

Throughout the fifties Langston and his fellows tried, with limited success, to set up organizations that could attract grassroots support. The first attempt was made in 1850 with the formation of the Ohio Colored American League, operated by a thirteen-member executive committee, of which Langston was a member, and with plans calling for the formation of leagues in every county. After a period of dormancy, the league was reconstituted in 1853 as the Ohio State Anti-Slavery Society, and again county auxiliaries were proposed. Five years later the society had to be revived and this time, due to the persistence and guidance of Langston, who drew up the plans for it and afterwards served as president and general agent, and his brother Charles, the recording secretary, it managed to stay in precarious being, with recurring financial problems, until the outbreak of war.[26]

At the conventions themselves Langston served as president in 1852 and again in 1857. As a frequent appointee to the business committee, particularly in the early years when major policies were laid down, he led in shaping goals and strategies. He co-authored the 1849 Declaration of Sentiments that promised on the one hand to "sternly resist" every form of oppression or proscription, and to disobey laws that curtailed the "natural rights of man," and, on the other, advocated such means of self-help as universal education, temperance societies, and better employment.[27]

Langston's forceful arguments, on the floor and inside committee rooms, were reflective of and probably had some influence upon the conventions' aggressive posture on various issues. The 1849 session resolved to purchase five hundred copies of *Walker's Appeal* and Garnet's Address, recently published back to back, for distribution throughout the state. In the following years the conventions adopted forceful resolutions on slavery, "the perfection of all wickedness and outrage," the American Colonization Society, "hollow hearted," "contemptible" and a "foul and filthy plague," and the Fugitive Slave Law, "a hideous deformity in the garb of law."[28]

Although Langston and the other leaders were able to attract the "literati" and aristocracy among black Ohioans, with more than two hundred persons attending at least one convention during the eleven years,[29] they failed to catch the interest of the black populace and, most strikingly, the black churches, whose support was crucial. Any measurable cooperation from the majority of Negroes was militated against by a corrosive mix of ignorance, indifference, fear, and the task of simply getting through each day.

Furthermore, even sympathetic whites seemed all but unaware of the movement, with interest seldom extending beyond a few observers at a convention or an occasional passing reference to convention proceedings in an antislavery paper. Of the state legislators, only Norton S. Townshend of Avon township consistently directed attention to the black man's self-help efforts. And, most discouragingly, white Ohio's prejudice, together with its misconceptions and ignorance of the black community, belied the prospect of any immediate significant change.

Given the formidable obstacles in their path, it was not to be expected that a handful of black leaders could bring about the revolution. From the beginning, and certainly as the decade wore on, most of them appeared to understand how difficult it would be to move the "mountains of prejudice" and to enlist the support of most Ohio Negroes. But they also appreciated how necessary it was that they try. Furthermore, if there was much to dismay Langston and his fellow workers, there was also much to encourage them. The comaraderie of men working toward a common goal was in itself inspiriting, as was the generally high level of debate within the conventions. Moreover, under the circumstances, it could be regarded as a victory of sorts that each year the conventions could be held at all. A sense of hope, not failure, marked their efforts. "Though defeated every day in the year," declared the preamble to the 1857 convention, black men must press on for their rights.[30]

During the fifties Langston was confronted with questions similar to those that concerned other black leaders across the North, emigration, self-help, civil and political rights, abolitionism, political involvement, and active resistance. His goals, however, remained constant. These were freedom for the slave and better conditions for the "half-free" Negro in the North or, as he put it in 1857, "a new order of things" to be characterized by "a democratic and Christian regard for the rights of all mankind, whatever their condition or complexion."[31]

He argued for emigration at the State Convention of Colored Citizens of Ohio in 1849, declaring that although he dearly loved his native land, it offered him no protection, and therefore he was willing to go wherever he could be free. So long as strong prejudice existed, and he saw "little hope for its removal," it was impossible for Negroes to have a nationality as Americans; and yet Negroes had to have a nationality "before we can become anybody." They must, therefore, leave the country; to remain would be humiliating, "virtually acknowledging our inferiority to the white man."[32]

But signs of amelioration in Ohio, in the form of some legislative victories,[33] along with his own involvement in reform activities, apparently made him change his mind. By 1854, and probably even earlier, what he called his "youthful enthusiasm" for emigration had passed, just at the time when many Negro leaders in the East were stepping up their proposals to emigrate to Africa or to other unsettled parts of America.[34]

Thereafter he viewed himself as an American; his destiny lay with this country. "We submit," he wrote in 1856, "that we are not Africans, but Americans, as much as any of your population. Here then is a great injustice done us, by refusing to acknowledge our right to the appellation of Americans, which is the only title we desire, and legislating for us as if we were aliens, and not bound to our country by the ties of affection which every human being must feel for his native land; which makes the Laplander prefer his snows and skins to the sunny skies and silken garb of Italy; which makes the colored American prefer the dear land of his birth, even though oppressed in it, to any other spot on earth."[35]

Integration with white America on equal terms, as Langston plainly stated on a number of occasions, was the end always to be kept in view. In an address prepared for delivery to the Ohio legislature (which his friend, state representative Norton Townshend, read to the legislators when he was denied permission to address them) Langston declared: "Now because a man is black, it is no reason why he should not kneel at the same altar, dine at the same table, ride in the same coach, be educated in the same school, and be buried, if he desires it, in the same graveyard by the side of his Anglo-American brother, and he who denies him the right, is either a heathen or a tyrant."[36]

At the same time, however, he believed that the foundation for racial advance was self-help for, as he told the Ohio black convention in 1851, the reforms they desired would have to be brought about "mainly if not entirely" by Negroes themselves.[37] He recognized that even those whites disposed to be sympathetic to their cause were chiefly interested in abolishing slavery, rather than in helping the free Negro attain civil and political rights. Throughout the decade, he urged a broad program of self-help correlated with economic advancement, the establishment of a black newspaper, education (in public schools if possible, in decent segregated schools if not), and enfranchisement.

Blacks must make a virtue of necessity, Langston contended, with self-help leading to an increased sense of dignity and pride. In his speeches he tried to bolster black self-respect by enumerating achievements in the professions and the arts that established "our unity and identity with the human family." Along with this, he strongly advocated temperance and personal morality. The theme was set during his speech from the floor of the 1849 convention. Quoting the black poet Terence, the Roman slave who wrote, "Homo sum atque nihil humani a me alienum puto," ("I am a man, and I think that nothing is estranged from me which pertains to humanity"), Langston declared: "The spirit of our people must be aroused, and they must feel and act as men."[38]

In company with convention colleagues, he called on Negroes to leave the horse stables, washtubs, and other menial employment, and go into agriculture, business or the professions. As a delegate to the Colored National Convention at Rochester in 1853, the most significant of the pre-Civil War conventions, he asked: "Where are our ships, our counting houses, our business connections with the world. They are wanting; and only because we have never fixedly resolved to have them." The Ohio conventions repeatedly recommended various schemes, some of them well-conceived, at least on their face, to pool economic resources.[39] However, black Ohioans, like Negroes across the North, were too harassed by the difficulties of maintaining a daily existence to come together for this purpose.

Langston was the major advocate in the conventions for the publication of a newspaper by black Ohioans. Frederick Douglass's newspaper, he argued (justifiably), failed to provide coverage of the activities of western Negroes. Thus they were left without a medium through which to express their "insults and wrongs." Langston headed a committee which drew up the recommendation for the establishment of a paper; and in 1853 *The Aliened American* (masthead: "Educate Your Children — And Hope for Justice") with William Howard Day, Oberlin graduate and Cleveland journalist, as editor, made its appearance. Surviving just over two years, it was succeeded in 1855 by the *Herald of Freedom,* but the twin factors that plagued the earlier paper, lack of money and failure to retain interest, brought about its early demise.[40]

Education, termed by Langston "the glory of any people — the sure palladium of their liberty," was one of his chief concerns. The number of schools for Ohio's Negro children, most established through private efforts, was pitiably small. The state had not opened public school education to Negroes (and then on a segregated basis) until 1848, and in effect made no serious effort to deal with the problem before the middle fifties. Besides prodding the state to recognize its responsibility in this area, the black conventions urged Negroes to establish their own schools. In 1852, a convention committee chaired by Langston proposed that Negroes "strive" to build school houses and to hire teachers who had the "requisite intellectual and moral qualifications" and "a deep interest in the welfare of the communities" as well.[41]

The previous fall, acting on his own initiative, Langston had called a meeting of Oberlin students and townspeople, at which he proposed that an agent be appointed to visit Negro schools, establish others wherever necessary, and see to it that they were supplied with teachers. The gathering unanimously elected Langston to serve as the agent, and shortly afterwards formally organized itself, with eighty-five members, as the Oberlin Young Men's Anti Slavery Society. Until Langston's graduation from theological school in 1853, the society met from time to time, generally to hear Langston's reports and to entertain visiting speakers, including John P. Hale, the Free Soil presidential candidate.

As the school agent Langston traveled the state, collecting nickels and dimes, surveying the "conditions and prospects" of Negro education, and seeking to bring some order from the chaos. Where teachers were needed, he tried to supply them.

Probably he called upon Oberlin students to teach during their long winter vacations, as he himself had once been taught and, indeed, as he himself had once taught. Where schools were lacking, he tried to organize local groups to build them. It was a meagre beginning. Records are not available to measure success, but that Langston remained in the work at least as late as 1854 is clear from this urgent plea written by a friend: "In this village of Putnam, we have over 100 children. Help us can't you."[42] Langston was one of the small group of citizens who urged that Oberlin establish a public high school, and in 1860 such a school was opened. Langston was subsequently elected secretary of the School Board, a position he retained until he took up residence elsewhere in 1871.[43]

Langston's highest priority was the removal of remaining restrictions on Negroes in the Ohio constitution and statutes, especially their disfranchisement. As the most active of the lecturers sent out by the state convention movement, he crisscrossed the state, month after month, year after year, seeking to tell "the story of our wrongs in plain unvarnished phrase." In preparing his brief for Negro suffrage (for that was what it came to be), he engaged in extensive research. He compiled the arguments of pioneer Negro activists Paul Cuffee, James Forten and Alexander Crummell, and the resolutions of state and national Negro conventions. He familiarized himself with constitutional documents, legal opinions, and historical precedents, subscribed to at least a half dozen abolitionist papers, solicited the views of such prominent men as Senator William Seward.[44] Additionally, he used the statistics he had been compiling since early in the decade on the Ohio Negro. Black abolitionist and historian William C. Nell, after observing him in 1856, called him a "walking and talking encyclopedia" of the Negro's aspirations and capacities. Nell further noted that his young colleague presented "arguments, appeals, facts and statistics" in "such a fearless, eloquent and irresistible manner as to leave the friend proudly satisfied and our enemies evidently confused."[45]

In written addresses, petitions, and speeches Langston demanded the franchise on democratic, legal, and moral grounds. The guarantees of the Declaration of Independence were not contingent upon "the curl of a man's hair, the projections of his lips, the color of his skin. . . . They are a constituent element of manhood — whether that manhood be encased in ebony or ivory." Caste legislation violated the Constitution, in which the word "white" was nowhere found; rather, therein every man was regarded as a man, as the "possessor of rights which civil society ought to respect and protect." The policy of the Founding Fathers in many states, Langston further noted, was to permit Negro electors. Moreover, the Negro was a native born inhabitant and, therefore, a citizen, as was agreed by "all standard writers on law." The Negro was a taxpayer, and it was a basic teaching of the Fathers of the Republic that "taxation and representation are inseparable." The Negro was a soldier, and had "stood cheek by jowl" with the white man in every war.[46]

The rights of citizenship were deserved by black Ohioans, Langston argued, and black Ohioans were determined to win them. In his address to the state Legislature in 1857 he declared: "Let us assure you . . . that no unjust and oppressive legislation shall ever drive us from this State. We are here, and here we intend to remain. Our position is as fixed and immovable as the pillars of the great state. Your history and your destiny shall be ours. And while cruel and despotic statutes disgrace our State Legislation, we will express, in every possible manner, our dissatisfaction and disapproval of them."[47]

In his abolitionist role Langston (like his older colleague Douglass) struck out with an independence equalled by few, black or white. No label or dogma bound him, no organization or individual dominated him. He was neither a moral abolitionist of the Garrisonian stripe, nor a pragmatic abolitionist committed to political action, nor a direct action militant like Garnet and Douglass. He was rather his own man, free to choose the features he considered best of all three approaches.

He operated largely without the assistance of white abolitionists and, except in Oberlin where he was regarded as a prominent citizen, he had little social or personal contact and only limited communication with them. Partly this resulted from differing emphasis: Langston's commitment was to equal rights for Ohio blacks, white abolitionists' concern, for the most part, with ending slavery. And partly it resulted from the sometimes ambivalent attitudes of the sympathizers, who were unable to escape prejudice toward those to whose uplift they were committed. For example, antislavery newspapers, in state and out, devoted few columns to Langston's work, or indeed, to any Ohio Negro activities.[48] Moreover, it was one thing for a Negro to be invited to speak to an organizational meeting or bazaar, quite another for him to have a close relationship with any of the members of that organization. Langston exchanged few letters with white abolitionists. Aside from his Oberlin friends, lawyer Philemon Bliss of Elyria, and Norton Townshend of Avon township, an antislavery state legislator, he seems to have had only a superficial relationship with the white antislavery people.[49]

When the Ohio State Anti-Slavery Society, with Langston as its president and general agent, was set up by the state Negro convention meeting late in 1858, for the announced purposes of organizing blacks for concerted efforts to secure "the immediate and unconditional abolition of American Slavery and the removal of the legal and social disabilities under which we suffer," it was greeted with mixed feelings by white abolitionists. An editorial in the *Anti-Slavery Bugle,* published at Salem, Ohio, noted: "It is a fact full of encouragement, that the colored people of Ohio, hitherto too apathetic or opposed, . . . strike for the rights of the slave, as the only effective means of securing their own." (The writer chose to disregard nine years of activity by the black convention movement, with a continuing anti-slavery emphasis.) However, enthusiasm was tempered. "Especially we doubt," the editorial read, "whether separate anti-slavery societies will tend most effectually to break down caste and otherwise secure their object. We should have been grateful if these friends could have cooperated with the society already in existence, which emphatically knows no distinction of creed or caste or race. . . ."[50]

Furthermore, although Langston and his colleagues had hoped to raise money from white sympathizers as well as blacks, and sent out appeals to the public, including letters to newspapers, and lecturers into fifty counties of the state in 1859, apparently few responded. A year later only $221.62 had been raised, scarcely enough for basic expenses. According to plans drawn up by Langston, the society was operated from a permanent office, for which rent had to be paid, with a small monthly stipend for Charles Langston, who acted as recording secretary, and payments and expenses for the lecturers. Except for contributions solicited by passing the hat, the lecturers had to go unpaid, and the older Langston took a much reduced salary. Still, antislavery pamphlets and the expenses of printing petitions and addresses had to be paid for. Until the beginning of the war, the society managed to scrape by financially, but certainly without any significant white support.[51]

Langston's talents were used rather sparingly by white abolitionists and he received little promotion nationally. Beyond the attitudes of white abolitionists toward their black counterparts, his limited appearance on the white antislavery scene may be explained by his own attitudes, heritage and training. His fierce insistence on being his own man, wedded to no one antislavery philosophy, was, of course, of primary importance. Further, his light complexion worked against his being accorded the symbolic stature that abolitionists gave other black orators. His skin was so light that he could be mistaken for a white man, leading some to accept him more readily but allowing others to attribute his competence to his white blood. As even a friendly visitor to Oberlin observed: "I certainly was fond of hearing him discourse on his true subject; his enunciation of English was especially excellent. But for me he was not the typical Negro of Oberlin; moreover, he was half white."[52]

His education, too, was liability as well as asset, especially in the eyes of those abolitionists who preferred that Negro orators be living demonstrations of slavery's oppression. He spoke "as eloquent language as is often heard upon the floor of . . . Congress," a Cleveland newspaper reported following his address to a mass meeting after the Oberlin-Wellington rescue. "The listeners forgot that he was a black man — he spoke a white language such as few white men can speak." Most importantly, perhaps, he had never been a slave, and however much he might say and mean, "I stand here today with invisible manacles upon me," he could not be so effective a symbol for white antislavery workers as he might have been had the manacles been real.[53]

If the relationships were less than intimate and his personal characteristics limiting, still the white abolitionists now and again called on his services. Several Garrisonian outposts in the West invited him to lecture at their annual meetings. In 1852 and again in 1853 he addressed the Cincinnati Anti Slavery Bazaar, a large spring gathering sponsored by the Cincinnati Ladies Sewing Society, who tried, despite their Garrisonian leanings, to bring together all ranges of antislavery thought. On both occasions Langston was accorded polite recognition with his election as one of the convention secretaries. In 1856 he addressed the Western Anti Slavery Society in Salem, Ohio, for nearly two hours in the morning and again for one and a half hours in the afternoon, with the result, according to Nell, that his "most radical sayings were enthusiastically applauded."[54]

In 1855 he was a featured speaker at the anniversary exercises of the American Anti Slavery Society in New York, where he shared the platform with Garrison, Wendell Phillips, and Antoinnette Brown, and for which he was paid fifty dollars (the first time, he noted somewhat ruefully in his autobiography, that he ever received remuneration for a lecture). During the course of his thirty-minute speech he made it a point to praise the antislavery movement in general, without mention of parties or organizations.[55]

Langston punctuated his antislavery speeches with themes made famous by Garrison and his followers: slavery's threat to the civil liberties of everyone, the features and strengths of prejudices against color, the pretentious and corrupt policy of the American Colonization Society, the proslavery nature of clergy and church, the destruction of the intellect and the will and the morality of the slave.[56] He outlined "obstructions" in the way of abolitionists, in pencilled notes for an essay or speech, as "(1) pecuniary interests, (2) commercial interests, (3) the church theology, (4) prejudice against color."[57]

"I am anxious every word I utter, shall be as a colored man," he began, in his address to the 1853 Cincinnati Anti Slavery Bazaar. "Yet on account of my complexion I do not ask your sympathy. The great contest is between liberty and slavery. I thank God that in this contest I am of necessity placed on the side of anti-slavery. . . . I stand as the advocate of the American slave, and from my connection with him, can speak with some freedom and boldness."

From a condemnation of American slavery as the "sum of all villainies," and an enumeration of its "outrages," he passed into a discussion of oppressive legislation in the North. "I stand here to-day with invisible manacles upon me"; he declared, "I have not the freedom that you desire me to have. . . . For we have all the virtues and vices of other men. Yes, we have helped to support your poor, but you have refused to support ours. We have done the same for your blind and insane, but you have not for ours."

"American slavery doesn't stop with striking down the colored man in the North," he continued, but also puts statesmen and churchmen "in fetters." As often in Negro state conventions, he spoke with especial harshness of clergymen who, he said, were "so cowardly and unmindful of the trust imposed upon them, . . . that they make it [slavery] a divine institution, and say that Christ and Paul gave it sanction."

Finally, he exhorted, "Labor for the overthrow of Slavery, or it will overthrow you and everything else. We must come to the rescue of our country from this great curse."[58]

Political involvement, Langston believed, in a departure from Garrison's way, was an absolute necessity for abolitionists and black people. His greatest efforts, as was noted earlier, were directed toward securing the vote for black Ohioans for, as he wrote to *Frederick Douglass' Paper*, "What we so much need just at this juncture, and all along in the future, is political influence; the bridle by which we

can check and guide, to our advantage, the selfishness of the American dema-
gogues."[59]

Throughout the decade, in addition to holding public office, as the elected clerk
of Brownhelm township and later, for two terms, as the clerk of Russia township,
he attended political conventions, supported and actively campaigned for both the
Free Soil and, later, the Republican parties, and strongly denounced the Democratic. On the eve of war he was one of the initiators of a "wide awake" Republican
Club in Oberlin.[60]

From his earliest public appearance Langston articulated, besides moral and
political suasion, a third approach, that of active resistance. He spoke out in favor
of, indeed practiced on occasion, the doctrine of a higher law. With many of his
colleagues he endorsed the calls of David Walker and the Reverend Henry Highland
Garnet for slaves to rise up and overthrow those masters who refused to free them.[61]

Langston and several others, with the approval of the 1856 black state convention, strongly hinted that violent resistance applied equally well for the North as
for the South. Expressing a sentiment rarely voiced publicly by northern blacks,
he joined with nine convention delegates to warn the Ohio legislators: "If we are
deprived of education, of equal political privileges, still subjected to the same
depressing influences under which we now suffer, the natural consequences will
follow; and the State, for her planting of injustice, will reap her harvest of sorrow
and crime. She will contain within her limits a discontented population — dissatisfied, estranged — ready to welcome any revolution or invasion as a relief, for they
can lose nothing and gain much."[62]

Langston drew up the resolution, approved by the 1860 convention, that ex-
tolled John Brown and his men as the "Heralds and Prophets of that new lesson,
the lesson of Insurrection." It is possible that he found two black recruits for
Brown's Harper's Ferry movement, as he claims in his autobiography, but there
is no evidence to substantiate this.[63] The right and duty of resistance by force of
arms "whenever it was feasible," was advocated by him and two other convention
allies in 1858, to render the Fugitive Slave Act null and void.[64]

Seeing to the care and lodging of fugitive slaves was a duty Langston gladly
performed as clerk of Russia township. On September 13, 1858, a fugitive, John
Price, fell into the hands of three deputy United States marshalls, but was quickly
rescued by indignant white and black Oberliners, including the visiting Charles
Langston. The Oberlin-Wellington rescue, along with the Shadrach, Thomas Sims,
Anthony Burns and Jerry rescue cases, received national attention, stirring antislavery sentiment across the North. While the case was in the courts (of thirty-seven
men indicted only two, one of them Charles Langston, were actually convicted, both
receiving light sentences), John Langston addressed rallies in the Western Reserve,
urging Americans to reinstate the Declaration of Independence and the Constitution, the former struck down by slavery and the latter by the Fugitive Slave Law.
Discharging this obligation would involve sacrifice, he told an Oberlin audience.

It might mean going to prison or to the battlefield. If so, he predicted that blacks and whites would march to battle together. He himself longed to take the field as "common soldier or in a more exalted rank," and "strike" for his country.[65]

Soon after, swept into the vortex of Civil War, black men in the North would center their protest for equal rights on the demand that they be allowed to fight to help free their brothers in the South, as well as themselves. Langston would press hard for this privilege and, when it was finally granted, spend his energies recruiting black troops for the Union armies.

Eleven years of struggle to bring about change in their status had produced little enough that Langston and his fellows could point to directly as solid achievement. Even as North prepared to fight against South, black men in Ohio were still discriminated against, still segregated, still without the right of franchise. And yet, the speaking tours, the attempts at organizing, the work with black groups and white had left Langston not defeated but determined. Despite the overwhelming odds against them, he and the other black leaders of Ohio, encouraged by a few white friends, never acquiesced in their debasement. Rather they mounted a continuing outcry against it. Toward the end of the decade, Langston expressed his belief in final victory, perhaps not in the streets or courtrooms of Ohio, but in the realm of the mind and spirit. He wrote: "Our deep love of liberty, our intelligent veneration for the precepts of Christianity, and our abiding determination to obey God rather than man, no prosecution, however oppressive, no irksome confinement in gloomy dungeons, no illegal and unjust confiscation of our property, can ever overthrow and destroy."[66]

Notes

[1] A few exceptions should be noted: Benjamin Quarles, *Black Abolitionists* (New York, 1969); Leon Litwack, "The Emancipation of the Negro Abolitionist," in Martin Duberman (ed.), *The Antislavery Vanguard* (Princeton, 1965), pp. 137–155; Leon Litwack, *North of Slavery* (Chicago, 1961); August Meier and Elliott M. Rudwick, *From Plantation to Ghetto* (New York, 1966), pp. 94–122.

[2] In *Black Abolitionists*, Quarles makes two casual references to Langston's speaking engagements and includes a paragraph citing several of his efforts to gain the right to vote for black people in Ohio. Litwack, in *North of Slavery*, a study of the northern free Negro, mentions Langston's name once, in a listing of nine black militant leaders. He is cited only twice, once as an organizer of a black antislavery society in Ohio and again as a colonization advocate, in Meier and Rudwick, *From Plantation to Ghetto*, pp. 111, 122. Other standard works make no reference to Langston as abolitionist or protest leader. Louis Filler, *The Crusade Against Slavery, 1830–1860* (New York, 1960); Dwight Lowell Dumond, *Antislavery* (Ann Arbor, 1961); John Hope Franklin, *From Slavery to Freedom* (New York, 1967); Martin Duberman (ed.), *The Antislavery Vanguard*.

[3] John Mercer Langston, *From Virginia Plantation to National Capitol* (Hartford, 1894), pp. 1–22 and *passim;* Petersburg, Va., *Index-Appeal,* Oct. 17, 1890; Louisa County, Va., *Will Book 9,* 110–111.

[4] For young Langston's deep emotional involvement with William Gooch and his family, see his autobiography, *Virginia Plantation,* pp. 37–53, 68–71; also the "Interview with John Mercer Langston," San Francisco *Weekly Post,* Apr. 5, 1877, in John Mercer Langston Scrapbooks, Moorland Room, Howard University.

[5] Langston, *Virginia Plantation,* pp. 54–76.

[6] *Ibid.,* pp. 55, 59, 66–67, 74–75.

[7] *Ibid., passim;* Langston to Henry [Howe], Apr. 10, 1854, John Mercer Langston Papers, Fisk University; Langston to James W. Fairchild, Jan. 5, 1895, James W. Fairchild Papers, Oberlin College Library; Robert Samuel Fletcher, *A History of Oberlin College* (Chicago, 1943), *passim.*

[8] Elyria *Independent-Democrat,* Oct. 20, 1852, Jan. 19, 1859; *Anti Slavery Bugle,* Oct. 25, 1856; Cleveland *Leader,* Aug. 1857; May 25, 1859.

[9] Elyria *Independent-Democrat,* Oct. 25, 1853; Langston, *Virginia Plantation,* pp. 117–124; *Anti Slavery Bugle,* Apr. 28, 1855.

[10] Howard H. Bell, "A Survey of the Negro Convention Movement, 1830–1861," (Ph.D. dissertation, Northwestern University, 1953), *passim.*

[11] Franklin Johnson, *The Development of State Legislation Concerning the Free Negro* (New York, 1948), p. 161; *State Convention of the Colored Citizens of Ohio, Columbus, January 10–13, 1849* (Oberlin, 1849).

[12] John L. Myers, "American Anti-Slavery Society Agents and the Free Negro, 1833–1838," *Journal of Negro History,* LII (July, 1967), 200–219; Allan Peskin (ed.), *North Into Freedom, The Autobiography of John Malvin, Free Negro, 1795–1880* (Cleveland, 1966), pp. 65–67.

[13] Francis P. Weisenburger, *The History of the State of Ohio* (Columbus, 1941), pp. 173, 471–473.

[14] *State Convention of the Colored Citizens of Ohio, 1849; Minutes of the State Convention of the Colored Citizens of Ohio . . . 1850* (Columbus, 1850); *Minutes of the State Convention of the Colored Freemen of Ohio . . . 1852* (Cincinnati, 1852); *Official Proceedings of the Ohio State Convention of Colored Freemen . . . 1853* (Cleveland, 1853); *Proceedings of the State Convention of Colored Men . . . 1856* (Cleveland, 1856); *Proceedings of the State Convention of the Colored Men of the State of Ohio . . . 1857* (Columbus, 1857); *Proceedings of a Convention of the Colored Men of Ohio . . . 1858* (Cincinnati, 1858); *Proceedings of the First Annual Meeting of the Ohio State Anti-Slavery Society . . . 1860* (Cleveland, 1860). All conventions to be cited hereafter as *State Convention,* followed by the date. For other conventions, see *Anti Slavery Bugle,* Feb. 22, 1851; *Frederick Douglass' Paper,* Oct. 1, 1852; Elyria *Independent-Democrat,* Oct. 25, 1853.

[15] Langston to Francis Barry, Jan. 15, 1855, in *Frederick Douglass' Paper,* Jan. 26, 1855.

[16] *Russia Township, Township Records, 1855–1869,* Oberlin College Library.

[17] *The Record of Deeds,* Lorain County, Ohio, Elyria Courthouse, Elyria, Ohio, contains many listings of property bought and sold by Langston. For his payment of tuition for an Oberlin Negro student, see "Miscellaneous Receipts," Langston Papers.

[18] William Wells Brown, *The Rising Son* (Boston, 1876), p. 448.

[19] Langston ms., Mar. 25, 1854, Langston Papers.

[20] Brown, *The Rising Son,* p. 448.

[21] W. C. Nell to William Lloyd Garrison, Nov. 10, 1856, in *The Liberator,* Nov. 14, 1856.

[22] *Anti Slavery Bugle,* Aug. 17, 1850; interview with Mrs. Nettie Mathews (Langston's granddaughter), Nov. 24, 1960.

[23] Langston, *Virginia Plantation,* pp. 137–139. For his oratorical style, see Langston, "Address to the Union Society" and "Action of the Federal Government," both in Langston Papers; "Address to the Cincinnati Anti Slavery Bazaar," in *Anti Slavery Bugle,* Apr. 10, 1853; "A Plea for Freedom," in *Annual Report presented to the American Anti Slavery Society* (New York, 1855); "The World's Anti Slavery Movement" (lecture delivered at Xenia and Cleve-

land, Ohio, Aug. 2 and 3, 1858), in Langston, *Freedom and Citizenship, Selected Lectures and Addresses* (Washington, 1883), pp. 41–64; Oberlin *Evangelist*, Jan. 19, 1859.

[24] Julia Griffiths (ed.), *Autographs for Freedom* (Rochester, 1854), pp. 147–150; Langston, "The Oberlin Wellington Rescue," *The Anglo-African Magazine*, I, 1, (Jan., 1859).

[25] For mention of the State Central Committee, see, in addition to the State Convention reports, *Anti Slavery Bugle*, Dec. 18, 1852, Oct. 1, 1853; *The Liberator*, Feb. 15, 1856; W. R. Burnham to Langston, Feb. 6, 1854 and Peter H. Clark to Langston, Jan. 22, 1854, both in Langston Papers.

[26] *State Convention*, 1850; *State Convention*, 1853; Oberlin *Evangelist*, Feb. 2, 1853; *State Convention*, 1858; Elyria *Independent-Democrat*, Dec. 1, 1858; Cleveland *Leader*, Feb. 15, 1859; *State Convention*, 1860.

[27] *State Convention*, 1849.

[28] *Ibid.; State Convention*, 1852; *State Convention*, 1856; Langston, "Address to the Legislature of Ohio," *State Convention*, 1857.

[29] *State Convention*, 1849; *State Convention*, 1850; *State Convention*, 1851.

[30] *State Convention*, 1857.

[31] *Ibid.*

[32] *State Convention*, 1849.

[33] In addition to the removal of many of the Black Laws in 1849, the Ohio legislature passed bills in 1848, 1849, and 1852 relating to public school education for Negroes.

[34] *Proceedings of the National Emigration Convention of Colored People, held at Cleveland, Ohio . . . the 24th, 25th, and 26th of August, 1854* (Pittsburg, 1854); Bell, "A Survey of the Negro Convention Movement, 1830–1861," *passim*.

[35] *State Convention*, 1856.

[36] Langston ms., Mar. 25, 1854, Langston Papers.

[37] *State Convention*, 1851.

[38] *State Convention*, 1850; *State Convention*, 1853; *State Convention*, 1849.

[39] *State Convention*, 1850; *Proceedings of the Colored National Convention, Rochester, July 6–8, 1853* (Rochester, 1853); *State Convention*, 1851; *State Convention*, 1853.

[40] *State Convention*, 1850; *State Convention*, 1851; I. Garland Penn, *The Afro-American Press* (Springfield, Mass., 1891), p. 76.

[41] *State Convention*, 1852.

[42] Oberlin Young Men's Anti Slavery Society Records, Oberlin College Library; W. H. Burnham to Langston, Feb. 6, 1854, Langston Papers.

[43] On Langston's various services to Oberlin education, see Russia Township, Board of Education Records, 1842–1871; *Historical Sketches of Public Schools in Ohio* (General Assembly of Ohio, 1876); *Lorain County News*, Mar. 19, 1862, Mar. 21, 1866, Sept. 21, 1871.

[44] Langston, "Address to the Legislature of Ohio," *State Convention*, 1857; Langston Speech, "Action of the Federal Government in Behalf of Slavery,"; "Miscellaneous Notes," both in Langston Papers.

[45] W. C. Nell to William Lloyd Garrison, Nov. 10, 1856, in *The Liberator*, Nov. 14, 1856.

[46] Langston, "Address to the Legislature of Ohio," *State Convention*, 1857.

[47] *Ibid.*

[48] *The Liberator* and the *Anti Slavery Bugle* contain few articles and only rare editorials on the activities of the Negroes of Ohio. The Elyria *Independent-Democrat*, the Oberlin *Evangelist*, and the Cleveland *Leader* were sympathetic observers of the efforts of black Ohioans, but they, too, gave only limited coverage. The problem of tension between white and black abolitionists has been suggested elsewhere. See Litwack, *North of Slavery*, ch. 7; Litwack, "The Abolitionist Dilemma: The Antislavery Movement and the Northern Negro," *New England Quarterly*, XXXIV (Mar., 1961), 50–73; William and Jane Pease, "Antislavery

Ambivalence: Immediatism, Expediency, Race," *American Quarterly,* XVII (Winter, 1965), 682–695.

[49] Langston, *Virginia Plantation,* pp. 102, 117; *The Liberator,* Nov. 14, 1856. A broad combing of the papers of the major abolitionists and antislavery politicians has led me to conclude that only Gerrit Smith and Salmon P. Chase had any correspondence with Langston before the Civil War.

[50] *State Convention,* 1858; *Anti Slavery Bugle,* Dec. 4, 1858.

[51] Cleveland *Morning Leader,* Dec. 4, 1858; *State Convention,* 1860.

[52] Denton J. Snider, *A Writer of Books* (St. Louis, 1910), p. 100.

[53] Cleveland *Morning Leader,* May 25, 1859; *Anti Slavery Bugle,* May 7, 1853.

[54] *Anti Slavery Bugle,* May 8, 1852, Apr. 29, 1853, Aug. 2, 1856; W. C. Nell to William Lloyd Garrison, Aug. 4, 1856, in *The Liberator,* Aug. 15, 1856.

[55] *Annual Report presented to the American Anti Slavery Society, 1855;* Langston, *Virginia Plantation,* p. 145.

[56] *Anti Slavery Bugle,* Apr. 30, 1853; *Annual Report presented to the American Anti Slavery Society,* 1855; *State Convention,* 1852; *State Convention,* 1850.

[57] Pencilled notes in John Mercer Langston Scrapbook, Fisk University.

[58] *Anti Slavery Bugle,* May 7, 1853.

[59] *Frederick Douglass' Paper,* reprinted in *Anti Slavery Bugle,* Apr. 28, 1855.

[60] Elyria *Independent-Democrat,* Sept. 1, 1852; Jan. 12, Sept 28, 1853; June 1, June 15, 1859; *Anti Slavery Bugle,* Dec. 4, 1858; *Lorain County News, June 13, 1860.*

[61] *State Convention,* 1849.

[62] *State Convention,* 1856.

[63] *State Convention,* 1860; Langston, *Virginia Plantation,* pp. 190–193.

[64] *State Convention,* 1858.

[65] *Russia Township, Township Records;* Fletcher, *Oberlin College,* I, 402–415; Cleveland *Leader,* Jan. 13, 1859.

[66] *The Anglo-African Magazine,* 216.

William Still and the Underground Railroad

Larry Gara

The writer of a popular account of the underground railroad in Pennsylvania stated in his preface that "it required the manhood of a man and the unflinching fortitude of a woman, . . . to be an abolitionist in those days, and especially an Underground Railroad agent."[1] He was referring to the noble minority who stood firm when the abolitionists were being "reviled and persecuted" in both the North and the South. Other underground railroad books — some of them written by elderly abolitionists — put similar emphasis on the heroic conductors of the mysterious organization. They reflected the history of the underground railroad from the vantage point of the abolitionist conductor. They also contributed to the growth of a favorite American legend, which is as much a part of folklore as of history. Two of the forgotten characters in the popular legend are the Negro members of various vigilance committees and the fugitives themselves. If it required some strong character to be an abolitionist, it took even more courage to become a hunted fugitive or one of his colored abettors. William Still's work with the Philadelphia vigilance committee called attention to both of these neglected groups.

William Still's parents were both born slaves, and they left slavery at considerable personal sacrifice: his father purchased his freedom, and his mother, after one unsuccessful attempt to escape, finally ran away with two of her four children. They later farmed a forty-acre plot in the New Jersey pines near Medford. William was born there on October 7, 1821, the youngest of eighteen children. With a bare minimum of formal schooling he continued his own education by extensive reading. When he was twenty he left home, and three years later he moved to Philadelphia. He held a number of jobs before joining the staff of the Pennsylvania Society for Promoting the Abolition of Slavery in the fall of 1847.[2]

Still began working with the abolition society as a combination janitor and mail clerk. After several years, both his duties and his salary were increased. He took a special interest in the society's efforts to assist slaves who had run away from the

From Larry Gara, "William Still and the Underground Railroad," *Pennsylvania History*, XXVIII, January 1961, pp. 33–44. Reprinted by permission of the publisher and author.

A grant from the Penrose Fund of the American Philosophical Society made it possible to complete the research upon which this article is based. A shorter version was read at the annual meeting of the Pennsylvania Historical Association on October 14, 1960.

South. They were often boarded at his home before resuming their journey towards Canada. For fourteen years Still served the society. During that time he worked with such well known anti-slavery advocates as Robert Purvis, who was also colored, Lucretia and James Mott, Sarah Pugh, Thomas Garrett, and J. Miller McKim, who was the agent in charge of the Philadelphia office.[3]

In 1838 Philadelphia abolitionists had organized a vigilance committee to assist fugitives coming into the city. There was some underground railroad activity in the area. Thomas Garrett of Wilmington, the more militant anti-slavery Quakers of Philadelphia and the neighboring counties, and the vigilance committee were primarily responsible for the work. Although there was a semblance of organization to these efforts, much of the aid given the fugitive slaves was on a haphazard basis. By 1852 even the vigilance committee had disintegrated. In December of that year a group of abolitionists reported that the old committee "had become disorganized and scattered" and that for several years its duties "had been performed by individuals on their own responsibility, and sometimes in a very irregular manner," causing "much dissatisfaction and complaint." The group decided to organize a new vigilance committee, with an acting committee of four members, which should have the authority to attend "to every case that might require aid," to raise necessary funds, and "to keep a record of all their doings," and especially of their receipts and expenditures. They appointed William Still chairman of the acting committee.[4]

One of the principal activities of the new Philadelphia vigilance committee was to extend financial aid to fugitives. The committee provided money to board fugitives with families of free Negroes, sometimes for as long as thirteen days but usually for only a few days. As a Negro, William Still easily gained the confidence of the new arrivals and knew where to find them board and lodging among the colored population of Philadelphia. The committee also purchased clothing, medicine, and the fugitives' railroad fares to Canada. It advertised anti-slavery meetings in the newspapers and on one occasion spent twenty dollars for handbills and other expenses of a meeting. Mostly, the committee spent money in small amounts; very few items in its financial reports involved more than five dollars.[5]

At times William Still and other members of the acting vigilance committee were very busy with their labor on behalf of the fugitives. Late in 1857 J. Miller McKim wrote another abolitionist, "Other rail-roads are in a declining condition and have stopped their semi annual dividends, but the Underground has never before done so flourishing a business." He further reported, "Exactly fifty — men, women and children — have passed through the hands of our Vigilance Committee in the last fortnight."[6] It was a dramatic time and a most unusual amount of work for the vigilance committee. According to the committee's journal it assisted approximately 495 fugitives between December, 1852, and February, 1857. In his later published account, covering eight years of vigilance committee activity, Still listed approximately eight hundred fugitives, including sixty children, who had received aid from the committee.[7]

Although a great deal of William Still's work was of such a routine nature as answering correspondence or meeting new arrivals at the railroad station, he had some moments of high adventure too. One arrival from the South, who had purchased his freedom, contacted Still for information about his family. Upon investigation he proved to be Still's own brother, left in slavery forty years earlier when his mother fled to the North. Still also witnessed the arrival of the famous Henry "Box" Brown, who had literally had himself crated and sent north via the Adams' Express Company, and of the clever William and Ellen Craft. The Crafts had traveled all the way from Georgia with the nearly-white Ellen disguised as an ailing planter and William playing the part of the faithful servant. Still observed a number of other unusual and interesting cases, though none got the public attention given to Henry "Box" Brown and the Crafts.[8]

One of William Still's duties was to ask the newly arrived slaves their names, the names of their masters and where they had come from, and to question them about their escape experiences and the severity of their servitude. In part the interrogation was meant to protect the vigilance committee from the imposters who not infrequently found the abolitionist easy prey for a handout. Still not only recorded the data but carefully preserved the records. In his book he wrote that he had kept the documents for possible use in helping to reunite relatives and friends.[9] In 1884 he told a meeting of aged abolitionists that he had kept them because they were interesting, and because his family had been connected with the underground railroad.[10] Possibly, too, the records were a protection for him in case any of the Philadelphia abolitionists had requested a detailed accounting of Still's work for the anti-slavery society. To Still the vigilance committee was synonymous with the underground railroad. In 1893 he informed historian Wilbur H. Siebert that his "were the only records that were kept of the U.G.R.R.," and that when he collected them he had never dreamed that they could be published in his lifetime.[11]

Still's voluminous record books were a rich source of indisputable evidence had the government been inclined to invoke the Fugitive Slave Law against him or the vigilance committee. He hid the records after the Harpers Ferry fiasco and for a while they were stored in the loft of the Lebanon Cemetery building.[12] In a number of instances he faced possible prosecution. It was Still and others at the anti-slavery office who had warned the Negroes of Christiana that warrants were out for two slaves hiding there. The slave hunt resulted in a mob scene in which the slaves' master was murdered and his nephew seriously wounded. Several abolitionists and thirty-four Negroes were indicted for treason but none were convicted.[13] Still was not indicted with the Christiana rioters but the government brought charges against him for helping to entice Jane Johnson away from her master, Colonel John H. Wheeler, the American minister to Nicaragua. Still was acquitted, but two of five other Negroes indicted were sentenced to a week in jail on a charge of assault and battery, and Passmore Williamson, a Philadelphia Quaker, spent three months in jail for contempt of court.[14] John Brown had confided his plans to William Still six months before his raid on Harpers Ferry and a memorandum found among the papers of Brown's lieutenant, John Henry Kagi, seemed to implicate Still in the scheme.[15] In all these cases Still avoided punishment, but when a woman sued him for libel in 1860 he was not so fortunate.

The woman, a Mrs. Ellen Wells, who was a former slave from St. Louis, was traveling throughout the country raising money to purchase her mother, her children, and several other relatives from slavery. She stayed at William Still's rooming house in Philadelphia, but he did not encourage her project. When a Boston abolitionist wrote for information about Ellen Wells, Still answered that she was an imposter and a prostitute. The letter fell into Mrs. Wells' hands and she sued Still for scandalous and malicious libel. He pleaded guilty to having written the letter and the court sentenced him to ten days in jail and fined him a hundred dollars. Boston abolitionists supported Still and paid the fine from the treasury of the Massachusetts Anti-Slavery Society.[16]

A year later, with the Civil War in progress, Still resigned his position with the Pennsylvania Anti-Slavery Society.[17] He had already ventured into some real estate transactions, and he then bought and managed first a store and later a very successful retail coal business. In 1872 he published *The Underground Rail Road*. The book was another of William Still's contributions to the progress of his race. His work with the fugitive slaves had impressed upon him the need for Negroes to take the initiative to improve their condition. In August of 1860 he told a Negro audience at Kennett Square celebrating the anniversary of West Indian emancipation, "The hundreds of heroic fugitives who yearly throw off their yokes, . . . seem to cry aloud in our ears — 'Hereditary bondmen! know ye not who would be free themselves must strike the blow?' "[18]

In 1855 William Still had visited the former slaves who had settled in Canada, and he later wrote a strong defense of their conduct and achievements, answering those who maintained that slaves could not meet the responsibilities of free citizens. In 1859 he initiated a successful eight-year campaign to secure equal service for Negroes in the Philadelphia streetcars. In 1861 he helped organize an association for the purpose of collecting and disseminating accurate information about the American Negro population in order to improve its position.[19] These and many other activities stemmed from Still's determination to help improve the status of the colored people.[20] So did his book. He wanted to make the underground railroad "a monument to the heroism of the bondmen under the yoke." Their "heroism and desperate struggles," said Still, as well as "the terrible oppression that they were under, should be kept green in the memory of this and coming generations." He also believed that books written by Negroes would prove their mental ability and provide an effective answer to those who argued that the colored people were inferior. "We very much need works on various topics from the pens of colored men to represent the race intellectually," he wrote.[21]

He received added encouragement from the Philadelphia abolitionists. At a meeting in May, 1871, the Pennsylvania Anti-Slavery Society passed a resolution requesting Still to publish his reminiscences relating to the underground railroad.

That same year there was a seven-months coal strike in Pennsylvania which made his business very dull but gave him the leisure he needed to prepare his material for publication. Still worked diligently in the preparation of his book, a task which was made more difficult by the bitter division in the anti-slavery movement. He corresponded with old acquaintances, put his own records in order and collected material from others. The Philadelphia abolitionists with whom he had worked were all Garrisonians, but he included the political abolitionist Lewis Tappan among those whom he asked for information. One of the difficult tasks was to write a sketch of J. Miller McKim, his superior in the anti-slavery office. When McKim asked Still to outline the material concerning him, Still tactfully replied that "it would not be just to confine [McKim] to any special department of the work but to represent [him] as a general laborer," with many services in the anti-slavery cause.[22] Frederick Douglass, however, got no mention in Still's book, except in material reprinted from a British pamphlet. In 1893 Douglass boasted of his long service in the underground railroad and claimed that Still had omitted him because he had criticized Still's conduct toward the fugitives.[23]

William Still's book on the underground railroad is unique in that it emphasized the courage and ingenuity of the fugitives. White conductors are the heroes in the accounts which the abolitionists recorded for posterity; in Still's account, the daring fugitives are the heroes. Scattered throughout the volume are legal documents, letters, and newspaper items, but the focus of the narrative is always on the slaves themselves. Still placed his sketches of the abolitionist conductors at the end of the book, after the great bulk of material on the passengers. The book's numerous illustrations also focus the spotlight on the absconding slaves and on their heroic struggle for freedom.

In Still's book the vast majority of the fugitive slaves came from the neighboring border states. Most of them were young men, of more than average intelligence, though there were some women and children too. Although they were all considered underground railroad passengers, many of them had received little or no assistance before they contacted the vigilance committee. Some passed as white or as free Negroes, some traveled on foot at night, some adopted clever disguises, and more than a few hid or were hidden on steamers running from southern ports. Much of the escape drama was a self-help affair.

Although never a slave himself, William Still hated the South's peculiar institution. Not only did he have the zeal of the abolitionists, but as a Negro he was able to identify himself emotionally with the bondsmen. "The half will never be told of the barbarism of Slavery," he wrote. He described one fugitive as a "decided opponent to the no-pay system, to flogging, and selling likewise." Still said he had taken care "to furnish artless stories, [and] simple facts," and had resorted "to no coloring to make the book seem romantic." He took great care to be factual but his bias was apparent throughout the book. In his preface Still commented that those who sought information regarding "the existence, atrocity, struggles and destruction of Slavery" would have no trouble finding the "hydra-headed monster ruling and tyrannizing over Church and State, North and South, white and black, without let or hindrance for at least several generations."[24]

The fugitives whom Still and the vigilance committee interviewed had confirmed his prejudice against the slave system. Although a few maintained that they had been treated well, the great majority testified to many hardships. Some were probably aware of the committee's preference for cruel and libertine masters. One slave from Maryland said that he had been "treated as bad as a man could be," another had been "allowed no privileges of any kind, Sunday or Monday," and a woman had "endured all outraged nature could endure and survive." The fugitives described their former owners with an abundance of such terms as "always a big devil — ill-grained," an "ill-natured man," and "a notorious frolicker." One described a cruel master who "made a common practice of flogging females when stripped naked." Still and the other committee members were also temperance advocates and duly noted in their records when a master was described as "given to 'intemperance' " and to "gross 'profanity,' " "a gambler and spree'r," and a man "devoted to card playing, rum-drinking and fox-hunting."[25]

Occasionally the committee sharply questioned fugitives whose stories did not seem plausible, but they sometimes took obviously exaggerated statements at face value. After trying to dispute her testimony, the committee gave "the benefit of the doubt" to Amarian, a good-looking girl of twenty-one who said she had always been treated very well. Similarly, they doubted Washington Somlor's description of inhuman treatment at the hands of a master who "believed in selling, flogging, cobbing, paddling, and all other kinds of torture. . . ." Yet they accepted the statements of William Jordon who said that he had lived three months in a cave "surrounded with bears, wild cats, rattle-snakes and the like." Theophilus Collins testified that he was brutally punished for attending a Sunday night religious meeting. His master called him in for a whipping and when he refused to remove his shirt, gave him twenty blows on the head with the butt of a cowhide, struck him on the head with fire-tongs, beat him with a parlor shovel until the handle broke, jabbed the shovel blade at his head with all his might, and when the slave tried to make for the door, stabbed him in the head and stomach with a pocket knife. Nevertheless, Theophilus escaped and ran sixteen miles carrying a part of his entrails in his hands for the whole journey.[26]

William Still believed that a book containing such thrilling tales as the one Theophilus told to the vigilance committee should certainly sell many copies. His previous business experience enabled him to plan and promote the sale of his book to good advantage. He decided to sell it only by subscription and carefully supervised his sales campaign.[27]

Prospective agents for a particular territory had to apply personally to Still. If no suitable person applied, Still preferred to leave the area temporarily unsolicited. He had two editions, one in plain English cloth which sold for five dollars, and a sheepskin edition priced at five-fifty. Still prepared a full set of instructions for his agents and sold each of them a kit with sample copies. He gave them forty or fifty per cent of the purchase price as commission, but they had to adhere strictly to his terms. During the financial panic of 1873 he permitted them to sell on the installment plan, but they were not to deliver the book until the last payment had been made. All of his agents had to submit weekly reports.[28]

Still preferred to hire colored men to sell his book, but he realized that few of his race had the necessary experience. He was confident it would be well received among the Negroes and among the Republicans, if the agents did their part well. "The book only needs to be presented by a man who appreciates and comprehends the value and importance of having our heroes and Martyrs under Slavery well represented in the history of our times — to make the work take exceedingly well," he wrote a representative in Kansas in 1873.[29] And the work took well indeed. A salesman in Pittsburgh cleared about a hundred dollars a week for six weeks. His best agent followed five others who had sold only a few copies in Baltimore, and at the end of six weeks he had more than three hundred subscriptions. In 1873 Still reported, "Agents are doing well with the U.G.R.R. this summer. East, West, North and South, wherever competent persons are presenting it." He first printed ten thousand copies but hoped to sell a hundred thousand before the demand ceased.[30] The first edition sold out completely, as did a second edition in 1879. In 1883 Still published a third edition with a new title, *Still's Underground Rail Road Records,* and with a sketch of the author written by James P. Boyd.

William Still's book undoubtedly circulated more widely than any other first-hand account of the underground railroad. In writing and distributing it Still proved that a Negro author could produce a creditable book and sell it on a large scale. He proudly exhibited it at the Philadelphia Centennial Exposition in 1876. It was a fitting tribute to his race. He hoped it would inspire other Negroes to greater efforts until they could exhibit such fruits "of their newly gained privileges" as "well-conducted shops and stores; lands acquired and good farms" well-managed, and "valuable books produced and published on interesting and important subjects."[31] It is not possible to evaluate the book's effect on American Negroes, but in one respect it failed to make its mark. William Still put the courageous fugitive slaves at the center of his stage. His book provided an excellent corrective for the many abolitionist-centered accounts. Yet in the popular mind, the white conductor of the underground railroad remains the leading figure in the drama. Despite Still's financial success, his message has been hidden under a mass of literature written by the abolitionists, their descendants, and admirers.

Notes

[1] Robert C. Smedley, *History of the Underground Railroad in Chester and the Neighboring Counties of Pennsylvania* (Lancaster, Pa., 1883), preface, xv.

[2] James P. Boyd, "William Still: His Life and Work to This Time," in William Still, *Still's*

Underground Rail Road Records (3rd ed., Phila., 1883), iii–xvii. The title page varied some-what in each edition of Still's book, but the pagination of the text remained the same.

[3] Boyd, "Still," in Still, *Underground Rail Road,* xviii.

[4] Still, *Underground Rail Road,* 611–12.

[5] *Journal of the Philadelphia Vigilance Committee, 1852–1857,* in the Historical Society of Pennsylvania.

[6] J. Miller McKim to Mrs. M. W. Chapman, November 19, 1857, in the Weston Papers in the Boston Public Library. McKim's letter was published in the 1858 edition of the *Liberty Bell.*

[7] *Journal of the Philadelphia Vigilance Committee;* Still, *Underground Rail Road, passim.*

[8] Lucretia Mott to Joseph and Ruth Dugdale, March 28, 1849, in the Lucretia Mott MSS in the Friends Historical Library of Swarthmore College; Still, *Underground Rail Road,* 81–86, 368–377.

[9] Still, *Underground Rail Road,* preface; Boyd, "Still," in Still, *Underground Rail Road,* xxxiv.

[10] *Commemoration of the Fiftieth Anniversary of the Organization of the American Anti-Slavery Society, in Philadelphia* (Philadelphia, 1884), 39–40.

[11] William Still to Wilbur H. Siebert, November 18, 1893, in scrapbook "The Under-ground Railroad in Pennsylvania, vol. 3," in the Wilbur H. Siebert Papers in the Ohio Historical Society.

[12] Boyd, "Still," in Still, *Underground Rail Road,* xxiii, xxxiv.

[13] Still, *Underground Rail Road,* 348–368.

[14] Still, *Underground Rail Road,* 86–95.

[15] Boyd, "Still," in Still, *Underground Rail Road,* xxii–xxiv.

[16] J. Miller McKim to R. S. Webb, June 23, 1860, and Samuel May, Jr., to McKim, May 23, 1860, in the Garrison Papers in the Boston Public Library; New York *National Anti-Slavery Standard,* April 28, May 5, 1860.

[17] Boyd, "Still," in Still, *Underground Rail Road,* xxx.

[18] New York *National Anti-Slavery Standard,* August 18, 1860.

[19] Boyd, "Still," in Still, *Underground Rail Road,* xxv–xxviii, li–lvii; Harrod G. Villard, "William Still," in the *Dictionary of American Biography,* 18:23.

[20] For Still's other activities see Alberta S. Norwood, "Negro Welfare Work in Phila-delphia, Especially as Illustrated by the Career of William Still, 1775–1930," unpublished thesis in the Library of the University of Pennsylvania (1931).

[21] William Still to Dr. Henry Charles, June 6, 1873, to J. W. Jones, November 4, 1873, and to J. C. Price, June 3, 1873, in the William Still Papers in the Historical Society of Pennsylvania.

[22] Boyd, "Still," in Still, *Underground Rail Road,* xxxv; William Still to J. Miller McKim, November 10, 1871, in the J. Miller McKim Papers in the New York Public Library.

[23] Frederick Douglass to Wilbur H. Siebert, March 27, 1893, in scrapbook, "The Under-ground Railroad in New York, vol. 2," in the Siebert Papers in the Ohio Historical Society.

[24] William Still, *The Underground Rail Road* (Philadelphia, 1872), 144, 290, preface, 3, 5. This preface appears only in the first edition.

[25] Still, *Underground Rail Road,* 185, 260, 307, 383, 388, 416, 480, 519, 533, 754.

[26] *Ibid.,* 130, 304, 435, 495–496.

[27] Boyd, "Still," in Still, *Underground Rail Road,* xlvi–xlix, lxi–lxii.

[28] Still to T. L. W. Titus, January 7, 1874, to W. D. Teister, June 10, 1873, to Robert Furnas, June 18, 1873, to James E. Thompson, July 9, 1873, and to J. C. Price, June 23, 1873, all in the Still Papers.

[29] Still to Thomas E. Franklin, April 9, 1874, and the Rev. J. C. Embry, October 14, 1873, in the Still Papers.

[30] Still to W. H. Jones, June 3, 1873, the Rev. Jones, November 12, 1873, and to E. Sanborn, June 11, 1873, in the Still Papers.

[31] William Still, *The Underground Rail Road* (Philadelphia and Cincinnati, 1879), preface. This preface appears in the second and third editions.

The Abolitionist Movement: The Negro's Role

2

The Negro in the Organization of Abolition

Charles H. Wesley

The Abolition Movement was an organized activity in which representatives of both races participated. Negroes were allied with anti-slavery organizations as delegates and members, and by themselves initiated independent activities for the freedom of the slave population. The opinion which has prevailed that Negroes were not aggressive in the struggle for their own freedom is not corroborated by the facts and their logical interpretation. There were Negroes who organized societies for abolition purposes and joined with the group efforts for freedom in their local communities. Others manifested active interest in abolition in its national phase and shared in the rise of its epoch of immediatism.

When the first public step in the announcement of a new Abolition Movement was taken with the publication of *The Liberator* in Boston on January 1, 1831, William Lloyd Garrison addressed a statement to his "free colored brethren." He stated that their advancement would be a leading object of the paper and he expressed the hope that "some patronage" would be given to the paper by them. That this assistance was granted was admitted by Garrison when he later said that he struggled through the first year of the existence of *The Liberator* with about fifty white subscribers and four hundred colored subscribers.[1] Of its first four agents three were Negroes, Messrs. Philip A. Bell of New York City, Joseph Cassey of Philadelphia and William Watkins of Baltimore.

The announcement of the publication of this paper in August, 1830, attracted the attention of Negroes and their response showed their interest. On December 31, 1830, James Forten, wealthy Negro sailmaker of Philadelphia, wrote to Garrison at Boston, stating that he was happy to learn that *The Liberator* was to be established and that he hoped that it would be "the means of exposing more and more the odious system of slavery and of raising up friends to the oppressed and degraded people of colour throughout the Union."[2] Forten sent with this letter fifty-four dollars and the names of twenty-seven subscribers. One month after *The Liberator* was issued Forten again wrote that the paper was highly valued by all and enclosed twenty dollars for additional subscriptions.[3] It seemed probable that "a significant part of

From Charles H. Wesley, "The Negro in the Organization of Abolition," *Phylon,* II, 3rd Quarter, 1941, pp. 223–235. Reprinted by permission of the publisher.

the indebtedness of *The Liberator"* was carried by Forten.[4] From Pittsburgh, John B. Vashon, Negro proprietor of a public bath house and the organizer of an anti-slavery society in this city, sent fifty dollars during the second year of *The Liberator.* This sum was acknowledged by Garrison.[5] On March 31, 1831, Forten wrote that he was pleased "to see how all the people of color, subscribers to *The Liberator,* speak in praise of it."[6]

This opinion was expressed by several groups. A meeting, described as an "enthusiastic" one, was held in Philadelphia on March 1, 1831. It was designated as "a convention of young men of color." Resolutions were adopted stating that they would give support to *The Liberator,* and accord was expressed with the views and sentiments of Garrison.[7] From Boston another group forwarded a letter pledging their support and sending with the letter "a very generous and seasonable donation." A meeting of Negroes in New York City resolved that they would use every effort to procure subscribers for *The Liberator.* Similar action was taken by Negroes in Rochester, New York, New York City and Middletown, Connecticut.[8]

Free Negroes were also contributors to the columns of *The Liberator.* They sent in reports of their meetings, letters and comments upon events affecting their condition. They purchased advertising space in the paper. As agents for its sale and distribution, they were especially active in Philadelphia, New York City and Boston.

The support of the free colored people was acknowledged in an appeal for assistance during the fourth year of the publication of *The Liberator.* A circular was issued in 1834 by Garrison and Knapp which stated that only one-fourth of the total number of subscribers were white. They added, "the paper then belongs especially to the people of color — it is their organ — and to them its appeal will come with peculiar force."[9] When a division arose in the ranks of the abolitionists, and the anti-Garrisonians had organized, Garrison issued an appeal addressed to "My Colored Brethren." He said, "Stand by me now, as you have hitherto done and we will soon scatter to the winds this lofty but fragile fabric of persecution, pride and cowardice."[10]

In response to the appeal for financial assistance, Henry Williams, an untutored Negro of New York, sent a request for aid to prominent Negro citizens of the District of Columbia, "in behalf of the committee to assist us (the coloured citizens of N.Y.), in the great and noble undertaking to save *our paper, The Liberator,* which is under a great embarrassment at this time."[11] The conclusion is inevitable that without the assistance of the free Negro population in the eastern urban centers, *The Liberator* would have been greatly reduced in its income and support.

A second step in the organization of immediate abolition was the formation of an anti-slavery society. After several unsuccessful meetings, finally on January 1, 1832, at a meeting in the schoolroom of the African Baptist Church in the Negro section of Boston, the New England Anti-Slavery Society was organized. An address was later published espousing the doctrine of immediate abolition, signed by seventy-two persons, about one-fourth of whom were Negroes.[12]

During the same year the New England Anti-Slavery Society adopted a resolution at its annual meeting inviting the Negroes "to form auxiliaries to this society."[13] This invitation was undoubtedly due to the fact that Negroes had already held three annual conventions, in 1830, 1831 and 1832 in Philadelphia, and these showed that Negroes had considerable power of organization.[14] These conventions were called by Negroes and conducted by them, although they were visited and addressed by Garrison, Lundy, Jocelyn, Tappan and other friends of the Negro people. The publication in New York City of *Freedom's Journal* in 1827, first Negro newspaper, and the distribution in 1828 of the incendiary pamphlet by David Walker of Boston, *Walker's Appeal,* were also indications of Negro militant attitudes prior to the rise of Garrisonian Abolition. It is significant that leading participants in these movements among Negroes were also organizers and supporters of the movement for the immediate abolition of slavery.

The first Negro association to take advantage of the invitation by the New England Anti-Slavery Society was the Massachusetts General Colored Association. A chief objective of this association was the abolition of slavery. A communication was sent by the association to the New England Anti-Slavery Society, which expressed approval of the objects of this Society and the desire to become an auxiliary to it. This association was accepted as an auxiliary organization.[15]

The mission of Garrison to England was encouraged and financed partly by donations from the free Negro population. On October 16, 1832, Joseph Cassey of Philadelphia, a Negro manufacturer of wigs and other decorations and also an agent for *The Liberator,* wrote a letter to Isaac Knapp, Garrison's associate, in response to a suggestion from Knapp, stating that Garrison was "a suitable person" for the mission of securing aid in England for the manual labor school for Negroes and of attacking the program of the Colonization Society. He agreed to send the letter without intimating that the suggestion had originated with Knapp.[16] Garrison secured the approval of the New England Anti-Slavery Society but he was without funds for such a journey and an appeal was issued to the "Friends of Emancipation."[17]

As a result of Garrison's appeal, contributions began to be sent in immediately and among them were funds from Negroes. Meetings were held for this purpose in Boston, Philadelphia, New York, Albany, Providence, Newark, and Brooklyn.[18] It was announced that about one-half of the amount collected, which was $624.50, was contributed by Negroes.[19] They were interested in his trip and also showed their esteem for him by giving him several presents. Notable among the organizations contributing gifts were the Colored Female Religious and Moral Society of Salem, the Juvenile Garrison Independent Society of Boston, the Mutual Relief Society, the Colored Female Literary Society and the Colored Female Tract Society, all of Providence.[20] Towards the expenses of his return trip, Garrison was loaned $200 by Nathaniel Paul, Negro clergyman, then in England for the purpose of raising funds to assist the Wilberforce Colony in Canada. Garrison acknowledged this loan and endeavored to repay it by a draft on Arthur Tappan. It is not clear that the loan was ever repaid.[21] Continuing this support, the Garrison Colored Society of

Boston in 1833 sent thirty dollars to the New England Anti-Slavery Society as a payment for life membership for Messrs. Garrison and Knapp.[22]

Numerous meetings of free Negroes were held between 1832 and 1834 and anti-slavery organizations were started by them. These meetings adopted resolutions against slavery and African colonization. Resolutions were reported from meetings in New York City, Rochester, Boston, Nantucket, New Bedford, Salem, Baltimore, Washington, D.C., Brooklyn, Middletown, New Haven, Lynn, Philadelphia, Columbia, Lewistown, Pittsburgh, Harrisburg, Wilmington, Providence, Trenton and other cities.[23]

While these organizations among Negroes were beginning their work, a New York committee, with Arthur Tappan as the leading spirit, was planning the formation of a national anti-slavery society. They launched a weekly paper, *The Emancipator*, which began publication in May, 1833. Negroes were interested in its publication and gave it their support. Negro agents were selected for it. These agents were David Ruggles of New York City, who was the general agent; John D. Closson, Newark, New Jersey; Thomas Van Rensslear, Princeton, New Jersey; Abraham D. Shadd and John Carlisle of Pennsylvania.[24] David Ruggles, who was a bookseller and publisher, advertised for additional agents to distribute anti-slavery papers.[25]

Meetings were held for the purpose of arousing interest in anti-slavery papers. One of these meetings was held in New York City, July 17, 1831. It was resolved to increase subscribers for *The Liberator* and *The Genius of Universal Emancipation*.[26] Another assembled in Philadelphia in June, 1833. It was held for the purpose "of encouraging and extending the patronage of *The Emancipator.*" David Ruggles and others addressed this meeting. Resolutions were adopted expressing approval of the paper and subscriptions were received for both *The Emancipator* and *The Liberator*.[27]

The result of subscriptions to these papers was an increased interest by Negroes in the approaching convention to form a national anti-slavery society. The meeting of the proposed society, the American Anti-Slavery Society, was held in Adelphi Hall, Philadelphia, December 4, 5 and 6, 1833. The following Negroes were among the delegates from the anti-slavery societies: James G. Barbadoes, of Massachusetts; James McCrummell, Robert Purvis, James Forten, John B. Vashon and Abraham D. Shadd, of Pennsylvania; and Peter Williams of New York. Among the sixty-two signers of the Declaration of Sentiments were the three Negro delegates, James G. Barbadoes, Robert Purvis and James McCrummell and the Declaration was prepared at the home of McCrummell.[28] The Board of Managers included James G. Barbadoes, Peter Williams, Robert Purvis, James McCrummell, John B. Vashon and Abraham Shadd. These men were capable persons and possessed talents readily discernible. For instance, Robert Purvis who was placed on a committee to nominate officers for the Society, was said to be a man of some means, of rare gifts as a speaker and of public spirit. He once served as a presiding officer of the American Anti-Slavery Society.[29]

Following the first meeting of the American Anti-Slavery Society the formation of anti-slavery societies by Negroes continued. One at Rochester, New York, was organized in January 1834,[30] and another at Newark, New Jersey, the Colored Anti-Slavery Society, was established in May, 1834.[31] Still another society, organized in this year, was the Colored Female Anti-Slavery Society of Middletown, Connecticut. It was organized on April 2, 1834, both as an anti-slavery society and for "mutual improvement and increased intellectual and moral happiness."[32]

This, however, was not the first colored female society. One of the earliest was organized in November, 1831, in Philadelphia, and between this date and 1834, others were organized in Providence, Rhode Island, Nantucket and Salem, Massachusetts, and Rochester, New York.[33]

It is evident that Negro women as well as men joined with the movement for the organization of abolition. Susan Paul of Boston became a life member of the Massachusetts Anti-Slavery Society in 1835 and was counsellor of the Boston Female Anti-Slavery Society. Sarah Douglass was one of the central committee of the Anti-Slavery Women of New York, assembled in convention at New York in May, 1837. The published appeal of this committee contained a poem by Sarah Forten.[34]

There was anti-slavery sentiment among the Negroes of Western Pennsylvania and Ohio. The racial situation in Ohio, resulting from the presence of pro-slavery sympathizers and its location near the scene of slavery, did not favor the active participation of Negroes in these organized efforts.[35] There was also opposition which expressed itself in riots and disturbances in New York, Philadelphia and other places in the East, but the Negroes there seemed undaunted by these and continued their activity in abolition.[36]

Even some so-called friends of the cause seemed to oppose the participation by Negroes in abolition organizations in the East. Garrison criticized William Ellery Channing because he expressed the belief that "we ought never to have permitted our colored brethren to unite with us in our associations."[37] In reply to this type of criticism, a resolution was adopted by the Massachusetts Anti-Slavery Society at its meeting on January 20, 1836, stating that the Anti-Slavery cause was "the cause of Philanthropy, with regard to which all human beings, white men and colored men, citizens and foreigners, men and women, have the same duties and the same rights."[38]

In New England and the eastern middle states the active participation of Negroes in abolition was a regular part of the convention activities in these sections. The New England Anti-Slavery Society met in Boston, May 27–29, 1834. The committee of arrangements included James G. Barbadoes of Boston. Other colored members of the convention were Joshua Easton and John T. Hilton. Barbadoes seconded the motion that the interests of the anti-slavery cause "demand that special efforts be made to multiply the subscribers to *The Liberator.*" Barbadoes also made a motion that "Messrs. Garrison and Knapp deserve the gratitude of the colored people and their friends, for their persevering exertions in pleading the cause of the oppressed." John T. Hilton moved that "having put our hands to the plow of liberty we give our sacred pledge never to look back, until every root and branch of the noxious principle of slavery shall be exterminated from the American soil."[39] The adjourned meeting of this society on October 9 of this year was addressed by John T. Hilton and Joshua Easton, among other speakers.[40]

The meeting of the American Anti-Slavery Society on May 6, 1834, placed several Negro delegates on its Board of Managers. They were James G. Barbadoes of Massachusetts; Theodore S. Wright, Christopher Rush, Peter Williams and Samuel E. Cornish of New York; Robert Purvis, Joseph Cassey, James McCrummell, John B. Vashon and Abraham D. Shadd of Pennsylvania. Cornish, Williams and Wright were elected to the Executive Committee of twelve members with Arthur Tappan as chairman. James Forten was named as one of the vice-presidents of the society. This society adopted a motion which attracted the support of Negroes. With its declarations against slavery, an invitation was also extended to Negroes "to a participation with us in all those happy and elevating institutions which are open to others."[41]

Negroes were now well represented in conventions. At the second annual meeting of the American Anti-Slavery Society in New York, May 12, 1835, Negroes were listed in the membership of the convention. Theodore S. Wright, Samuel Cornish, Christopher Rush and Peter Williams were from New York; Abraham Shadd, James Forten, Robert Purvis, John B. Vashon, James McCrummell were from Pennsylvania, and James G. Barbadoes was from Boston, Massachusetts. The address of the Executive Committee of ten delegates again included the names of Wright and Cornish and an address was issued signed by these members. Among the five names selected as delegates to the New England Anti-Slavery Convention was the name of Theodore S. Wright.[42] David Ruggles attended the meeting of the New York Anti-Slavery Convention at Utica, October 21, 1835.[43]

While continuing this type of cooperation Negroes were conducting their own societies. The Negro Anti-Slavery Societies active at this time included the following: Lexington (Ohio), Colored Anti-Slavery Society, Job Pears, President, Jonas Crosby, Secretary; Middletown (Connecticut), Colored Female Anti-Slavery Society, Mrs. Nancy Beman, President, Mrs. C. M. Beman, Secretary; Nantucket (Massachusetts), Colored Anti-Slavery Society, William Harris, President, Edward J. Pompey, Secretary; Newark (New Jersey), Colored Anti-Slavery Society, Henry Drayton, President, A. B. Ray, Secretary; Newark (New Jersey), Juvenile Anti-Slavery Society and Rochester (New York), Colored Female Anti-Slavery Society, (officers not reported); The Albany (New York) Colored Anti-Slavery Society, Nathaniel Paul, President, John C. Stewart, Secretary.[44] The New York Committee of Vigilance, organized in 1835 to aid fugitive slaves, was another militant Negro organization in opposition to slavery.[45] This is a small list of societies among the hundreds of other societies, but it is significant that Negroes had any such organizations in this period of their subjection as slaves and proscription as free men.

On the contrary, there were Negroes who were aware of abolition organizations but did not participate in their activities. These persons were criticized by more aggressive Negroes. An instance of this kind occurred in Boston, July 22, 1834, when a meeting of Negroes adopted a resolution, stating that they regarded "all persons of color who were not anti-slavery men in principles and practice as the greatest enemies of our cause, our elevation and our happiness."[46]

The anti-slavery societies of New York, Pennsylvania and New England had Negro representatives in their work during this period. Negro delegates attended the meeting of the New York Anti-Slavery Society at Utica, New York, on October 19, 1836. Among these delegates were Theodore S. Wright, Henry Highland Garnet and William Johnston.[47] A circular addressed "To the Friends of Immediate Emancipation in the State of New York" was signed, among others, by Cornish and Wright.[48] Similar activities were carried on by the Negroes of Pennsylvania when a circular was issued by the State Society "to the Friends of Immediate Emancipation in the State of Pennsylvania." This circular was signed by twelve Negroes.[49] The Ladies Anti-Slavery Society of Philadelphia was addressed by James Forten, Jr. on April 14, 1836. This address was later printed.[50] Theodore S. Wright urged the members of the New England Anti-Slavery Society, meeting May 24–26, 1836, to speak out for those of his race whose minds and bodies were in chains and who had "no power to speak for themselves."[51]

At the third annual meeting of the American Anti-Slavery Society on May 10, 1836, the Board of Managers included James Forten, Robert Purvis, Joseph Cassey, James M. McCrummell, John S. Vashon, Abraham D. Shadd of Pennsylvania and Samuel E. Cornish and Theodore S. Wright of New York. Robert Purvis presented a resolution commending the results of the experiment in the West Indian Islands in which the system of apprenticeship was rejected and asserting that these results were proof of the salutary effects of emancipation. Theodore S. Wright led in the proposal of a motion requesting the auxiliary societies to appoint committees to plan the introduction of the colored people to useful arts, especially those who were desirous of learning the arts and becoming regular apprentices.[52] Wright was appointed one of the eight delegates to the New York Anti-Slavery Society. He also served as traveling agent for the Society. Cornish and Wright were again on the Executive Committee of twelve of the American Anti-Slavery Society. An appeal "To the People of the United States" was issued by this committee, signed also by Cornish and Wright.[53]

By the year 1837,[54] Negro participation and activity were well recognized facts in abolition organization, and it was not unusual for several Negroes to be present at conventions. The appointment of agents to work among the Negroes was said to be creating "a new impulse" to the movements already in operation in this year.[55]

When the Fourth Annual Meeting of the American Anti-Slavery Society was held in New York on May 9, 1837, Negro representatives were again present. Cornish and Wright were re-elected to places on the Executive Committee. An address was delivered at this meeting by Rev. Charles Gardner of Philadelphia, a Negro Presbyterian pastor. The sentiments of his speech revealed the attitude of the Negro abolitionist. He presented and supported the motion that "sufficient evidence had been given to the world to convince the enlightened public that the immediate emancipation of colored people is morally right and politically safe." He defended this statement by references to the achievements of the colored people. He said that in Philadelphia alone there were at least fourteen congregations of colored people owning several churches worth between twenty-five and fifty thousand dollars. He cited the fact that these Negroes were educating and elevating themselves morally and mentally and that there were several "pay schools" maintained by the colored people and at least sixty beneficial societies. He praised the activities of the colored people for their demonstrations against slavery and colonization, and declared that when Garrison was "a mere child," Negroes had assembled in different parts of the United States "to wage a combat against removal to another country." This address was declared by an observer to be "the most eloquent" of the convention.[56]

The state and local anti-slavery conventions in this year had their Negro participants. The sessions of the Fourth New England Anti-Slavery Convention in Boston in 1837 were attended and addressed by several Negroes. The same activities by Negroes were manifested at the annual meetings in 1837 of the Massachusetts Anti-Slavery Society, the New England Anti-Slavery Society, the New York Anti-Slavery Society and the Pennsylvania Anti-Slavery Society. At the second annual meeting of the Ohio Anti-Slavery Society, M. M. Clark, a Negro, presented a report on the condition of the Negro in Ohio. This resulted in the adoption of resolutions concerning the improvement of the Negro's status in Ohio.[57] The United Anti-Slavery Society meeting in New York, with Thomas Van Rensslaer presiding, appointed five Negro delegates to the Fourth Anniversary meeting of the American Anti-Slavery Society.[58]

Free Negroes were thus associated with the organizers of immediate abolition. They had organized themselves both with and without the invitation or persuasion of white friends. Northern abolitionists have been characterized within recent periods as individuals who not only placed the South upon the defensive but also as those who aroused Negroes, who were satisfied with their condition.[59] This opinion has been due largely to the belief in the South that Northern whites, through their speeches and writings, were responsible for the insurrections and desires for freedom by Negroes.[60] This view has some historical truth in it. But it seems never to have occurred to persons of this opinion, so far as their writings reveal, that Negroes might desire and seek, as have other human beings, freedom for and of themselves.

The comprehensive and definitive treatment of the history of abolition requires attention to its origins and support by Negroes. The neglect of these facts will continue to produce a narrow and biased treatment of this important movement in our history. For historical records reveal that representative Negroes were active with other Americans, as organizers, supporters and participants, both on the local and national scenes where anti-slavery organization was being undertaken. Their efforts gathered momentum in the succeeding decades after 1837 and outstanding individuals among them, Frederick Douglass, William Wells Brown, Samuel R.

Ward, Sojourner Truth and others, became well-known lecturers and agents in the rising tide of freedom.

Notes

[1] *The Liberator*, Vol. I, No. 1, January 1, 1831, p. 3; vol. V, No. 1, January 3, 1835; *Proceedings of the Fourth New England Anti-Slavery Convention held in Boston May 30, 31 and June 1 and 2, 1837.* Boston, 1837, pp. 48–49. For a brief discussion of the number of subscribers to *The Liberator*, see Gilbert Hobbs Barnes, *The Anti-Slavery Impulse*, New York, 1933, pp. 50–51.

[2] *James Forten to William Lloyd Garrison*, December 31, 1830 (mss). William Lloyd Garrison, 1805–1879, *The Story of His Life told by His Children*, Vol. I, p. 223; For a sketch of Forten's life, see William C. Nell, *The Colored Patriots of the American Revolution, with sketches of several colored persons.* Boston, 1855, pp. 166–181. (Garrison Papers, Boston Public Library).

[3] *Forten to Garrison*, February 2, 1831 (mss). Garrison Papers, Boston Public Library.

[4] William Lloyd Garrison, 1805–1879, *The Story of His Life told by His Children.* Vol. I, p. 433 n. New York, 1885–1889.

[5] *Garrison to Vashon*, December 2, 1832 (mss). Concerning Vashon, see Nell, *op. cit.*, pp. 181–188. Garrison Papers, Boston Public Library.

[6] *Forten to Garrison*, March 31, 1831 (mss). Garrison Papers, Boston Public Library.

[7] *The Liberator*, Vol. I, No. 11, March 12, 1831, p. 43.

[8] *Ibid.*, Vol. I, No. 29, July 16, 1831, p. 115; No. 30, July 31, 1831, p. 117; No. 36, September 3, 1831, p. 143. These actions were due in part to Garrison's addresses to the colored people interpreting his purposes. See Garrison, *An Address delivered before the Free People of Color in Philadelphia, New York and other cities during the month of June, 1831.* Boston, 1831.

[9] Garrison and Knapp, *Shall the Liberator Die?* (A Circular. Boston, 1834).

[10] *The Liberator*, Vol. V, No. 6, February 7, 1835, p. 23.

[11] *Henry Williams to Mr. F. Datcher, J. F. Cook, A. Price, D. Carroll, A. Waring and others.* New York, June 23, 1834 (mss). The original of this letter is in the possession of Professor J. Welford Holmes, Winston-Salem Teachers College, Winston-Salem, N.C.

[12] William Lloyd Garrison, *Boston Anti-Slavery Days.* A paper read to the Bostonian Society Council Chamber, Old State House, May 10, 1905, p. 86; *William Lloyd Garrison, 1805–1879, The Story of His Life told by His Children*, Vol. I, p. 282; *The Liberator*, Vol. V, No. 1, January 3, 1835, p. 3.

[13] *The Constitution of the New England Anti-Slavery Society*, with an *Address to the Public*, Boston, 1832, p. 6.

[14] "First Colored Convention." *The Anglo-African Magazine*, Vol. I, No. 10, October, 1859, pp. 305–310; *Minutes of the First Annual Convention of the People of Color.* Philadelphia, 1831; *Minutes and Proceedings of the Second Annual Convention for the Improvement of the Free People of Color in the United States. Held by adjournments in the City of Philadelphia, from the 4th to the 13th of June, inclusive, 1832.* Philadelphia, 1832.

[15] The communication was signed by Thomas Dalton, president; William C. Nell, vice-president, and James C. Barbadoes, secretary. *First Annual Report of the Board of Managers of the New England Anti-Slavery Society, presented January 9, 1833.* Boston, 1833, p. 7; *The Abolitionist*, Vol. I, No. 2, February, 1833, p. 20; *The Liberator*, Vol. I, No. 22, May 28, 1831, p. 87.

[16] *Joseph Cassey to Isaac Knapp.* October 16, 1832, (mss); *Second Annual Report of the*

Board of Managers of the New England Anti-Slavery Society presented January 15, 1834. Boston, 1834, p. 10. Garrison Papers, Boston Public Library.

[17] *The Liberator.* Vol. III, No. 10, March 9, 1833, p. 39; *ibid.,* No. 11, March 16, 1833, p. 43.

[18] *Ibid.,* Vol. III, No. 12, March 23, 1833, p. 47; No. 15, April 13, 1833, p. 59; No. 19, May 11, 1833, p. 74; No. 21, May 25, 1833, p. 83. William Lloyd Garrison, *Address on the Progress of the Abolition Cause, delivered to African Abolition Freehold Society of Boston, July 16, 1832.* New York, 1832; *Genius of Universal Emancipation,* Vol. III, No. 6, Third Series, April, 1833, p. 82.

[19] *The Liberator,* Vol. III, No. 22, June 1, 1833, p. 86. The largest amounts reported were received from Negroes. Negroes in Philadelphia through Joseph Cassey sent $100; from New York they sent $124; from Providence, $80 and from Boston $25. *The Abolitionist,* Vol. I, No. 6, June, 1833, p. 96.

[20] *The Liberator,* Vol. III, No. 10, March 9, 1833, P. 39. In the Boston Public Library there is a silver medal presented to Garrison on his departure for England by the Juvenile Garrison Independent Society, an organization of Negro children. Tappan Collection, Manuscript Division, Library of Congress.

[21] *Garrison to Lewis Tappan,* Brooklyn, December 17, 1835; February 29, 1836 (mss); Austin Steward, *Twenty-two Years a Slave — Forty Years a Freeman.* Rochester, 1861, p. 341, quoting a letter of Garrison denying the loan, dated Boston, June, 1865.

[22] *The Abolitionist,* Vol. I, No. 12, December, 1833, p. 192.

[23] *First Annual Report of the Board of Managers of the New England Anti-Slavery Society.* Presented January 9, 1833, Boston, 1833, pp. 36–40; *The Liberator,* Vol. II, III and IV, *passim; The Emancipator and Journal of Public Morals,* Vol. II, No. 21, May 27, 1834.

[24] *The Emancipator,* Vol. I, No. 6, June 8, 1833, p. 21.

[25] *Ibid.,* Vol. II, No. 32, August 12, 1834; Vol. 2, No. 19, May 13, 1834. For experiences of an agent see Amos Dresser, *The Narrative of Amos Dresser.* New York, 1836; *Human Rights,* Vol. I, No. 4, October, 1835; *The Emancipator and Journal of Public Morals,* Vol. II, No. 21, May 17, 1834.

[26] *The Liberator,* Vol. I, No. 34, August 20, 1831, p. 133. Subscriptions by Negroes were noted for other publications of the American Anti-Slavery Society and among these were *Human Rights, The Anti-Slavery Record, The Slave's Friend,* and *The Quarterly Anti-Slavery Magazine.*

[27] *The Emancipator,* Vol. I, No. 11, July 13, 1833, p. 43; Vol. I, No. 19, September 7, 1833, p. 75; *The Abolitionist,* Vol. I, No. 6, June, 1833, p. 96.

[28] *The Abolitionist,* Vol. I, No. 12, December, 1833, pp. 177–184; *Declaration of Sentiments and the Constitution of the American Anti-Slavery Society.* Philadelphia, 1833; *The Liberator,* Vol. III, No. 50, December 14, 1833, p. 198; *The Emancipator,* Vol. I, No. 33, December 14, 1833, p. 130.

[29] *The Abolitionist* states in a footnote to the report of the convention that Mr. Purvis was "a colored gentleman of Philadelphia, whose talents and gentlemanly deportment have won the esteem of all who know him." Vol. I, No. 12, December, 1833, p. 183 n. He was said to have been well educated and an owner of considerable property; William Wells Brown, *Rising Son,* Boston, 1874, p. 469; W. C. Nell, *Colored Patriots of the American Revolution, with Sketches of Several Distinguished Colored Persons.* Boston, 1855, p. 347; Samuel J. May, *Some Recollections of our Anti-Slavery Conflict.* Boston, 1869, pp. 288–289.

[30] *The Liberator,* Vol. IV, No. 2, January 11, 1839, p. 6. Garrison Papers, Boston Public Library.

[31] *The Emancipator and Journal of Public Morals.* Vol. II, No. 21, May 27, 1834.

[32] *The Emancipator and Journal of Public Morals.* Vol. II, No. 15, April 15, 1834.

[33] *James Forten to William Lloyd Garrison.* July 28, 1832 (mss); *The Liberator,* Vol. II, No. 46, November 17, 1832, p. 183; Vol. IV, No. 10, March 8, 1834, pp. 37, 38.

[34] W. C. Nell, *Colored Patriots of the American Revolution, with sketches of Distinguished*

Colored People. Boston, 1855, pp. 346–347, 351; *Annual Report of the Boston Female Anti-Slavery Society,* 1836, p. 84; *Third Annual Report of the Board of Managers of the New England Anti-Slavery Society presented January* 21, 1835, Boston, 1835, p. 22.

³⁵ When a colored man was invited to participate in an anti-slavery meeting in Ohio, some of the colored people told Theodore Weld that they thought that it was best for him not to sit in the convention as it might bring reprisals upon them. Weld was of the opinion, nevertheless, that "to make a distinction between a white man and a black man on account of their color in organization is the very principle of slavery." An effort was made by anti-abolitionists, in Cincinnati, Ohio, to show that Negroes were not sympathetic with the abolition program. It was reported that the Cincinnati Union Society of colored persons had adopted resolutions disclaiming all connection with the abolitionists and calling upon James G. Birney and his associates to cease their efforts in their behalf. It was declared that the publication of abolition papers tended to incite "angry feelings" and "personal violence." Thirty-five names were signed to these resolutions. A few days later a disclaimer, signed by twenty-eight of these persons, appeared in the *Cincinnati Gazette.* This statement declared that their names were used without their knowledge or consent. Advantage had been taken of the Negroes so that it might appear that they were opposed to the purposes of the abolitionists and were contented with their condition. Gilbert H. Barnes and Dwight L. Drummond, *Letters of Theodore Weld, Angelina Grimke Weld and Sarah Grimke, 1822–1844,* Vol. I, p. 274; *Narrative of the Late Riotous Proceedings Against the Liberty of the Press in Cincinnati: Address to the People of Ohio by the Executive Committee of the Ohio Anti-Slavery Society.* Cincinnati, 1836, pp. 44–45. Tappan Collection, Manuscript Division, Library of Congress.

³⁶ *The Liberator,* Vol. V, No. 33, August 15, 1835, p. 131; Samuel R. Ward, *Autobiography of a Fugitive Slave,* London, 1855, p. 46.

³⁷ Garrison to Lewis Tappan, December 17, 1835 (mss). Instances of such opposition are not difficult to find. See Elizabeth Buffum Chase, *Anti-Slavery Reminiscences,* Central Fall, R.I., 1891, pp. 16–17.

³⁸ This resolution was sponsored by Professor Charles Follen of Harvard University. In reporting this resolution he said, "We have been advised if we really wished to benefit the slave and the colored race generally, not unnecessarily to shock the feelings, though they were but prejudices, of the white people by admitting colored persons to our anti-slavery meetings and societies." In the following year, another evidence of this attitude was manifested when the Anti-Slavery Women of New York in their convention were reported to have declared that "Those societies that reject colored members, or seek to avoid them, have never been active or efficient." W. C. Nell, *op. cit.,* p. 350; *Fourth Annual Report of the Board of Managers of the Massachusetts Anti-Slavery Society, January* 20, 1836, Boston, 1836, p. 49; W. C. Nell, *op. cit.,* p. 351; *The Liberator,* Vol. VI, No. 4, January 23, 1836, p. 15.

³⁹ *Proceedings of the New England Anti-Slavery Convention held in Boston on the 27th, 28th and 29th of May,* 1834. Boston, 1834, pp. 3, 5, 8, 13, 14, 18.

⁴⁰ *The Liberator,* Vol. IV, No. 41, October 11, 1834, p. 163.

⁴¹ *First Annual Report of the American Anti-Slavery Society . . . ,* May 6, 1834, New York, 1834. pp. 15, 34, 35, 36, 47, 61.

⁴² *Second Annual Report of the American Anti-Slavery Society, with the Speeches Delivered at the Anniversary Meeting, held in the City of New York, on the 12th May,* 1835, *and the Minutes of the Meetings of the Society for Business.* New York, 1835. pp. 23, 25, 26, 27; *The Liberator,* Vol. V, No. 22, May 30, 1835, p. 87; *The Emancipator — Extra,* June 16th, 1835.

⁴³ *Proceedings of the New York Anti-Slavery Convention held at Utica, October* 21, 1835, *etc., Utica,* 1835, p. 45.

⁴⁴ *Second Annual Report of the American Anti-Slavery Society,* 1835, *op. cit.,* pp. 83–86; *The Liberator,* Vol. V, No. 1, January 3, 1835, p. 3; *Human Rights,* Vol. I, No. 11, May, 1836.

⁴⁵ *First Annual Report of the New York Committee of Vigilance, for the year* 1837, *together with Important Facts Relative to their Proceedings.* New York, 1837.

⁴⁶ *The Emancipator and Journal of Public Morals.* Vol. II, No. 32, August 12, 1834.

[47] *Proceedings of the First Annual Meeting of the New York State Anti-Slavery Society, convened at Utica, October* 19, 1836. *Utica,* 1836.

[48] *Human Rights.* Vol. I, No. 4, October, 1835.

[49] *The Liberator.* Vol. VI, No. 45, November 5, 1836, p. 179. Tappan Collection, Manuscript Division, Library of Congress.

[50] James Forten, Jr., *An Address Delivered before the Ladies Anti-Slavery Society of Philadelphia on the Evening of the 14th of April,* 1836. Philadelphia, 1836. Copy in possession of Dr. Luther Jackson, Virginia State College.

[51] *Proceedings of the New England Anti-Slavery Society Convention held in Boston, May* 24, 25, 26, 1836. Boston, 1838, pp. 20–21. Wright spoke on two other occasions during this convention, pp. 48, 55.

[52] *Third Annual Report of the American Anti-Slavery Society, with the Speeches Delivered at the Anniversary Meeting, held in the City of New York, on the 10th May,* 1836, *and the Minutes of the Meetings of the Society for Business.* New York, 1836. pp. 22, 23, 25, 27. This idea of introducing Negroes to the useful arts had been considered earlier in correspondence between James G. Birney and Lewis Tappan. Birney had written, "Our members are now so great and our occupations so various that it can be easily effective if we have but the disposition to effect it." *James G. Birney to Lewis Tappan,* March 17, 1836. (mss); *The Emancipator,* Vol. I, No. 1, April 23, 1836, p. 3.

[53] To the People of the United States; or, To Such Americans as Value Their Rights, and Dare to Maintain Them in Behalf of the American Anti-Slavery Society." New York, American Anti-Slavery Society, 1836. *The Anti-Slavery Examiner,* Vol. I, No. 1, August, 1836, p. 8; *The Colored American,* Vol. I, December 16, 1837.

[54] Garrison and Knapp announced in 1837 that they had served a "regular apprenticeship in the cause of liberty" and were then "prepared to advocate it upon a more extended scale." *The Liberator,* Vol. VII, No. 5, December 15, 1837, p. 203.

[55] *Proceedings of the Pennsylvania Convention Assembled to organize a State Anti-Slavery Society at Harrisburg on the 31st of January and the 1st and 2nd of February.* Philadelphia, 1837, p. 56.

[56] *The Liberator,* Vol. VII, No. 21, May 19, 1837, p. 82; June 2, 1837, p. 90; June 9, 1837, p. 95; *Fourth Annual Report of the American Anti-Slavery Society, with the Speeches Delivered at the Anniversary Meeting held in the City of New York on the 9th May,* 1837, *and the Minutes of the Meetings of the Society for Business.* New York, 1837. pp. 17, 18, 21, 28, 131; *Zion's Watchman,* Vol. 2, No. 79, July 8, 1837.

[57] *Proceedings of the Fourth New England Anti-Slavery Convention.* Boston, May 30, 31, and June 1 and 2, 1837. pp. 47, 48, 66–69; *Proceedings of the Massachusetts Anti-Slavery Society at its Fifth Annual Meeting,* January 25, 1837, p. XXXIX; *Proceedings of the Pennsylvania Convention, assembled to organize a State Anti-Slavery Society at Harrisburg,* January 31, February 1–3, Philadelphia, 1837, p. 56; *Report of the Second Anniversary of the Ohio Anti-Slavery Society held in Mount Pleasant, Jefferson County, Ohio, April* 27, 1837. Cincinnati, 1837; *The Liberator,* Vol. VII, No. 42, p. 165; *The Colored American,* Vol. I, October 4, 1837.

[58] *The Colored American,* Vol. I, April 29, 1837.

[59] For support of this view, see Arthur Young Lloyd, *The Slavery Controversy,* Chapel Hill, 1939, particularly Chapter II, "The Extreme Abolitionist Attack" and Chapter IV, "Southern Defense"; and Avery Craven, *The Repressible Conflict.* Louisiana State University Press, 1939.

[60] *The National Intelligencer,* September 15, 1831, quotes the *Tarborough Free Press* which stated that *The Liberator* was "published in Boston or Philadelphia by a white man, with the avowed purpose of inciting rebellion in the South." See also editorial in *The National Intelligencer,* September 30, 1831, entitled "Incendiary Publications." An example of this opinion in reference to other anti-slavery papers has been recently extracted from the files of the Clerk's Office at Norfolk, Virginia, by Dr. Luther P. Jackson of Virginia State College.

This citation is as follows: "Incendiary Papers: *Human Rights* and *The Emancipator,* papers published in the northern states have been forwarded to the Post Office addressed to free persons of color. Believing that papers of this character are calculated to stir up a spirit of disobedience and dissatisfaction among the free Negroes and slaves — court asks mayor to call on the Post Master and ask, in so far as he is authorized, to withhold the delivery of such or similar papers addressed to free Negroes and other colored persons." July 28, 1835. *Corporation Court, Norfolk, Virginia, Order Book* (*MS*) 31, p. 30 (Clerk's Office).

The Emancipation of the Negro Abolitionist

Leon F. Litwack

When William Lloyd Garrison launched his antislavery offensive, Negro aboli-tionists responded with warm enthusiasm. It "has roused up a Spirit in our Young People," one Negro leader wrote, "that had been slumbering for years."[1] En-couraged by this emergence of antislavery militancy among whites, Negroes helped to sustain *The Liberator*, joined the newly formed abolition societies, and cheered the announced intention of white abolitionists to establish a Negro industrial col-lege. It appeared to be an auspicious beginning of effective interracial cooperation for mutual goals. But the attempted coalition, though not unproductive, was to reveal to the abolitionists — white and black — fundamental differences in assump-tions, goals, and emphasis. "Thus, was the cause espoused," Negro leader Martin R. Delany wrote in 1852, "and thus did we expect much. But in all this, we were doomed to disappointment, sad, sad disappointment. Instead of realizing what we had hoped for, we find ourselves occupying the very same position in relation to our Anti-Slavery friends, as we do in relation to the proslavery part of the com-munity — a mere secondary, underling position." The time had come, he insisted, for Negroes to break the chains of this bondage.[2]

The Negro's initial enthusiasm was readily understandable. Several years of independent Negro agitation had produced few results. And now, in the wake of the Nat Turner insurrection, new racial tensions gripped large sections of the country, for not only the South but the North, too, was forced to consider the possible consequences of a disgruntled racial minority in its midst. Both sections embraced the prevailing image of the Negro as an inferior race, incapable of assum-ing any of the responsibilities of citizenship, but in the North the Negro could at least challenge this assumption and strive to improve his position. Thus Garrison's antislavery debut had come at an opportune moment. Subjected to incessant harass-ment and racist propaganda, the Negro found encouragement in the advent of a movement which forcefully challenged the colonizationists, the doctrine of racial inferiority, and any antislavery which did not include as an objective the elevation

From Leon Litwack, "The Emancipation of the Negro Abolitionist," in *The Antislavery Vanguard: New Essays on the Abolitionist,* ed. Martin Duberman, pp. 137–155. Copyright © 1965 by Princeton University Press; Princeton Paperback, 1968. Reprinted by permission of Princeton University Press.

of the free Negro — politically, socially, and economically. The publication of *The Liberator,* Garrison declared, had "operated like a trumpet-call" on the Northern Negro community. "They have risen in their hopes and feelings to the perfect stature of men: in this city, every one of them is as tall as a giant."[3]

Notwithstanding some opposition or misgivings, most of the white abolition societies admitted Negroes, and some elevated them to positions on the executive committee. The Negro's most important function, however, was that of an antislavery lecturer, for "eloquent" Negro speakers were able to draw "in most places far larger" audiences than their white counterparts. "The public have itching ears to hear a colored man speak," one abolitionist wrote to Garrison, "and particularly *a slave.* Multitudes will flock to hear one of this class speak."[4] Such was the response to Frederick Douglass, for example, that he soon became a leading abolitionist orator. The Negro who committed himself to the abolitionist cause incurred obvious risks. If the average white man expected anything of the Negro, it was that he acquiesce in the racial status quo and act the clownish, childish, carefree, irresponsible Uncle Tom that whites had long presumed him to be. But the Negro abolitionist betrayed the white man's trust and confidence; more than that, he confounded by his very example the white man's rationale for a benevolent guardianship over an inferior and helpless race. Rare, indeed, was the Negro abolitionist who did not have to face a hostile mob at some point in his antislavery career; it was the price he paid for having committed the most unpardonable sin of all — impudence.

In a society racked by racial tensions, misunderstanding and suspicion were almost bound to precipitate divisions between white and black abolitionists. Such questions as Negro membership in abolition societies and race mixing at antislavery functions, for example, provoked considerable debate among white abolitionists.[5] Many feared that a bold defiance of prevailing customs might endanger the eventual success of the antislavery cause. Outside of official gatherings, such intercourse also posed challenges to well-meaning white abolitionists. Sarah Forten, a Philadelphia Negro, recalled a white friend who told her that when walking with a Negro "the darker the night, the better Abolitionist was I." Nevertheless, she was willing to forgive such conduct on the ground that abolitionists were often forced to make "great sacrifices to public sentiment." Still, it was disconcerting. "Many, very many anxious to take up the cross," she lamented, "but how few are strong enough to bear it."[6] Less forgiving was the Rev. Theodore S. Wright, who entreated white abolitionists to "annihilate in their own bosoms the cord of caste. We must be consistent — recognize the colored man in every respect as a man and brother." And this must be applied, he said, to "the church, the stage, the steamboat, the public house, in all places."[7]

Equally annoying to Negroes was the patronizing attitude of some white abolitionists and the application of a double standard which strongly suggested the Negro's inherent inferiority. After exiling himself to England, along with his white wife, Negro abolitionist William G. Allen wrote to Garrison that the English had treated him warmly, in contrast to the "patronizing (and, of course, insulting) spirit, even of hundreds of the American abolitionists," who had always seemed so overly conscious of color differences.[8] More pointedly, however, some Negroes complained that white abolitionists tended to establish different standards by which to judge the respective abilities of the two races. Thus whites expected less of Negro students in the classroom, spoke exultantly of the academic work of Negroes which would have been barely passable if performed by whites, and willingly tolerated Negro ministers and teachers who fell far short of the qualifications of whites for the same positions. "Our white friends," commented a Negro newspaper, "are deceived when they imagine they are free from prejudice against color, and yet are content with a lower standard of attainments for colored youth, and inferior exhibitions of talent on the part of colored men. This is, in our view, the worst feature of abolitionism — the one which grieves us most. It is the highest rock of danger; the only one on which we fear a shipwreck of our high and holy cause."[9]

But that was not all. Of what use, asked Negroes, was the right to vote, attend school, and enter the homes of abolitionists if it was still impossible to gain access to any but the most menial employment. The economic condition of the Negro was at best deplorable, and the new waves of immigrants, competing for many positions which Negroes had long monopolized, only made matters worse. Although some white abolitionists had agitated vigorously in the areas of civil rights and educational opportunities, little had been done in the way of economic assistance, except to call upon Negroes to improve themselves. Perhaps this simply reflected the dominant middle-class ideology of self-help which affected abolitionists, like other whites, but Negroes found little encouragement in such a doctrine and appealed to the antislavery movement to meet this true test of its stated determination to elevate the free Negro.

That the Negro should have placed considerable emphasis on the economic question is understandable. To many Negroes, in fact, this was a key point if they were ever to achieve the respect of white society. The abolitionist, then, was called upon to render practical assistance. But when the *Colored American* reviewed the economic plight of the Negro in the wake of the Panic of 1837, it noted that not one local abolitionist had placed a Negro in any conspicuous position in his business establishment; in fact, it could not even find a Negro in the offices of the New York Anti-Slavery Society. The newspaper beseeched abolitionists to correct this grievous situation, and preferably not by passing a resolution at their next convention.[10] In the absence of any measurable progress along these lines, Negro delegates to an abolition convention in 1852 charged that the antislavery movement had failed in its responsibility. Proposals had been made to leading abolitionists to employ Negroes in their commercial establishments but the appeal had been largely in vain. True, one delegate conceded, Negroes had found employment in Arthur Tappan's department store, but, he added, only in a menial capacity. "Wherever the colored man is connected with the houses of these gentlemen, it is as the lowest drudges."[11]

In demanding economic assistance, the Negro denied any desire for preferential treatment; he simply wanted an equal opportunity to compete for respectable employment. And since many white abolitionists were in a position to make this possible, they were asked to give practical implementation to their antislavery professions. After all, one Negro leader argued, the struggle for equal rights cannot be won on "the bare ground of abstract principles"; abolitionists must strive not only to abolish chattel slavery but "that other kind of slavery" which doomed the free Negro to economic dependence and pauperism; indeed, he deplored the preoccupation of abolitionists with such reforms as capital punishment, temperance, and women's rights, while they refused in their own establishments to afford equal economic opportunities to depressed Negroes.[12] But such strictures yielded few concrete results, thus prompting a Negro convention delegate to charge that some of those who professed to be "the strongest abolitionists" have refused to grant Negroes anything but sympathy; they have persistently evaded a more practical application of their principles. True, some "might employ a colored boy as a porter or packer," but most abolitionists "would as soon put a hod-carrier to the clerk's desk as a colored boy, ever so well educated though he be."[13] It was left to Frederick Douglass to issue a more direct challenge to the abolitionists: "What boss anti-slavery mechanic will take a black boy into his wheelwright's shop, his blacksmith's shop, his joiner's shop, his cabinet shop? Here is something *practical;* where are the whites and where are the blacks that will respond to it?"[14] The response was difficult to discern. This "is not the song that anti-slavery sung," wrote the disillusioned Delany, "in the first love of the new faith, proclaimed by its disciples."[15]

Perhaps the Negro had been unrealistic in his expectations. By the late 1830's, at any rate, Negro leaders began to reassess their role in the antislavery movement; increasing factional quarrels among the whites made such a reappraisal all the more necessary. Although some Negro abolitionists, such as Robert Purvis and Charles Remond, remained loyal Garrisonians, a growing restlessness within the Negro abolitionist camp manifested itself in more frequent demands for ideological and political independence; moreover, as Negroes became more articulate themselves, they tended increasingly to voice their own aspirations and to question the white abolitionist's prerogative to speak for them. "As long as we let them think and act for us," the *Colored American* warned in 1839, "as long as we will bow to their opinions, and acknowledge that their word is counsel, and their will is law; so long they will outwardly treat us as men, while in their hearts they still hold us as slaves."[16]

Under the editorial supervision of Charles B. Ray and Philip A. Bell, the *Colored American* was the most prominent voice of this quest for independent expression. Published in New York, the newspaper first took to task the recently formed American Moral Reform Society, dominated largely by pro-Garrison Philadelphia Negroes, for its criticism of separate Negro conventions and the term "colored people," both of which allegedly implied degradation. To the *Colored American,* such positions not only were preposterous but they ignored the primary problems facing the Negro in a hostile society. "[W]hile these sages are frightened half to death, at the idea of being called colored, their FRIENDS and their FOES, in the convention, in the Assembly and in the Senate; through the pulpit and the press, call them nothing else but NEGROES, NEGROES, THE NEGROES OF PENNSYLVANIA."[17]

But the *Colored American* found even more distasteful the destructive factional warfare among abolitionists, for it threatened to undermine the antislavery effort. "The controversy," the newspaper asserted, "has . . . engrossed all their powers, and been prosecuted with a spirit wholly unworthy the character of the brethren engaged in it. . . . There is nothing to be gained by brother contending with brother."[18] That was heresy enough, in the eyes of some Garrisonians, but what followed must have confirmed their suspicions. Accepting political action as a legitimate antislavery weapon, the *Colored American* urged qualified Negroes to vote. When the Garrisonians then attacked the newspaper for abandoning the true faith (which deprecated political action), the editors affirmed their right to take an independent position. Notwithstanding the noble motives of most abolitionists, the *Colored American* insisted that they had no right to dictate antislavery doctrine to the Negro. "Sooner than abate one jot or tittle of our right to think, speak and act like men, we will suffer our enterprise to perish, and the *Colored American* will be numbered with the things that were."[19]

When the Garrisonian press claimed that separate Negro conventions perpetuated the idea of segregation, the *Colored American* and its supporters reaffirmed their defense of independent action. The multiplicity of wrongs inflicted on the Negro, Samuel Ward argued, made frequent meetings and independent organization indispensable; his white friends, he thought, would appreciate this need if they had "worn a colored skin from October '17 to June '40, as I have, in this pseudo-republic." Although conceding some valuable service by the white antislavery men, Ward was still dissatisfied, especially with those "abolitionists in *profession*" who had yet to conquer prejudice within themselves. "Too many," he regretted, ". . . best love the colored man at a distance."[20]

If there remained any doubts as to the determination of Negroes to voice their opinions, regardless of prevailing antislavery creeds, Henry Highland Garnet quickly dispelled them in 1843 when he told a national Negro convention that slaves would be justified in using violent means to win their freedom.[21] The convention refused by a single vote to endorse the address; nevertheless, the issue had been permanently raised and the narrow vote suggested a growing impatience among Negroes with the traditional reliance on moral force to conquer slavery. But the aftermath of this debate was in many ways even more revealing. Condemned by *The Liberator* for his militant appeal to the slaves and for his endorsement of the Liberty Party, Garnet accepted the challenge. "If it has come to this," he replied, "that I must think and act as you do, because you are an abolitionist, or be exterminated by your thunder, then I do not hesitate to say that your abolitionism is abject slavery."[22] Six years later, an Ohio Negro convention ordered the "gratuitous" circulation of Garnet's convention address;[23] and by this time Frederick Douglass, who had opposed Garnet at the convention, was on the verge of breaking with the Garrisonians and adding his considerable force and prestige to the cause of independent Negro expression and agitation.

The Douglass heresy, made public at the American Anti-Slavery Society convention of 1851, struck particular dismay into the Garrisonian camp, for he had been their principal Negro spokesman. The estrangement stemmed from Douglass' revised position on the dissolution of the Union, political action, nonresistance, and the nature of the Constitution. In each case, he broke with prevailing Garrisonian ideology. To seek the dissolution of the Union, he now argued, was to violate his duty as an abolitionist, for it left the slave helpless; to abstain from voting was to ignore "a legitimate and powerful means for abolishing slavery"; and to hold that the Constitution was a proslavery document was to distort both its letter and spirit.[24] The Garrisonians, Douglass charged, had abandoned the original purposes of the antislavery movement. "It started to free the slave," he contended. "It ends by leaving the slave to free himself. It started with the purpose to imbue the heart of the nation with sentiments favorable to the abolition of slavery, and ends by seeking to free the North from all responsibility of slavery." To Douglass, this was not practical antislavery; his alleged apostasy, he insisted, was not from "the Anti-Slavery Cause, for all know that I am as faithful to that cause as I ever was," but from "Garrisonism."[25]

Even before these ideological differences, there had been indications that Douglass was growing restive in the Garrisonian camp. When he first began to lecture, his white friends told him to confine his remarks to his experiences as a slave, for that was what the audiences wanted to hear. "Give us the facts," an abolitionist remarked to Douglass, "we will take care of the philosophy."[26] But Douglass soon found it impossible to confine himself in this way; indeed, his rapid intellectual development had already created some concern among his friends. "People won't believe you ever were a slave, Frederick, if you keep on this way," one abolitionist exclaimed, and another added, "Be yourself and tell your story. Better have a little of the plantation speech than not; it is not best that you seem too learned."[27]

When Douglass went to England in 1846 on a lecture tour, a Boston abolitionist, Mrs. Maria W. Chapman, expressed her concern to an English friend that Douglass might not be able to withstand the pressure of the anti-Garrison faction. Hearing of this letter, Douglass wrote Mrs. Chapman that "if you wish to drive me from the Anti-Slavery Society, put me under overseership and the work is done."[28] Three years earlier, Douglass had objected to abolitionist John Collins' injection of utopian socialism into antislavery meetings, for it imposed "an additional burden of unpopularity on our cause"; reprimanded by Mrs. Chapman for his remarks, Douglass later recalled that this "first offense against our antislavery Israel" had been "a strange and distressing revelation to me, and one of which I was not soon relieved."[29]

When the still restive Douglass decided to establish a newspaper in Rochester, despite the contrary advice of his Garrisonian friends, the subsequent break was almost assured, for he now had an independent means of expression. The newspaper project, Douglass contended, was no reflection on the quality of existing antislavery journals; the time had come, however, for Negroes to demonstrate their own capabilities, to produce their own authors, editors, and journals, and to be their "own representatives and advocates, not exclusively, but peculiarly — not distinct from, but in connection with our white friends."[30] But since independence also involved divergence in antislavery creed, it was insufferable to the Garrisonians. Before long, Garrison and Douglass were engaged in a vituperative editorial war, while other abolitionists looked on in dismay. To Douglass, it was ironic that the proved champions of human freedom — the Garrisonians — should presume to suppress dissent within their own movement. Apparently the only true faith was that proclaimed in Boston. "They talk down there," he wrote to Gerrit Smith, "just as if the Anti-Slavery Cause belonged to them — and as if all Anti-Slavery ideas originated with them and that no man has a right to 'peep or mutter' on the subject, who does not hold letters patent from them."[31] Such subordination was more than an ex-slave could accept.

Whatever the merits of the conflicting abolition doctrines, Douglass' actions, when combined with those of various state and national Negro conventions, dramatized the increasing demand of Negro abolitionists for a greater voice in the tactics, strategy, and creed of the movement. And this reflected not only conflict over doctrine but considerable dissatisfaction with the pace of the equal rights struggle in the North. Some Negroes questioned whether or not racial equality had been relegated to a position of secondary importance in the abolition crusade. "I have seen constitutions of abolition societies," one Negro leader charged, "where nothing was said about the improvement of the man of color! They have overlooked the great sin of prejudice. They have passed by this foul monster, which is at once the parent and offspring of slavery."[32] Pursuing this subject, the *Colored American* charged that the American Anti-Slavery Society had made "secondary and collateral what ought to have been the primary object of all their efforts. In their strong zeal and fiery indignation against slavery in the South, they half overlooked slavery in the North." Indeed, more is known of slavery in the Carolinas "than of the deep and damning thralldom which grinds to the dust, the colored inhabitants of New York."[33] On the eve of the election of 1860, Douglass noted with regret that the equal suffrage movement in New York was almost exclusively in the hands of Negroes, for neither abolitionists nor Republicans "seem to care much for it."[34] But these differences in emphasis were perhaps inevitable and never effectively reconciled; the black abolitionist was generally moved by compelling personal need, his white cohort acted more from the abstractions of conscience; for one, the primary problem was the Negro; for the other, the slave. Each sought, in his own way, to enlarge the area of freedom.

During the crucial decade of the 1850's, the Negro abolitionist grew ever more restive and impatient. The Fugitive Slave Act, the resurgence of the American

Colonization Society, the unsuccessful attempts to win equal suffrage, and, finally, the Dred Scott decision, impressed many Negroes with the increasing helplessness of their position in the face of the white man's apparent determination to maintain racial supremacy. Despite two decades of militant antislavery, the Negro's position seemed little improved. Moreover, the emergence of the Republican party made the very term "antislavery" difficult to define with any precision. If the Republican party was "antislavery," why did it refuse to move against racial oppression in the free states? and why in some areas did it proclaim principles of white supremacy? If the Kansas free staters were, indeed, "antislavery," how does one account for their determined efforts to keep all Negroes out of the territory? The answer was obvious: it was possible to be both "antislavery" and anti-Negro, to proclaim both free soil and white supremacy. "Opposing slavery and hating its victims," Douglass observed, "has come to be a very common form of abolitionism."[35] Disillusioned with Republican pronouncements, an Illinois Negro leader was moved to declare that he cared "nothing about that antislavery which wants to make the Territories free, while it is unwilling to extend to me, as a man, in the free States, all the rights of a man."[36] Of course, many white abolitionists had come to an identical conclusion about the "cowardly and contemptible" antislavery of the Republican party. When Stephen S. Foster accordingly called for a convention to reorganize the abolitionist movement, Douglass enthusiastically endorsed the proposal. Reviewing the history of the antislavery struggle, the Negro leader contrasted the heroic beginnings of militant abolitionism with the "Sentimental Abolitionism" of the Republican party, the "fratricidal conduct" of the American Anti-Slavery Society, and the political impotency of the Liberty party. If the "noble objects" of Foster's convention were put into effect, abolitionists — white and black — might once again unite into "one solid abolition organization" which would agitate for the exercise of Federal and State power to abolish the institution of slavery. Thus might the confusion between Republican antislavery and true abolitionism be ended.[37]

But in the absence of any such unified movement, the Negro abolitionist continued to advance an increasingly independent position. Tired of exhortations to be patient and await that "impartial and just God" who would inevitably rid the nation of slavery, Negroes began to talk of organized insubordination, slave insurrections, the use of physical force to resist the newly passed Fugitive Slave Act, the organization of state leagues to combat repressive legislation, and, in view of the Dred Scott decision, some even argued that Negroes no longer had any obligation to the United States and should welcome the overthrow of the government if necessary to exterminate slavery.[38] The vindication of the Negro's rights now seemed to demand a position more advanced than that of moral suasion. "Every slavehunter who meets a bloody death in his infernal business," Douglass wrote, "is an argument in favor of the manhood of our race."[39] Had not John Brown demonstrated, a Boston Negro leader asserted, that physical force might prove more effective than the "gradual diffusion of anti-slavery gospel." Although he hoped that slavery might be abolished peaceably, "if, as appears to be the case, there is no use in crying peace, then let us not shrink from the responsibility. My motto has always been, 'Better die freemen than live to be slaves.' "[40]

The espousal of increasingly radical measures mirrored the Negro's deepening sense of alienation from American society. The antislavery crusade had not altered the image of the Negro in the eyes of white America, nor measurably improved his position. "We are slaves in the midst of freedom," Delany wrote, "waiting patiently, and unconcernedly — indifferently, and stupidly, for masters to come and lay claim to us, trusting to their generosity, whether or not they will own us and carry us into endless bondage. . . . I must admit, that I have no hopes in this country — no confidence in the American people."[41] The movement which Delany advocated in the 1850's, that of emigration, began to attract more Negroes; it enunciated a vigorous race nationalism, rejected the democratic pretensions of white Americans, questioned the motives and effectiveness of white abolitionists, and urged the establishment of an independent Negro state. To remain any longer in the United States was to remain "the dupes of, and deluded by the whites, even our most professed anti-slavery friends." The Negro must find his own identity, apart from that of the whites. "The truth is," an emigration convention declared, "we are not identical with the Anglo-Saxon or any other race of the Caucasian or pure white type of the human family, and the sooner we know and acknowledge this truth, the better for ourselves and posterity."[42] Although most Negroes rejected emigration, they did so uneasily, for the logic of the argument seemed difficult to refute.

The emigrationists had challenged the assumption of most white and Negro abolitionists that racial equality was a realizable goal in the United States and that some day Negroes would attain the level of the white man's civilization. But some Negroes chose to question that level. Were white standards of success worthy models for the Negro? Did success in war and material gain, for example, truly constitute "the great ends of human existence"? Was there any other standard of excellence than that "which revolves around the almighty dollar"? In raising these questions, *The Anglo-African Magazine* regretted the fact that most Negroes wanted only to reach the level of the white man; the apparent ideal is "comfortable subsistance; with many, a comfortable room and bedroom, on the same floor, in a front building; with many, in addition, a handsome carpet, a few mahogany chairs, a sofa, and a piano." Most Negro men, it found, would be well satisfied with a "Morphy cap, one well-fitting suit of clothes, patent-leather boots of the latest fashion, an ingot or two of gold in the form of a chain hanging over their breast, a long nine and a sherry cobbler at the St. Charles." And the ideal for Negro women "reaches no higher than the polka and redowa, and agreeable flirting at a picnic." Such goals, the magazine argued, were unoriginal, "imitative and artificial." The Negro must seek a higher goal; despite his present degradation, he must "look up, above, and beyond the whites, and determine to whip, to beat, to excel them. . . . Once bent upon beating this Yankee Nation, who are beating all creation, and there will come upon us an inspiration, a power, hitherto unknown — hitherto unfelt by any other men, or race of men." The nature of this higher ideal was not indicated, except to suggest that it would not be money; economic changes, the magazine concluded, were already anticipating a day when "wealth will cease to be God of the American heart" and give way to some "nobler idolatry."[43]

On the eve of the Civil War, most Negroes aspired no higher than the goal of incorporation into white American society. Nevertheless, a strong undercurrent of race pride and consciousness, made explicit in the emigration movement, was clearly present, and white reformers would henceforth have to contend with its implications. Although the "wealth, the intellect, the Legislation (State and Federal), the pulpit, and the science of America" still tended to dismiss the Negro "as something less than a man," one Negro journal prophesied in 1859 that such arguments would become increasingly insupportable and that "this great black sluggard" may yet "shake the pillars of the commonweal."[44] In the meantime, the Negro had begun to produce his own spokesmen and media of expression; he had achieved increased recognition within the antislavery movement, and though he continued to express his appreciation of the efforts and sacrifices of white abolitionists, he made it clear that they were no longer to dominate the cause or confine its limits. The entire question of racial equality was at issue, not merely the elimination of chattel slavery. "The time is come," a Negro conference announced in 1854, "when our people must assume the rank of a first-rate power in the battle against caste and Slavery; it is emphatically our battle; no one else can fight it for us, and with God's help we must fight it ourselves. — Our relations to the Anti-Slavery movement must be and are changed. Instead of depending upon it we must lead it."[45]

Notes

[1] James Forten to William Lloyd Garrison, March 21, 1831, Garrison Papers, Boston Public Library.

[2] Martin R. Delany, *The Condition, Elevation, Emigration, and Destiny of the Colored People of the United States* (Philadelphia, 1852), p. 27.

[3] Garrison to Samuel Joseph May, February 14, 1831, Garrison Papers.

[4] Theodore Weld to Gerrit Smith, October 23 [1839], in Gilbert H. Barnes and Dwight L. Dumond, eds., *Letters of Theodore Dwight Weld, Angelina Grimké Weld and Sarah Grimké, 1822–1844* (2 vols., New York, 1934), II, 811; John A. Collins to Garrison, January 18, 1842, quoted in Philip S. Foner, *The Life and Writings of Frederick Douglass* (4 vols., New York, 1950–55), I, 46.

[5] See Leon F. Litwack, *North of Slavery: The Negro in the Free States, 1790–1860* (Chicago, 1961), pp. 216–22.

[6] Sarah Forten to Angelina Grimké, April 15, 1837, in Barnes and Dumond, eds., *Weld-Grimké Letters,* I, 380.

[7] *Address of the Rev. Theodore S. Wright before the Convention of the New York State Antislavery Society, . . . held at Utica, Sept. 20, 1837,* in Carter G. Woodson, ed., *Negro Orators and Their Orations* (Washington, D.C., 1925), p. 91.

[8] William G. Allen to Garrison, June 20, 1853, in *The Liberator*, July 22, 1853.

[9] *The Colored American*, November 4, 1837.

[10] *Ibid.*, July 28, 1838.

[11] *The* [12th] *Annual Report of the American and Foreign Anti-Slavery Society, presented at New York, May 11, 1852* (New York, 1852), pp. 29–30.

[12] Charles L. Reason, "The Colored People's 'Industrial College,' " in Julia Griffiths, ed., *Autographs for Freedom* (Second Series, Auburn, Rochester, 1854), pp. 12–15.

[13] *Frederick Douglass' Paper*, May 18, 1855.

[14] *Ibid.*, March 4, 1853.

[15] Delany, *The Condition, Elevation, Emigration, and Destiny of the Colored People*, p. 28.

[16] *Colored American*, October 5, 1839.

[17] *Ibid.*, August 26, September 2, 9, 1837; March 15, 1838.

[18] *Ibid.*, October 7, 1837.

[19] *Ibid.*, October 5, 1839.

[20] New York *National Anti-Slavery Standard*, July 2, 1840.

[21] Reprinted in Woodson, ed., *Negro Orators and Their Orations*, pp. 150–57.

[22] Henry Highland Garnet to Mrs. Maria W. Chapman, November 17, 1843, in Carter G. Woodson, ed., *The Mind of the Negro as Reflected in Letters Written During the Crisis, 1800–1860* (Washington, D.C., 1926), p. 194.

[23] *Minutes and Address of the State Convention of the Colored Citizens of Ohio, convened at Columbus, January 10th, 11th, 12th, and 13th, 1849* (Oberlin, 1849), p. 18.

[24] Frederick Douglass, *Life and Times of Frederick Douglass* (Boston, 1892), p. 322; see also Foner, *Life and Writings of Frederick Douglass*, II, 52–53, 149–50, 152–53, 155–57.

[25] Foner, *ibid.*, pp. 350, 425.

[26] Douglass, *Life and Times*, p. 269.

[27] *Ibid.*, pp. 269–70.

[28] Frederick Douglass to Maria W. Chapman, March 29, 1846, in Foner, *Life and Writings of Frederick Douglass*, I, 144.

[29] Douglass, *Life and Times*, pp. 282–83. See also Douglass to Chapman, September 10, 1843, in Foner, *Life and Writings of Frederick Douglass*, I, 110–12.

[30] *The North Star*, December 3, 1847.

[31] Douglass to Gerrit Smith, August 18, 1853, in Foner, *Life and Writings of Frederick Douglass*, II, 270.

[32] *Address of the Rev. Theodore S. Wright . . . Sept. 20, 1837*, in Woodson, ed., *Negro Orators and Their Orations*, pp. 90–91.

[33] *Colored American*, May 18, 1839.

[34] *Douglass' Monthly*, November 1860.

[35] *Frederick Douglass' Paper*, April 5, 1856.

[36] *The Liberator*, July 13, 1860.

[37] *Douglass' Monthly*, October 1860.

[38] See, for example, the speeches of Dr. John S. Rock and Robert Purvis, as reported in *The Liberator*, May 22, 1857; March 16, May 18, 1860, and H. Ford Douglass, in Herbert Aptheker, ed., *A Documentary History of the Negro People in the United States* (New York, 1951), pp. 366–68; *Proceedings of a Convention of the Colored Men of Ohio, held in the City of Cincinnati, on the 23d, 24th, 25th and 26th Days of November, 1858* (Cincinnati, 1858), pp. 6–7; *Proceedings of the Second Annual Convention of the Colored Citizens of the State of California* (San Francisco, 1856), pp. 14, 19.

[39] *Frederick Douglass' Paper*, June 2, 1854.

[40] *The Liberator,* March 16, 1860.

[41] Delany, *The Condition, Elevation, Emigration, and Destiny of the Colored People,* p. 155; Delany to Garrison, May 14, 1852, in Woodson, ed., *Mind of the Negro,* p. 293.

[42] *Proceedings of the National Emigration Convention of Colored People; held at Cleveland, Ohio, . . . the 24th, 25th, and 26th of August, 1854* (Pittsburgh, 1854), pp. 5, 40.

[43] "A Word to Our People," *The Anglo-African Magazine,* I (1859), pp. 293–98.

[44] "Apology," *ibid.,* p. 1.

[45] *Frederick Douglass' Paper,* May 18, 1855.

The Negro: Innately Inferior or Equal?

James McPherson

One of the most formidable obstacles to the abolition of slavery and the extension of equal rights to free Negroes was the widespread popular and scientific belief, North as well as South, in the innate inferiority of the Negro race. Most white Americans took it for granted that Negroes were by nature shiftless, slovenly, childlike, savage, and incapable of assimilation as equals into white society. Since the beginning of the antislavery movement abolitionists had been confronted by arguments that Negroes belonged to a separate and inferior species of mankind; that they would work only under compulsion; that they could not take care of themselves in freedom and would revert to barbarism; and that emancipation would bring economic and social ruin to the South and the nation.[1]

For thirty years abolitionists had worked tirelessly but without much success to combat these arguments. When war came in 1861 and emancipation became an imminent possibility, the debate about the Negro's racial character reached new heights of intensity and bitterness. Conservatives urged their thesis of Negro inferiority and unfitness for freedom with desperate energy; abolitionists argued from the pulpit, platform, and press that a hostile environment, not innate inferiority, had created the servile, comic creature that was the American concept of the Negro in 1860. The abolitionists affirmed that if this environment were transformed by the abolition of slavery and of racial discrimination, the Negro would prove himself a constructive, capable, and creative member of society.

Abolitionists were well aware that the common belief in the Negro's racial inferiority constituted one of the main justifications for slavery. In the final analysis, wrote Sydney Howard Gay in 1860, slavery was based "upon the assumed fact that the negroes are an inferior race, over whom the whites possess not merely an artificial superiority dependent upon the existing circumstances of their mutual position, but a natural superiority, which exists and ever must exist." Frederick Douglass said, "In truth, this question is at the bottom of the whole [slavery] controversy." Until the doctrine of the diversity and inequality of races was dis-

From James McPherson, *Struggle for Equality: Abolitionists and the Negro in the Civil War and Reconstruction,* pp. 134–153. Copyright © 1964 by Princeton University Press; Princeton Paperback, 1967. Reprinted by permission of Princeton University Press.

credited, abolitionists reasoned, the theory and practice of slavery would remain strongly entrenched in America. "We cannot expect," said Gilbert Haven, the militant, red-headed Methodist clergyman, "the complete removal of this curse from our land until we stand boldly and heartily upon the divine foundation — the perfect unity of the human race."[2]

With the coming of war in 1861 and the impending prospect of emancipation, proslavery advocates roused themselves to even greater efforts to show that bondage was the normal and only possible condition of the Negro. When the emancipationist drive was gathering momentum at the end of 1861, the *New York Journal of Commerce* published a concise summary of the conservative argument against abolition. "A year ago, no thoroughly sane man in America would have consented to a decree of absolute emancipation," declared the *Journal*, and the war was no reason why the nation should suddenly go insane. "Let no man say this is a base and sordid view of a question of personal freedom." It was a matter of racial common sense. The Negro simply could not take care of himself in freedom. "Unless the reformer can, with his emancipation scheme, introduce new and superhuman industry, economy, thrift and perseverance into the negro, it will result that he will not earn a support for himself alone, much less for his family." The attempt "to make use of the war for the purposes of emancipation," concluded the *Journal*, "is virtually a proposition to plunge the South into the depths of poverty."[3] The northern proslavery press echoed these sentiments throughout the war.

The abolitionist attack on the concept of racial inequality centered on two fronts: one, an attempt to demonstrate, from the Bible, from science, from history, and from observed facts, the essential unity and equality of races; and two, an attempt to show that the unfavorable environmental conditions of slavery and segregation, rather than natural inferiority, had caused the vices and disabilities of the American Negro.

The antebellum generation was fond of quoting the Bible as a weapon in the slavery controversy, and abolitionists could point to several passages of scripture which "proved" the unity of the human race. The book of Genesis told the story of the creation of *man* (not men) in God's own image. In his famous sermon on Mars Hill, St. Paul told the people of Athens that God "hath made of one blood all nations of men for to dwell on the face of the earth." Gilbert Haven contended that the Bible sanctioned the complete equality and fraternity of the races. Solomon treated the Queen of Sheba, an Ethiopian, "with the utmost respect and cordiality." Moses married an Ethiopian; a Negro was called by God to be one of the prophets and teachers of the Church at Antioch. "More than this," declared Haven, "the Bible constantly proclaims the absolute oneness of the race of man, in Adam, Noah, and Christ."[4]

By 1860, however, the Bible argument was pretty well played out. Thirty years of controversy had only shown that the Bible could be quoted effectively on both sides of the slavery issue. Science, especially ethnology and anthropology, commanded a large and growing influence in the mid-nineteenth century. Ethnology in the hands of Josiah Nott, Louis Agassiz, Samuel G. Morton, and George Gliddon (a group that came to be known as the "American School" of anthropology), who taught that the various races of mankind constituted separate species with the Negro at the bottom of the scale, had become a major weapon in the defense of slavery. Abolitionists realized that to combat these teachings they must themselves use the weapons of ethnology. Few abolitionists had any formal anthropological training, but as a group they were well educated and highly literate; and given the rather crude state of nineteenth century ethnological knowledge, the industrious layman could become almost as well informed as the professional scientist.

Several abolitionists made intensive studies of the question of race. To refute the "American School" of anthropology, abolitionists quoted prominent European naturalists who argued for the unity and equality of races. In 1861, for example, the *Anti-Slavery Standard* published a review of *L'Unité de l'Espèce Humaine,* by M. de Quatrefarges, professor of natural history and ethnology at the Museum of Natural History in Paris. Using the classifications of Linnacus and Lamarck, M. de Quatrefarges defined mankind as a single species; racial differences were the result of varieties within the species developed by conditions of environment and transmitted by heredity. M. de Quatrefarges used his vast knowledge to deny the existence of any fundamental and immutable differences in the mental capacities of various races.[5]

Abolitionists cited several other outstanding European scientists who maintained the unity and equality of races: Dr. R. G. Latham, the British ethnologist; Dumont d'Urville, the French geographer and navigator; George Louis Leclerc Buffon, the brilliant naturalist; and finally, most important of all, the renowned Alexander von Humboldt, who wrote: "Whilst we maintain the unity of the human species, we at the same time repel the depressing assumption of superior and inferior races of men." Through Humboldt, said Charles Sumner, "Science is enlisted for the Equal Rights of All."[6]

Sumner may have overstated his case, since American science, at least, spoke overwhelmingly for inequality. But the ethnologists of the world spoke with a discordant and divided voice on the subject of race in 1860. Abolitionists argued forcefully and accurately that science had failed to *prove* the racial inferiority of the Negro. "You may read Prichard, and Pinkerton, and Morton, and Pickering, and Latham, and all the rest — the whole library of Ethnology," said Theodore Tilton in 1863, "and in the confusion of knowledge you will find one thing clear — and that is, science has not yet proved, in advance, that the negro race is not to be a high-cultured, dominant race — rulers of their own continent, and perhaps dictators to the world."[7]

The endless refinements of the scientific racial arguments probably passed over the heads of the general public. The average man was more interested in concrete examples; and the advocates of Negro inferiority thought they had one incontrovertible example to show him: the supposed barbarous and uncivilized condition of Africa. What contribution to civilization and progress had Africa ever made, asked proslavery writers derisively?

This was a potentially damaging argument, and abolitionists advanced boldly to meet it. Negro abolitionists were in the forefront of the struggle to vindicate Africa. The central theme of their argument was that the inhabitants of ancient Egypt, fountainhead of western civilization, were a Negroid or partially Negroid race. "The ancient Egyptians were not white people," declared Frederick Douglass, "but were, undoubtedly, just about as dark in complexion as many in this country who are considered Negroes." Their hair "was far from being of that graceful lankness which adorns the fair Anglo-Saxon head." William Wells Brown, a prominent Negro abolitionist, lecturer, and author, said in 1862, "I claim that the blacks are the legitimate descendants of the Egyptians." While the ancestors of the proud Anglo-Saxons were roaming the forests of northern Europe as savages, declared Brown, Africa had created the foundations of western civilization and passed on this precious heritage to the Jews, Greeks, Romans, and ultimately to western Europe.[8] Martin Delany, another Negro abolitionist, cited the historians Herodotus and Diodorus Siculus in support of his contention that the world was indebted to ancient Egypt and Ethiopia "for the propagation of that glorious light of progressive civilization — religion, philosophy, arts, science and literature in general, which now illuminate the world." In reply to a derisive reference to Negroes by Senator William L. Yancey of Alabama, William Wells Brown told a group of Boston abolitionists in 1860: "When Mr. Yancey's ancestors were bending their backs to the yoke of William the Conqueror, the ancestors of his slaves were revelling in the halls of science and learning. If the Hon. Senator from Alabama wants antecedents, he shall have them; and upon such, I claim a superiority for the negro. (Loud applause)"[9]

These arguments were most vigorously advanced by Brown in a book entitled *The Black Man, His Antecedents, His Genius, and His Achievements*, published in 1863. Brown wrote the book for the express purpose of dispelling popular notions about the Negro in order to help mobilize popular support for Lincoln's newly adopted emancipation policy. The book was an immediate success; the first edition was sold out soon after publication, and in the next three years ten printings came off the presses. "Such a rapid sale of a book devoted entirely to an exhibition of the genius, the talent and the heroism of the hated Negro," said the *Anti-Slavery Standard*, "shows that a great change has come over the minds of the American people, and that justice to a long injured race is not far off." Lewis Tappan exclaimed, "This is just the book for the hour. It will do more for the colored man's elevation than any work yet published."[10]

But the glories of ancient Ethiopia were not sufficient to convince many skeptics of the inherent equality of Negroes. Modern Africa stood in the way. Most nineteenth century Americans considered Africa a backward, barbaric continent, devoid of any trace of civilization or culture. Most world travelers who visited the dark continent concurred with Bayard Taylor's opinion that the Negro was "the lowest type of humanity on the face of the earth." Not being world travelers themselves, abolitionists perforce obtained much of their information on Africa from such unflattering sources. Consequently they admitted that contemporary Africa stood low in the scale of civilization, but they advanced a kind of cyclical theory of history, by which nations rose and fell, and would rise again. At one time Africa was the center of learning and culture, said Gerrit Smith, but in the course of events she declined in importance. Africa's "inherent, inborn faculties," however, "are neither multiplied nor diminished because developed in one age, and undeveloped in another. . . . Changes of circumstances, along with other causes, alternately lift up and depress a people." Theodore Tilton asked in 1863:

Do you call the negro race inferior? No man can yet pronounce that judgment safely. How will you compare races, to give each its due rank? . . . You must compare them in their fulfillments, not in their beginnings. . . . How will you estimate the rank of the Roman people? By its beginnings? By its decline? By neither. You rank it at the height of its civilization. . . . The Germans, today, give philosophy to Europe — but you can count the years backward when the Germans, now philosophers, were barbarians. . . . No man can now predict the destiny of the negro race. That race is yet so undeveloped — that destiny is yet so unfulfilled — that no man can say, and no wise man pretends to say, what the negro race shall finally become.[11]

Some abolitionists, moreover, did not entirely accept the dark portrait of modern Africa drawn by most travelers. Several months after the outbreak of the Civil War a remarkable little book, written anonymously and entitled *Record of an Obscure Man,* was published in Boston. It purported to be the memoir of a man who had visited a friend in the South in 1842 and had talked with him about the capabilities of the Negro race. In reality it was a fictional essay by Mrs. Mary Putnam, elder sister of James Russell Lowell and an abolitionist sympathizer. Mary Putnam asserted that most travelers who visited Africa penetrated no farther than the coastal areas, whose inhabitants had been subjected to debasing contact with rapacious slave traders, "to which their degradation is to be attributed, rather than to inherent depravity or stupidity." Travelers who had ventured into the interior of Africa found people of finer appearance, gentler manners, greater industry and honesty. "When Central Africa has been fully laid open to the world," she argued, "we shall be called upon to revise many of our opinions."[12]

Displaying great learning, Mrs. Putnam quoted from world-famous travelers and explorers who had ventured into Central Africa: Hugh Clapperton, Mungo Park, and Dixon Denham. "Read what Denham says of the inhabitants of the interior," she urged; "of their industry, their skill in weaving and dyeing, of their love of music and poetry." Denham described the natives as "hospitable, kind-hearted, honest, and liberal." Anticipating the findings of modern scholars, Mrs.

Putnam decried the notion that Negroes had been civilized and uplifted by slavery and Christianity. Slavery, she said, had only suppressed their native virtues and intelligence.[13]

In one of the best expressions of "cultural relativism" to come out of the nineteenth century, Mary Putnam warned against accepting at face value the somber descriptions of Africa by certain westerners. "All men are prone to judge the manners of other countries by the standard of their own," she wrote, "and the civilized world views from its own stand-point that which it calls savage. We find the Africans barbarians, wherever customs differ from ours; but they are on the road to civilization, when their nonsense suits our nonsense."[14]

Abolitionists praised Mary Putnam's little book. "Such a studied tribute to the negro, in this way, we have never had the fortune to see," said Garrison in his review of *Record of an Obscure Man*. "The African is contemplated as a man apart from his accidents, and heavy must be the load of prejudice against color that is not lightened by the spirit and the truthfulness with which his claims are urged."[15] Abolitionists adopted many of Mrs. Putnam's arguments in their crusade for emancipation and equal rights.

The advocates of racial equality did not have to confine their researches to Africa to find persuasive examples of the manhood, ability, and achievements of the Negro race. There were plenty of authentic black heroes in the western hemisphere. By all odds, the greatest of these was Toussaint L'Ouverture, the Haitian liberator who led his people out of slavery and defeated the armies of Napoleon when the French tried to reenslave the Caribbean island. One of Wendell Phillips' most powerful and compelling lectures was a biography of Haiti's warrior statesman. In 1862–63 Phillips gave this lecture to dozens of audiences throughout the Northeast as a means of dramatizing the Negro's fitness for freedom. "The negro race, instead of being that object of pity and contempt which we usually consider it, is entitled, judged by the facts of history, to a place close by the side of the Saxon," said Phillips. Did anyone doubt the Negro's courage? "Go to 50,000 graves of the best soldiers France ever had, and ask them what they think of the negro's sword." Could the Negro take care of himself in freedom? "Hayti, from the ruins of her colonial dependence, is become a civilized state, the seventh nation in the catalogue of commerce with this country, inferior in morals and education to none of the West Indian isles. Toussaint made her what she is. Courage, purpose, endurance — they are the tests." The *Semi-Weekly New York Tribune* printed a special edition containing Phillips' speech on March 13, 1863, for circulation among the troops in the Union army.[16]

The Negro had proved his physical courage in Haiti, in the American Revolution and War of 1812, and would soon prove it again in the Civil War; but what about mental ability and intellectual achievement? It was while asking himself this question that Moncure Conway stumbled across the remarkable story of Benjamin Banneker. Conway did some research on Banneker's life and published an article on him in the *Atlantic Monthly* at the end of 1862. A free-born, self-taught Maryland

Negro, Banneker had devoted all his spare time to scientific research. He corrected some of the errors of the greatest astronomers of his age; in 1790 he compiled an accurate almanac based on his studies, and continued to publish annual almanacs until shortly before his death in 1804. His work was praised by Jefferson and internationally acclaimed by scientists. "History must record," concluded Conway, "that the most original scientific intellect which the South has yet produced was that of the pure African, Benjamin Banneker."[17]

Abolitionists industriously gathered statistics on the intellectual, professional, and business achievements of free Negroes. The American Anti-Slavery Society's *Annual Report* for 1859 pointed to the Negro actor Ira Aldridge, who was delighting European audiences with his portrayal of Othello; to three young Haitian students who had won highest honors at the concourse of all French colleges in Paris; to the New York Negro, Ditz, who had submitted a plan for a Broadway railroad; and the Philadelphia Negro, Aaron Roberts, who had developed a new and improved fire-extinguishing apparatus. These and many other accomplishments by Negroes demonstrated "the black man's capacity for mental culture and improvement . . . wherever a fair chance to test it has been given." In the business world Negroes boasted George T. Downing of Rhode Island and Stephen Smith of Philadelphia, both of them wealthy men by any standards. Some Negro lawyers of mark were John Mercer Langston of Ohio, and Robert Morris and John Rock of Boston. Frederick Douglass was one of the foremost orators in America, and in the pulpit the Reverend Henry Highland Garnet of New York and the Reverend J. Sella Martin of Boston ranked high. In sum, wrote William Wells Brown, the Negroes of the North, though "shut out, by a cruel prejudice, from nearly all the mechanical branches, and all the professions," had "learned trades, become artists, gone into the professions. . . . If this is not an exhibition of capacity, I don't understand the meaning of the term."[18]

Many abolitionists, while arguing vigorously for the inherent equality of the Negro race, nevertheless believed in racial *differences.* "It is a mistake to speak of the African as an inferior race to the Caucasian," said James Freeman Clarke. "It is doubtless *different* from this, just as this is also different from the Malay, the Indian, the Mongolian. There are many varieties in the human family." This was an accurate statement by today's ethnological standards, but Clarke parlayed it into a more questionable thesis: that the Negro was innately inferior to the Caucasian in some respects and superior in others. He stated:

The colored man has not so much invention as the white, but more imitation. He has not so much of the reflective, but more of the perceptive powers. The black child will learn to read and write as fast or faster than the white child, having equal advantages. The blacks have not the indomitable perseverance and will, which make the Caucasian, at least the Saxon portion of it, *masters* wherever they go — but they have a native courtesy, a civility like that from which the word "gentleman" has its etymological meaning, and a capacity for the highest refinement of character. More than all, they have almost universally, a strong religious tendency, and that strength of attachment which is capable of any kind of self-denial, and self-sacrifice. Is this an inferior race — so inferior as to be only fit for chains?[19]

Several other abolitionists subscribed to the notion of the Negro's superiority in the realm of manners, religion, and the arts, and inferiority in certain aspects of the hard-headed, practical business world. In an effort to convince readers of the Negro's ability to make positive contributions to American culture, Moncure Conway penned an article for the *Boston Commonwealth* in 1862, signing himself "A Native of the South." Negroes were a graceful people, he said, full of exuberance and picturesque charm. It was the Negro who gave to the South its warmth and radiance. The colored people had fertile, poetic imaginations. They had contributed much to southern culture, and would contribute more in freedom. "In our practical, anxious, unimaginative country, we need an infusion of this fervid African element, so child-like, exuberant, and hopeful," wrote Conway. "We ought to prize it, as we do rare woods and glowing gems imported from the gorgeous tropics." One year later, writing for an English audience, Conway stated that Negroes "seem to me to be weaker in the direction of the understanding, strictly speaking, but to have strength and elegance of imagination and expression. Negro sermons, fables, and descriptions are in the highest degree pictorial, abounding in mystic interpretations which would delight a German transcendentalist. My belief is, that there is a vast deal of high art yet to come out of that people in America. Their songs and hymns are the only original melodies we have."[20]

In his widely publicized speech on "The Negro," Theodore Tilton proclaimed the Negro "the most religious among men. Is not the religious nature the highest part of human nature? Strike out the negro then, and you destroy the highest development of the highest part of human nature." It was a mistake, thought Tilton,

to rank men only by a superiority of intellectual faculties. God has given to man a higher dignity than the reason. It is the moral nature. . . . In all those intellectual activities which take their strange quickening from the moral faculties — processes which we call instincts, or intuitions — the negro is superior to the white man — equal to the white woman. The negro race is the feminine race of the world. . . .

We have need of the negro for his . . . aesthetic faculties. . . . We have need of the negro for his music. . . . But let us stop questioning whether the negro is a man. In many respects he is a superior man. In a few respects, he is the greatest of men. I think he is certainly greater than those men who clamor against giving him a chance in the world, as if they feared something from the competition.[21]

Among American natural scientists of the mid-nineteenth century, Louis Agassiz was foremost in prestige and authority. His adherence to the "American School" of anthropology gave it an influence it could not otherwise have commanded. As a Harvard Professor, Agassiz had many acquaintances in Boston's intellectual circles; several of these acquaintances were abolitionists, and Agassiz's racial ideas could not help but have some effect on their thinking. Samuel Gridley Howe was one such friend. In 1863–1864 Howe served as a member of the American Freedmen's Inquiry Commission. In connection with his research for the Commission, Howe asked Agassiz for his views on the effect of race on the problems of emancipation and reconstruction. Agassiz replied that he welcomed the prospect of emancipation, but warned against granting equal political and social rights to freedmen. He reviewed the history of the Negro in Africa and the western hemisphere, and concluded that Negroes were "indolent, playful, sensual, imitative, subservient, good-natured, versatile, unsteady in their purpose, devoted and affectionate." The Negro had never shown himself qualified for self-government. "I cannot," concluded Agassiz, "think it just or safe to grant at once to the negro all the privileges which we ourselves have acquired by long struggles. . . . Let us beware of granting too much to the negro race in the beginning, lest it become necessary hereafter to deprive them of some of the privileges which they may use to their own and our detriment."[22]

Howe was torn between his respect for Agassiz's learning and his own equalitarian principles. "I would not only advocate entire freedom, equal rights and privileges," he told Agassiz, but "open competition for social distinction." Howe was nevertheless influenced by some of Agassiz's notions regarding the mental inferiority of Negroes. In a book on Canadian Negroes published in 1864, Howe lamented that the younger generation, who had never known slavery and who enjoyed equal civil and political rights in Canada, had failed to produce as many outstanding individuals, in proportion to their numbers, as the white community. Howe took into account the prejudice, discrimination, and lack of opportunity that might account for this failure, but concluded that even with these disabilities the Negro community should have produced more superior men. Teachers to whom he talked testified that Negroes learned just as fast as whites in the lower grades, but fell behind at the higher levels "when they come to studies which tax the higher mental powers, or the reasoning and combining faculties." Colored people, thought Howe, were "quick of perception; very imitative; and they rapidly become intelligent. But they are rather knowing, than thinking people. They occupy useful stations in life; but such as require quick perceptions, rather than strong sense."[23]

To the modern reader familiar with the view of contemporary anthropology that there is no proof of significant differences in the mental capacities of various races, the opinions of Howe and other abolitionists who thought like him appear to border on racism. Even the belief of Tilton, Conway, and others in the inherent superiority of the Negro in the "feminine" virtues — religion and the arts — imply an assumption of Negro *inferiority* in the "masculine" virtues of reason and enterprise. Thus a case of modified racism could be made out against certain of the abolitionists, but only by ignoring the fact that in the contemporary spectrum of opinion on race, the abolitionists were far in the liberal vanguard. The remarkable fact about the abolitionists was not that as champions of the Negro *some* of them believed in racial differences, but that in a nation where popular belief *and* scientific learning overwhelmingly proclaimed the Negro's absolute inferiority, there were men and women who dared to affirm their faith in the innate equality of all men, regardless of race.

Then as now, one of the most explosive aspects of the race question was the issue of intermarriage. "Would you like your daughter to marry a nigger?" was the derisive question hurled at abolitionists hundreds of times through the years. It is not recorded whether any daughter of a white abolitionist did marry a Negro, but it is known that the abolitionists did not shrink from discussing the issue. In the face of popular odium and violence, abolitionists struggled to remove laws barring intermarriage from the statute books of Massachusetts and other states. Marriage "is a personal and private matter, with which neither Congress nor any other law-makers have aught to do," said Gerrit Smith. "When a man and woman want to be married it is *their* business, not mine, nor anybody's else," declared Theodore Tilton. "But to read what some newspapers say of the 'monstrous doctrine of amalgamation,' one would think it consisted in stationing a provost-marshal at street corners, to seize first a white man and then a black woman, and to marry them on the spot, against their will, for a testimony to human equality." Tilton pointed out the obvious fact, usually ignored by proslavery partisans, that amalgamation occurred under slavery, not freedom, at the bidding of the white man, not the Negro. Tilton declared that "a slave-woman's master, who makes himself the father of her children, is in honor bound to make himself her husband. So far from denouncing the marriage of blacks and whites, I would be glad if the banns of a hundred thousand such marriages could be published next Sunday."[24]

Abolitionists Louisa May Alcott, Lydia Maria Child, and Anna Dickinson defended intermarriage in short stories and novels. Gilbert Haven frequently vindicated amalgamation from his pulpit.[25] Moncure Conway proclaimed boldly that "I, for one, am firmly persuaded that the mixture of the blacks and whites is good; that the person so produced is, under ordinarily favourable circumstances, healthy, handsome, and intelligent. Under the best circumstances, I believe that such a combination would evolve a more complete character than the unmitigated Anglo-Saxon," because it would combine the best traits of both races. "Amalgamation!" exclaimed Wendell Phillips dramatically. "Remember this, the youngest of you; that, on the 4th of July, 1863, you heard a man say, that in the light of all history, in virtue of every page he ever read, he was an amalgamationist to the utmost extent. (Applause)" Phillips had no hope for the future "but in that sublime mingling of races which is God's own method of civilizing and elevating the world. (Loud applause) Not the amalgamation of licentiousness, born of slavery, . . . but that gradual and harmonizing union, in honorable marriage, which has mingled all other races, and from which springs the present phase of European and Northern civilization."[26]

Most modern sociologists and psychologists agree that discrimination, segregation, and "cultural deprivation" rather than innate inferiority are responsible for the inferior status which the Negro occupies in American society. Abolitionists advanced this argument more than a century ago. Like modern sociologists, they maintained that environment, not racial deficiency, was the cause of the Negro's inferiority.

"I well remember what amazement was excited when Mr. Garrison and his partner first took a black boy as an apprentice in the office of 'The Liberator,' " wrote Oliver Johnson in his memoirs. "It was declared on every side that no 'nigger' could learn the art of printing, and it was held to be evidence of arrant folly to try the experiment. If the negroes, under such circumstances, sometimes seemed dull and even stupid, who can wonder? What race or class of men is strong enough to keep its feet under such a load of prejudice and contumely?" Theodore Tilton agreed that discrimination was responsible for the Negro's disabilities. "We put a stigma upon the black man's color, and then plead that prejudice against the commonest fair dealing," he stated. "We shut him out of schools, and then bitterly inveigh against the ignorance of his kind. We shut up all learned professions from his reach, and withhold the motives for ordinary enterprise, and then declare that he is an inferior being, fitted only for menial services."[27]

Prejudice and discrimination against the free Negro were debilitating enough, but the effects of slavery were worse still. "Take any race you please, French, English, Irish, or Scotch," said Frederick Douglass; "subject them to slavery for ages — regard and treat them every where, every way, as property. . . . Let them be loaded with chains, scarred with the whip, branded with hot irons, sold in the market, kept in ignorance . . . and I venture to say that the same doubt would spring up concerning either of them, which now confronts the negro." It was little wonder that "the colored people in America appear stupid, helpless and degraded. the wonder is that they evince so much spirit and manhood as they do." Theodore Tilton conceded that "slavery has reduced the blacks to the lowest point of ignorance and humiliation of which humanity . . . is capable." The "peculiar institution" had produced some singular effects on the Negro, making him childlike and dependent, lacking in initiative and self-respect. "Man is, to a certain extent, the creature of circumstances," argued Tilton, "and two centuries of slavery must needs have molded the character of the slave. . . . The faults of the slave . . . come of training, rather than of natural endowment."[28]

In the *New York Tribune* of February 5, 1863, Sydney Gay presented a cogent and eloquent summary of the environmentalist argument. "We have never supposed that the liberation of so many human beings, heretofore irresponsible, would be without some embarrassments," he wrote in reply to proslavery arguments that slaves were not fit for freedom. "It is Freedom that fits men for Freedom. . . . The crime of slavery has been that it has found the incapacity of its victims an argument for the continuation of its emasculating influences, and has continually pointed to the ruin it has wrought as an apology for postponing reparation." Nobody in his right senses, continued Gay,

has expected to find the Freedman . . . a miracle of virtue, a wonder of wit, a paragon of prudence, and a marvel of industry. In him who was yesterday a Slave, we should expect to find the vices of the Slave — the traces of that falsehood which heretofore had been his sole protection against cruelty — of that thievishness which may have saved him from the pangs of hunger, or guarded him from the inclemency of the elements — of that insubordination of the animal passions which his superiors in society have encouraged for their own profit and by their own example. . . . Emancipation will not remove the scars which Slavery has inflicted. There is many a brow from which the brand can never be erased. . . . So much the sooner should we, with all the courage of a genuine repentance, dock this entail of human misery, and at least turn the faces of future generations toward kindlier opportunities and less discouraging vicissitudes![29]

The effects of slavery and racial discrimination on the Negro's character, according to abolitionists, were felt primarily in three areas: intelligence, industry, and morals. The Negro's defects of intelligence, remarked Douglass, could be found among the peasants, laborers, and lower classes of all races. "A man is worked upon by what *he* works on. He may carve out his circumstances, but his circumstances will carve him out as well." Douglass recalled his trip to Ireland in the 1840's, where he found the population of the poorer districts much like plantation slaves in every respect save color. "The open, uneducated mouth — the long, gaunt arm — the badly formed foot and ankle — the shuffling gait — the retreating forehead and vacant expression — and, their petty quarrels and fights — all reminded me of the plantation, and my own cruelly abused people."[30]

Moncure Conway, born and raised on a Virginia plantation, recounted the story of a companion of his youth, a slave boy who was popular with the white boys of the neighborhood and excelled in telling stories, playing games, and so on. The boy had a great native intelligence. He accompanied young Moncure to school every day but of course was not allowed in the schoolroom. He wanted to know what happened in there, and when he found out he too wanted to learn to read. He could not understand why he was denied this privilege, and soon grew bewildered, then saddened, and finally rebellious, forcing Moncure's father to sell him South. Conway never forgot the boy. "I have dwelt upon this case," he wrote in his *Testimonies Concerning Slavery,* "because it is that which represents, in my own experience, one of the most tragical forms in which Slavery outrages human nature." On the basis of his experience, Conway also denied the theory that because of some natural disability, Negroes learned quickly until the age of ten or twelve, and then fell behind. "It has been my lot to have much to do with the poor whites of the South, and I have observed precisely the same arrest of development, both physical and mental, in those poor whites. . . . They learn well at first, even with a kind of voracity; but, at about the same age with the Negro child, they become dull." This was the result, not of inherent inferiority, but of the child's sudden realization of the cramped circumstances, limited opportunities, and unhappy future that faced the poor whites, as well as Negroes, of the South.[31]

The lazy, shiftless Negro who would work only under compulsion was a byword among those who defended slavery and ridiculed the idea of emancipation. Of course slaves were lazy, wrote Lydia Maria Child in her study of emancipation in the West Indies. Slavery "takes away the motive power from the laborers, who naturally desire to shirk as much as possible of the work, which brings them no pay. . . . It makes them indifferent to the destruction of property on estates, in whose prosperity they have no interest. . . . It kills their ingenuity and enterprise." She cited the testimony of planters and missionaries in the West Indies, who said that emancipation had "almost wholly put an end to sulking, or pretending to be sick. . . . Planters treat their laborers more like fellow-men, and that leads them to be respectful, in their turn. They have now a growing regard for character; a feeling unknown to them in the days of slavery."[32]

The alleged immorality, dishonesty and untruthfulness of the Negro were cited by proslavery propagandists as additional proofs of his inferiority. Of course the slave was immoral, replied abolitionists. Under slavery promiscuity was encouraged, marriage had no legal validity, and the father had no personal responsibility for his children, who belonged, not to their parents, but to their master. "Being regarded as animals, and treated like live-stock, [slaves] unavoidably lived like animals," wrote Mrs. Child. "Modesty and self-respect were impossible to their brutalized condition." In the West Indies, she contended, there was much less immorality a generation after emancipation than there had been under slavery.[33]

"To tell us that Slavery fosters in the enslaved habits of deception, is not to communicate to us any startling novelty," wrote Sydney Gay in 1862. Gay and Conway admitted that Negroes were prone to petty thievery, "but it should be remembered that the rights of property involve some very refined problems," said Conway. "If the Negro is inclined to sympathize with the views of Rousseau on such questions more than the English schools would approve, it must be admitted that the systematic disregard of his own right to his earnings is scarcely the best method of giving him better views. I have never heard yet of a slave who had managed to filch back so much as had been filched from him." Samuel Gridley Howe declared that "the offences against property, with which by public voice the [Negroes] are charged, . . . grow directly out of slavery. . . . The owner, in his daily practice, violates the most sacred right of property, by taking the slave's labor without pay; and the slave imitates him by violating the less sacred right of property, in stealing what he can lay his hands on." Upon the basis of his observations of free Negroes in Canada, Howe concluded that "with freedom and the ownership of property, the instinct of family will be developed, marriages will increase, and promiscuous intercourse decrease. . . . [Canadian Negroes] are, upon the whole, sober, industrious, and thrifty, and have proved themselves to be capable of self-guidance and self-support."[34]

"The difference between the Black and White," thought Sydney Gay, "is no other than the difference between the White and the White — differences occasioned by the accidents of location, and susceptible of removal by the opportunities of culture." Abolitionists realized, however, that these differences would not be wiped out in a year or two. "Men going from slavery to freedom cannot change their habits as they change their garments," wrote Howe. "The effects of Slavery will last more than one generation or even two," predicted Wendell Phillips. "It were a very slight evil if they could be done away sooner." The Negro was potentially the equal of the white man, but he had a long, hard road to travel before he reached that potentiality.[35]

In the final analysis, argued abolitionists, the question was not one of race, but of human rights. "I think races are of secondary importance," said Wendell Phillips in 1863. "I despise an empire resting its claims on the blood of a single race. My pride in the future is in the banner that welcomes every race and every blood, and under whose shelter all races stand up equal. (Applause)" Theodore Tilton proclaimed, "Looked at through the centuries, the question of races sinks into insignificance. The only generalization that will stand is, not that there are five races of men, or seven, or twelve, but only one — the universal human race in which all men are brothers, and God is father over all!"[36]

Notes

[1] The following studies treat this subject in considerable detail: William S. Jenkins, *Pro-Slavery Thought in the Old South* (Chapel Hill, 1935), 242–84; Guion G. Johnson, "A History of Racial Ideologies in the United States with Reference to the Negro," MS in the Schomburg Collection, NYPL; William R. Stanton, *The Leopards's Spots: Scientific Attitudes Toward Race in America, 1815–59* (Chicago, 1960). For a good example of the many pamphlets and books arguing the innate inferiority of the Negro, see J. H. Van Evrie, *Negroes and Negro "Slavery"; The First an Inferior Race — the Latter its Normal Condition* (New York, 1853).

[2] *New York Tribune,* Dec. 1, 1860; Philip S. Foner, *The Life and Writings of Frederick Douglass* (4 vols., New York, 1950–55), II, 294; Gilbert Haven, *National Sermons, Speeches, and Letters on Slavery and Its War* (Boston, 1869), 150.

[3] *New York Journal of Commerce,* quoted in *Liberator,* Jan. 3, 1862.

[4] Haven, *National Sermons,* 137.

[5] *N.A.S. Standard,* Nov. 9, 1861.

[6] Charles Sumner, *Works of Charles Sumner* (15 vols., Boston, 1870–73), XIII, 155–57. Curiously enough, none of the disputants in the racial controversy referred to Darwin before 1866, although *The Origin of Species* was known in America soon after its publication in 1859.

[7] Theodore Tilton, *The Negro* (New York, 1863), 5. This was a speech delivered by Tilton at the annual meeting of the American Anti-Slavery Society in 1863. Several thousand copies were published and distributed by the Society.

[8] Foner, *Douglass,* II, 296; *Liberator,* June 6, 1862, quoting speech by William Wells Brown.

[9] Martin Delany, *Principia of Ethnology: The Origin of Races and Color* (Philadelphia, 1879), 42–48; Brown was quoted in *Liberator*, Oct. 26, 1860.

[10] *N.A.S. Standard*, Aug. 1, 1863; Tappan was quoted in William Wells Brown, *The Rising Son* (Boston, 1874), introduction by Alonzo D. Moore, 24. See also *Commonwealth*, Oct. 30, 1863; and Samuel May, Jr., to Richard Webb, Sept. 19, 1865, Samuel May, Jr., Papers, BPL.

[11] Gerrit Smith to Montgomery Blair, Apr. 2, 1862, in *Liberator*, Apr. 18; Tilton, *The Negro*, 4–5.

[12] [Mary Putnam], *Record of an Obscure Man* (Boston, 1861), 91–92.

[13] *ibid.*, 92–96.

[14] *ibid.*, 123.

[15] *Liberator*, Nov. 29, 1861. The *Anglo-African*, a weekly newspaper published by Negroes in New York City, pronounced *Record of an Obscure Man* "the fullest and most satisfactory record it has been our fortune to meet with, after reading all we could find in print on the subject. . . . She recognizes in the negro an original, inherent germ force of his own, solemn, grand, endowed with energy and vitality enough to develop civil, social, and intellectual greatness out of his own resources." *Anglo-African*, Feb. 15, 1862.

[16] *New York Tribune* (Daily), Mar. 12, 14, 1863; *Semi-Weekly Tribune*, Mar. 13, 1863. In 1863 James Redpath edited and published an old biography of Toussaint by John R. Beard as a part of the effort to win public respect for the courage and resourcefulness of the Negro race. James Redpath, ed., *Toussaint L'Ouverture: a Biography and Autobiography* (Boston, 1863).

[17] Moncure D. Conway, "Benjamin Banneker, the Negro Astronomer," *Atlantic Monthly*, XI (Jan. 1863), 79–84.

[18] *Annual Report of the American Anti-Slavery Society for the Year Ending May 1, 1859* (New York, 1860), 77–78; Brown, *Black Man*, 49. This book contains short biographies of 57 eminent Negroes.

[19] James Freeman Clarke, *Slavery in the United States: A Sermon Delivered on Thanksgiving Day, 1842* (Boston, 1843), 24.

[20] *Commonwealth*, Oct. 18, 1862; Conway, *Testimonies Concerning Slavery*, 71. Conway had gone to England in 1863 as a sort of ambassador of good will from the American abolitionists. He liked London so well that he settled down and lived there for the next 20 years.

[21] Tilton, *The Negro*, 11–13.

[22] Howe to Agassiz, Aug. 3, 1863; Agassiz to Howe, Aug. 9, 10, 1863, in Elizabeth C. Agassiz, *Louis Agassiz: His Life and Correspondence* (2 vols., Boston, 1885), II, 591–608.

[23] Howe to Agassiz, Aug. 18, 1863, *ibid.*, 614; Samuel G. Howe, *The Refugees from Slavery in Canada West* (Boston, 1864), 81–82.

[24] Gerrit Smith to the Hon. John Gurley, Dec. 16, 1861, in *Liberator*, Jan. 3, 1862; Tilton, *The Negro*, 10.

[25] Louisa May Alcott, "M. L.," a short story published serially in the *Commonwealth*, Jan. 24, 31, Feb. 7, 14, 21, 1863; Lydia M. Child, *A Romance of the Republic* (Boston, 1867); Anna Dickinson, *What Answer?* (Boston, 1868); Haven, *National Sermons*, 146.

[26] Conway, *Testimonies Concerning Slavery*, 76; Phillips' speech quoted in *Commonwealth*, July 17, 1863.

[27] Oliver Johnson, *William Lloyd Garrison and His Times* (2nd ed., Boston, 1885), 101–02; *Independent*, May 29, 1862.

[28] Speech by Douglass in Cooper Union, Feb. 12, 1862, published in *New York Tribune*, Feb. 13; article by Tilton in *Independent*, Aug. 20, 1863.

[29] *New York Tribune*, Feb. 5, 1863. See also J. M. McKim to Gay, Jan. 28, 1863, Gay Papers, CU.

[30] Foner, *Douglass*, II, 304–05.

[31] Conway, *Testimonies Concerning Slavery,* 4–7, 65–66.

[32] Lydia Maria Child, *The Right Way the Safe Way* (2d ed., New York, 1862), 5–6, 15–16.

[33] Charles K. Whipple, *The Family Relation, as Affected by Slavery* (Cincinnati, 1858), passim; Child, *Right Way Safe Way,* 6.

[34] *New York Tribune,* Jan. 13, 1862; Conway, *Testimonies Concerning Slavery,* 70; Howe, *Refugees in Canada West,* 86–87, 103, 101.

[35] *New York Tribune,* Sept. 17, 1863; Howe, *Refugees in Canada West,* 86; speech by Wendell Phillips in Boston Music Hall, Dec. 16, 1860, in *New York Tribune,* Dec. 18.

[36] *Liberator,* May 29, 1863; Tilton, *The Negro,* 8.

Antislavery Ambivalence: Immediatism, Expedience, Race

William H. Pease

Jane H. Pease

Of constant distress to students of the American antislavery movement has been its ambivalence, especially its ambivalence over the term Immediatism. The term had originally defined a means to end British colonial slavery, but it failed to be similarly applicable to emancipation in the American South. Therefore the antislavery movement strained to give new meaning to emancipation *"instant and universal."* Did it not really mean gradual emancipation immediately begun or, perhaps, immediate emancipation gradually achieved? But no less than over immediatism, antislavery crusaders were beset by a fundamental ambivalence in their attitude toward the Negro himself. At the simplest level there was no issue. Slavery was sin; and the crusaders were moved to free the slave by a humanitarianism too genuine to be doubted.[1] Yet, sympathetic as they might appear and believe themselves to be toward the Negro, the abolitionists were, as Leon Litwack and others have shown, in part at least prejudiced against him.[2] And the variety of their response toward him demonstrates the ambivalence so characteristic of the antislavery movement as a whole.

Endemic was the abolitionists' tendency toward abstraction. Frequently they so abstracted both the "Negro" and the "Crusade" that they dealt not with people in a situation but only with intellectualizations in a vacuum. John Thomas has recently noted that William Lloyd Garrison failed "to understand people, black or white" and used them simply "as counters in the grim business of reform."[3] His analysis echoes publisher James Gordon Bennett's conclusion made one hundred years earlier that to Garrison "nothing [was] sacred . . . but the ideal intellect of the negro race."[4]

This preoccupation with the ideal is reflected by the American Anti-Slavery

William H. Pease and Jane H. Pease, "Antislavery Ambivalence: Immediatism, Expedience, Race," *American Quarterly*, XVII, Winter 1965, pp. 682–695. Copyright, 1965, Trustees of the University of Pennsylvania. Reprinted by permission of the publisher.

This article was read, in a slightly modified form, at the annual meetings of the Mississippi Valley Historical Association, April 1965.

Society, which, at its inception in 1833, resolved that to guarantee education to the Negro was more important than to end "corporeal slavery itself, inasmuch as ignorance enslaves the mind and tends to the ruin of the immortal soul."[5] And, on the very eve of Emancipation, Philadelphia antislavery leader James Miller McKim, although emphasizing the importance of slave rehabilitation and active in prosecuting it, thought that it was "not the place . . . of [the] abolitionists to descend to the details of th[e] work, teaching and the like; let this," he added, "be attended to by the neophytes and others. We are to continue to be what we always have been," he concluded, "a wheel within a wheel; an original motive power."[6] Thus for thirty years abolitionists, to a greater or lesser extent, heeded the kind of exhortation which Henry C. Wright enunciated so forcefully:

Watch, Sister, & pray that you enter not into temptation. *Watch, not* . . . for Abolition as an Organization, not even for our millions of crushed & bleeding slaves . . . , but watch *for* the eternal, immutable Principles of Justice & Right — watch for *Humanity*. . . . We are seeking an object that must command the respect of the world — i e *the redemption of man from the dominion of man.* This is Abolition.[7]

The abolitionists did, of course, at least partly understand their own position. They may not have realized just how fully they were depersonalizing the Negroes; but they were quite aware that they had difficulties in matching their protestations to their actions. "We are," said the Connecticut crusader Samuel J. May with a Zolaesque directness, "culpably ignorant of, or shamefully indifferent to the wrongs which are inflicted upon our colored brethren. . . . We are prejudiced against the blacks; and our prejudices are indurated . . . by the secret, vague consciousness of the wrong we are doing them. Men are apt to dislike those most, whom they have injured most."[8] And despite the teaching of the antislavery periodical, the *Abolitionist*, that the antislavery enthusiast ought "to banish from his own mind the unworthy feelings which would lead him to regard any human being with contempt merely on account of his color," New York abolitionist Lewis Tappan admitted "that when the subject of acting out our profound principles in treating men irrespective of color is discussed heat is always produced."[9]

This much, then, the abolitionists themselves perceived. But for the student of the antislavery movement it is also imperative to recognize that prejudice and abstraction were but the obvious symptoms of an ambivalence which gives to the antislavery crusade in the expediency and temporizing of its actions and in the complexity of its thought an architecture baroque in the richness of its variations.[10]

It was, for example, relatively simple to accept the humanity of the Negro; but then how did one account for his patently submerged position vis-à-vis the whites? Abolitionists like Lydia Maria Child of Northampton, Massachusetts, tried to link the two elements by admitting that, while all Negroes were not "Scotts or Miltons," they were *men*, capable of producing their proportions of Scotts and Miltons, if they could be allowed to live in a state of physical and intellectual freedom."[11] At the other extreme the New York Whig politician, William Henry Seward, defending the mentally deranged William Freeman in 1846, tried to subordinate intellectual lack to simple humanity and to separate it from race. He pleaded with the jury that

the color of the prisoner's skin, and the form of his features, are not impressed upon the spiritual, immortal mind which works beneath. In spite of human pride, he is still your brother, and mine, in form and color accepted and approved by his Father, and yours, and mine, and bears equally with us the proudest inheritance of our race — the image of our Maker. Hold him then to be a MAN.[12]

In denying, furthermore, that the apparent differences between Negroes and whites were not inherent the abolitionists became environmentalists. John Rankin, ex-slaveholder from Virginia and an ardent abolitionist, asserted with good will but dubious logic that, if racial inferiority were a valid criterion, then all Negroes would be inferior to all whites if but one was. Clearly this was not so. Therefore existing inferiority was explainable only in environmental terms.[13] Slavery it was, asserted German refugee Charles Follen of Boston, that debased and degraded the Negroes and generated among whites an "absurd and cruel prejudice against color."[14] The antislavery solution to prejudice was clear once the cause was thus linked to slavery. Charles Calistus Burleigh of Connecticut optimistically exhorted his fellow whites to "give [the Negro] his liberty, and as strong a motive to exertion as you have; — a prospect of reward as sure and ample; not only wages for his toil, but respect and honor and social standing according to his worth, and see what he can then become."[15]

Yet, for all their exuberance, for all their belief in equality, for all their efforts to raise the Negro above the debilitating influences of adverse environment, the abolitionists were never wholly convincing. Much of what they said betrayed an implicit and at times explicit belief in racial inferiority. Here again ambivalence emerged. That the abolitionists themselves were usually unconscious of their expression of prejudice and that they denied it when challenged should surprise no one. Nor, indeed, is the thoughtful student surprised to learn that such prejudice did in fact exist. Occasionally crude, more often hidden in underlying assumptions or in appeals to science, prejudice played a more pervasive role than the logic of consistency would admit.

Exasperated by poor printing, inferior paper and numerous misprints, and spurred on by his own literary pride, Edmund Quincy lashed out in a letter to Caroline Weston in 1846 at "Wendell's nigger," whom he held responsible for botching an Antislavery Report. Never, he urged, let the printing out to *"Smart people"*; they get things up so poorly.[16] Here clearly was not only a rather vulgar display of prejudice but also of a value structure in which the typography of a convention's report weighed more heavily than economic opportunity for the free Negro.

The acerbity of these outbursts may be attributed to Quincy alone. The subterranean import, however, was common property among antislavery people. As late as 1860 Theodore Parker, a backer of John Brown, observed that "the Anglo-Saxon with common sense does not like this Africanization of America; he wishes the superior race to multiply rather than the inferior."[17] His neighbor, Samuel Gridley Howe, known for his multiple reform interests, accepted Parker's assumptions but rejected his predictions by observing that, particularly among young Canadian refugee Negroes, many succumbed to "mesenteric and other glandular diseases" and suffered from "phthisical diseases" and a "softening of tubercles." "Many intelligent physicians," he stated, "who have practiced among both [white and Negro] classes, say that the colored people are feebly organized; that the scrofulous temperament prevails among them; that the climate tends to development of tuberculous diseases; that they are unprolific and short-lived."[18]

Whether feebly organized in physique or not, the Negroes were certainly docile in temperament. "It is paying a very poor compliment, indeed, to the courage and superiority of us whites," Richard Hildreth said through the sympathetically portrayed Mr. Mason in *Archy Moore*, "to doubt whether we, superior as well in numbers as in every thing else, could not inspire awe enough to maintain our natural position at the head of the community, and to keep these poor people in order without making slaves of them."[19] But, if Hildreth's Mason was fictional, the Lane Rebels were not. They had concluded, in their famous debates on slavery, that *"the blacks are abundantly able to take care of and provide for themselves";* but had added immediately that they *"would be kind and docile if immediately emancipated."*[20] This emphasis on docility is important, for quite openly it reduced the status of the Negro below that of the white man. J. Miller McKim, for example, negated American standards of self-reliance and manly independence when he praised Negroes for "their susceptibility to control."[21]

Not unreasonably, many Negroes actively resented this abolitionist presumption about their "susceptibility to control." During the 1850s, in fact, this resentment was in large part responsible for the growth and activity of the Negro Convention movement, whose purpose it was to do for the Negroes themselves what they feared the whites, at last, would not accomplish for them. Frederick Douglass and Henry Highland Garnet, two Negro leaders of marked undocility, both took umbrage at Maria Weston Chapman for her paternal concern about their appropriate behavior; and Douglass, disillusioned with radical abolitionism in the face of growing political antislavery activity and ambitious himself to assert his independence from white abolitionist domination, defied the Boston hierarchy by establishing his own newspaper in Rochester, New York. Likewise, Martin Delany, a successful Negro doctor, resented the Negroes' exclusion from antislavery leadership and was highly dubious about the abolitionists' touted support of economic opportunity for free Negroes. Delany's disillusionment led him to abandon America as a viable home for the Negro and in the late 1850s to sponsor projects for African colonization.[22]

Despite concepts of racial inferiority, further borne out by an almost universal preference for the lighter-skinned over the darker-skinned Negro,[23] abolitionists in fact did demand just and equitable civil liberties for colored persons. "The oppressive civil disabilities laid upon them in the non-slaveholding States, and the settled opposition to their education and elevation . . . ," said the Andover Theological Seminary antislavery society,

are but glaring indications of the prevalent spirit of slavery. The same contempt of the black man — the same disposition to trample on his rights and to lord it over his person, follows him, whatever *degree* of emancipation he may have obtained, and in whatever part of the nation he takes his refuge. Though we had in view only the wrongs of the colored people in New-England, we should feel ourselves compelled to take our present stand, and vindicate their rights as brethren, as men, and as Americans.[24]

Abolitionists everywhere asserted that Negroes and whites should be judged and treated according to the same standards in the apportioning not only of civil rights but also of economic and educational opportunities. In its Declaration of Sentiments the American Anti-Slavery Society announced in 1833 that

all persons of color who possess the qualifications which are demanded of others, ought to be admitted forthwith to the enjoyment of the same privileges, and the exercise of the same prerogatives, as others; and . . . the paths of preferment, of wealth, and of intelligence, should be opened as widely to them as to persons of a white complexion.[25]

Schools, like Oberlin College and the Noyes Academy in New Hampshire, which admitted Negroes on equal terms with whites,[26] bore out these principles as did Charles Sumner's argument in the Roberts Case in 1849 that separate schools were unequal and threatened cleavages in society.[27] And Samuel J. May, summing up the concept in a statement which avoided many of the pitfalls of prejudice into which his colleagues fell, averred that "all we demand for them is that Negroes shall be permitted, encouraged, assisted to become as wise, as virtuous, and as rich as they can, and be acknowledged to be just what they have become, and be treated accordingly."[28]

Yet these appeals to the efficacy of education and economic betterment reveal the middle-class values to which almost all abolitionists subscribed and which both compound and explain much of the ambivalence in the antislavery movement. As middle-class Americans, abolitionists, naturally enough, measured the Negroes against middle-class standards, and to those standards they expected the Negroes to conform — Negroes who were generally ex-slaves from the lowest and most abject class in America. Assuredly the American Anti-Slavery Society was eager to uplift them to "an equality with the whites" but only after carefully disclaiming that it approved any such non-middle-class shenanigans as adopting colored children, encouraging interracial marriages or "exciting the people of color to assume airs."[29]

It was expected, then, that the Negroes should adapt themselves to the values of the white community, should, as one abolitionist advised, submit to prejudice "with the true dignity of meekness" so that their critics might be stilled. Thus was fulfilled the stereotype of the malleable, willing and docile colored man. Still, on limited occasions, the same writer observed, the Negroes should take a positive stand. They should demand admission to the public schools, they should organize or join lyceum groups, they should acquire knowledge and education. And, he said in a condensed version of a middle-class *Poor Richard's*, they should organize uplifting visits to their poor and degraded brethren and teach them "temperance . . . cleanliness, neatness, strict honesty, and all that belong to good morality."[30] In addition to these virtues, the American Anti-Slavery Society agents were admonished to instill in the free people of color

the importance of domestic order, and the performance of relative duties in families; of correct habits; command of temper and courteous manners. Also the duty and advantages of industry and economy; promptness and fidelity in the fulfillment of contrasts or obligations, whether written or verbal; and encourage them in the acquisition of property, especially of real estate in fee simple, particularly dwellings for their own families. Present their duties and privileges as citizens, and encourage them to become voters, and to secure equal privileges with other citizens. . . .[31]

Others, varying little from the standard reforming attitudes of the day but less optimistic about raising the Negro to the middle-class, urged him to adopt their own conception of lower-class standards. He should learn a trade and become a mechanic. Since these abolitionists categorized the social strata in such a way that the hardy mechanic always fell comfortably below the solid middle class, the Negro was bracketed, at worst, with the Irish hod carrier, and at best only identified with the honest toiler.[32]

Sometimes in the abolitionists' arguments one discovers strong overtones of ordinary self-interest. The *Anti-Slavery Almanac* assured its readers, for example, that emancipated Negroes would not flock to the North. Let no one be perturbed, the *Almanac* urged in unctuous tone. "If the slaves are gradually set free, they must leave the place where they are (and will be likely to go to the north), that they may not interfere with the slavery which remains. But if they are all set free at once, they may continue where they are." Putting the argument in other terms, emancipated Negroes would be a great boon to the economy not only in the South but in the North as well.[33] "The southern laborers, when free and paid," C. C. Burleigh had said, "would buy of us many comforts and conveniences not allowed them now . . . which would give new activity to our shops and mills and shipping, and steadier employment, and, most likely, higher wages, to all kinds of labor here."[34] Thus emancipation would not inconvenience the North with a mass of freed slaves; it would rather prove quite profitable.

Still, there was the thorny issue of defining the social position of the Negro in a predominantly white society. Many of the same abolitionists who demanded so unfalteringly no association with slaveholders found it ticklishly difficult to espouse social intercourse with Negroes and almost impossible to champion holy wedlock with those of black skin. In theory and in conscience, of course, they deplored the bans on interracial marriage; yet in practice they as often betrayed an opposite sentiment.[35] For his own part, Garrison defended the ideal goal but reconciled it with practical reality. "At the present time," he said expediently, "mixed marriages would be in bad taste. . . ."[36] Elizur Wright, however, scornfully ridiculed such temporizing over prejudice. "Pray, what is the matter? we ask of a generous and enlightened public," he snapped viciously.

The reply is couched with quaking apprehension, in the appalling interrogatory; *would you have your daughter marry a negro?* And the utter slavery to which this tyrant prejudice has reduced everything that is noble and good in the land, is evinced by nothing more clearly than by the pains taking of even abolitionists to show that colored men *may be* enfranchised and elevated without bringing on the dreaded consequence.[37]

It seemed necessary, in the end, to plaster over the issue and to allay white fears. Mrs. Child, echoing the frequent antislavery assertion that there were scarcely enough abolitionists in the South to account for the evidences of miscegenation there, insisted that to say that abolitionists wished amalgamation was "a false charge, got up by the enemies of the cause, and used as a bugbear to increase the prejudices of the community." In fact, she added, "by universal emancipation we want to *stop* amalgamation."[38] More reassuring to those who hoped that the issues raised by social equality would fail to materialize was Samuel G. Howe's commentary made after a close study of Canadian Negroes. "Upon the whole," he observed,

. . . the experience of the Canadian refugees goes to show that there need be no anxiety upon the score of amalgamation of races in the United States. With freedom, and protection of their legal rights; with an open field for industry, and opportunities for mental and moral culture, colored people will not seek relationship with whites, but will follow their natural affinities, and marry among themselves.[39]

The social distance decreed by class identification provided perhaps the most common and satisfactory framework for abolitionists' contacts with free Negroes. Thus, steeped in middle-class values and having identified the Negroes with the laboring classes, the antislavery band frequently assumed the patronizing air of the uplifter and the saved toward the downtrodden and unwashed. James G. Birney, speaking for a slaveholding background, observed that without question emancipation would, "where the superior intelligence of the master was acknowledged, produce on the part of the beneficiaries, the most entire and cordial reliance on his counsel and friendship."[40] And Sumner, in the Roberts Case, urged that "the vaunted superiority of the white race imposes corresponding duties. The faculties with which they are endowed, and the advantages they possess, must be exercised for the good of all. If the colored people are ignorant, degraded, and unhappy," he asserted with a fine sense of noblesse oblige, "then should they be especial objects of care."[41]

Such paternalism was, to be sure, most benign. At times, however, it was most insufferable. "The more I mingle with your people," Angelina Grimké wrote to Sarah Douglass in a display of tactlessness as gargantuan as it was overbearing,

the more I feel for their oppressions and desire to sympathize in their sorrows. Joshua Leavitt threw out a new and delightful idea on this subject on our way to Bloomfield. He said he believed the Lord had a great work for the colored people to do, and that your long continued afflictions and humiliations was the furnace in which He was purifying you from the dross[,] the tin[,] and the reprobate silver, that you might come out like gold seven times refined. I Hav[e] thought of this and fully believ[e] you will after all get up abov[e] us and be the favored instruments [to?] carry pure and undefiled Religion to the Heathen World. May the Lord lift you from the dung hill and set you among princes. . . .[42]

Helping the Lord hoist the poor Negroes off the dung hill was, as it often turned out, an arduous and dangerous chore, but one which gave the abolitionists a chance many of them coveted to become martyrs in the cause. To defend the Negro in court, to speak on his behalf before hostile audiences, to be harried from town after town by the frenzied mob was the stuff of which martyrdom was made. And the genuine joy in the experience of such martyrdom only enhanced the rewards of protective guardianship, as those who braved the mob when Pennsylvania Hall was burned well knew. Confronting the hostile elements, the stalwart women of the Female Anti-Slavery Convention "maintain[ed] the perilled cause to the last." As they adjourned "the colored members of the convention were protected by their white sisters, and Oh! Shame to say," one of the white sisters wrote, "at both were thrown a shower of stones."[43] And then, Oh! Shame to say, the brand new hall was set ablaze and totally destroyed.

In their enthusiasm to elevate the Negro, the abolitionists frequently carried on their shoulders an early version of the White Man's Burden. They taught their children in heavily freighted moral tales that "negroes, even poor, degraded, despised slaves, are not without reason and understanding. [And that] many of them have a large share of sagacity." Go forth, they directed even the toddlers, instruct the poor and ignorant; become teachers, and help train the Negroes themselves to become missionaries that they may enlighten "their countrymen who are in ignorance and darkness."[44] The adults themselves set the initial example. When Helen Benson, daughter of Rhode Island abolitionist George Benson, was married to Garrison, she refused to allow cake at her wedding or to wear fancy clothes lest she be a poor model for the Negroes to follow.[45] Theodore Weld also cast himself as an exemplar of the good. "I attend Church with our colored friends," he wrote; "but," he honestly admitted, "I do it to cast my lot with them; and," he contentedly concluded, "tho not spiritually edified, I find joy and peace in it."[46]

It was, however, a far more difficult thing for the same abolitionists to follow through, unhesitatingly and courageously, the implications of their theories, to work unfalteringly and without equivocation, straight on to free the slave and obtain equality for the free Negro. Certainly the abolitionists were almost universally too forthright and too dedicated to be faithless to their ideals; certainly they did not knowingly forsake their plighted word. Still it was a constant fact of the antislavery crusade that it was clearly marked by the constant temporizing of its participants.[47] In Ohio, some Lane students objected when one of their number took up residence with Cincinnati Negro families while he was working among them because they thought it would be harmful to their project.[48] Throughout the North antislavery societies debated the questions "Ought abolitionists to encourage colored persons in joining Anti-Slavery Societies?" or "Is it expedient for Abolitionists to encourage social intercourse between white and colored families?" And their composite response was at best an equivocal "perhaps."[49]

This political temporizing was not, of course, without its reasons, particularly in the light of mobs and physical violence provoked by extremists. Some abolitionists, of course, merely thought of public relations and how best to draw support to the cause. Birney, for his part, thought it enough to strive for equal civil rights without, at the same time, trying for social equality. Too much too soon, he argued, would mean a denial of all rights to the Negro.[50] So too the American Anti-Slavery Society, after the serious antiabolitionist riots in New York in 1834, rejected charges that they supported amalgamation or attacked the Constitution. "We disclaim, and entirely disapprove," they asserted, "the language of a hand-bill recently circulated in this City the tendency of which is thought to be to excite resistance to the Laws. Our principle is, that even hard laws are to be submitted to by all men, until they can by peaceable means be altered."[51]

The abolitionists were painfully aware of their actions, yet in good conscience they believed that their course was the better part of wisdom and thus did not compromise their valor. Arthur Tappan for one was so fearful lest his earlier activities by misconstrued that he assured A. F. Stoddard of Glasgow in 1863 that "if . . . you should know of any one's charging me with any gross assault on the fastidiousness of the age, when I became the avowed friend of the colored man, you may set it down to the score of ignorance or malignant falsehood."[52] But Sarah Forten, member of the actively antislavery Negro family of Philadelphia, understood. "How much of this leaven still lingers in the hearts of our white brethren and sisters is oftentimes made manifest to us," she wrote, referring specifically to an abolitionist who was comfortable with Negroes only under cover of night; "but when we recollect what great sacrifices to public sentiment they are called upon to make," she generously added, "we cannot wholly blame them."[53]

Briefly, then, the antislavery movement was beset, throughout its history, by a fundamental ambivalence. Never could the abolitionists decide collectively, and infrequently individually, whether the Negro was equal or inferior to the white; whether social equality for the Negro should be stressed or whether it should be damped; whether civil and social rights should be granted him at once or only in the indefinite and provisional future; whether, in fact, social and civil rights should be granted or whether only civil rights should be given him. The abolitionists, furthermore, were torn between a genuine concern for the welfare and uplift of the Negro and a paternalism which was too often merely the patronizing of a superior class. And their forthright concern for the Negro was still more qualified by an unhappy degree of temporizing.

These are the hallmarks of a critical and fundamental ambivalence. When such a quandary existed over the position and treatment of the free Negro and over the very nature of the beings to be freed, abolitionist temporizing becomes understandable. When immediate emancipation as a plan of abolition was translated to mean only immediate repentance of the sin of slavery, the needs of the human beings who were slaves were ignored. The abolitionists had sought solace in abstractions about humanity. And their hesitancy and confusion about the question of race illuminate much of the contention and indecision within the antislavery movement — a movement baffled and torn by ambivalence.

Notes

[1] The abolitionists were defined and set off from their contemporaries by their opposition to slavery and their concern for the welfare of the slaves, a concern which usually embraced the free Negroes as well. This article is not, however, designed to compare abolitionists as a group with nonabolitionists but rather to explore the variations within the group.

[2] See, for example, Leon Litwack, "The Abolitionist Dilemma: The Antislavery Movement and the Northern Negro," *New England Quarterly*, XXXIV (1961), 50–73; and his *North of Slavery: The Negro in the Free States, 1790–1860* (Chicago, 1961). See also Larry Gara, Louis Filler, Gerda Lerner, Stanley Elkins for considerations of prejudice. For psychological probing see David Donald, Hazel Wolf, Clifford Griffin, Martin Duberman.

[3] John L. Thomas, *The Liberator, William Lloyd Garrison, A Biography* (Boston, 1963), p. 153.

[4] Quoted in Wendell Phillips Garrison and Francis Jackson Garrison, *William Lloyd Garrison, 1805–1879; The Story of His Life as Told by His Children* (4 vols.; New York, 1885–89), III, 283.

[5] American Anti-Slavery Society, *Proceedings of the Anti-Slavery Convention, Assembled at Philadelphia, December 4, 5, and 6, 1833* (New York, 1833), p. 19.

[6] James Miller McKim to Samuel J. May, May 20 [1862], in Samuel J. May Papers, Cornell University.

[7] Henry C. Wright to Maria Weston Chapman, May 2, 1839, in Weston Papers, Antislavery Collection, Boston Public Library.

[8] Samuel J. May, Sermon delivered May 29, 1831, in Boston, as reported in *Liberator*, July 23, 1831.

[9] *Abolitionist*, I (Jan. 1833), as quoted in Merton L. Dillon, "The Failure of the American Abolitionists," *Journal of Southern History*, XXV (1959), 167. Lewis Tappan, Diary entry [Apr. 1836], as quoted in Litwack, *North of Slavery*, p. 218. See also Garrison's July 4, 1829 oration (*Garrison* I, 133–34); Susan Cabot, *What Have We, as Individuals, to Do with Slavery* (American Anti-Slavery Society, *Anti-Slavery Tract No. 15*. New York, 1855), pp. 3–4; Beriah Green, *American Anti-Slavery Reporter*, I (June 1834), 88; and Birney to William Wright, June 20, 1845, in *Letters of James Gillespie Birney, 1831–1857*, ed. Dwight L. Dumond (2 vols.; New York, 1938), II, 947.

[10] This ideological ambivalence is reflected in the cleavages within the antislavery movement over the appropriate courses of action to be pursued. These cleavages have already been well examined in a variety of studies on antislavery published since 1935. Whether to take political action or to regard it as damaging to the requisite moral fervor, whether to expend time and funds on schools, give aid to fugitives and buy freedom for individual slaves or to work exclusively to propagate the antislavery faith are debates not only about means but also about the basic concepts of antislavery.

[11] Lydia Maria Child, *An Appeal in Favor of that Class of Americans Called Africans* (orig. ed. 1833. New York, 1836), p. 171.

[12] William Henry Seward, *Argument in Defense of William Freeman on His Trial for Murder . . .* (4th ed.; Auburn, N.Y., 1846), pp. 8–9. See also C. T. C. Follen, *Works, with a Memoir of His Life* [by Mrs. E. L. Follen] (5 vols.; Boston, 1841), I, 627–28.

[13] John Rankin, *Letters on American Slavery Addressed to Mr. Thomas Rankin . . .* (5th ed.; Boston, 1838), pp. 10–11. See also Lewis Tappan, *The Life of Arthur Tappan* (New York, 1870), p. 131; James A. Thome and J. Horace Kimball, *Emancipation in the West Indies. A Six Months Tour in Antigua, Barbadoes, and Jamaica in the Year 1837* (American Anti-Slavery Society, *Anti-Slavery Examiner No. 7*. New York, 1838), p. 75; and Sallie Holley to Gerrit Smith, Nov. 17, 1865, in the Smith Miller Papers, Syracuse University.

[14] Charles Follen, "The Cause of Freedom in Our Country," *Quarterly Anti-Slavery Magazine*, II (Oct. 1836), 65.

[15] Charles Calistus Burleigh, *Slavery and the North* (New York [1855]), p. 4. Rankin essentially held the same view, but thought that it would take a long time to raise the Negro; see *Letters on American Slavery*, pp. 10–11.

[16] Edmund Quincy to Caroline Weston, Feb. 1, 1846, in Weston Papers. A year later Quincy complained about Frederick Douglass' independence (what he thought was Douglass' overcharging the *American Anti-Slavery Standard* for copy supplied) by observing that "These niggers, like Kings, are kittle cattle to shoe behind." Quincy to Caroline Weston, July 2, 1847, in Weston Papers.

[17] Theodore Parker, *John Brown's Expedition Reviewed in a Letter from Theodore Parker, at Rome, to Francis Jackson, Boston* (Boston, 1860), p. 14.

[18] Samuel Gridley Howe, *The Refugees from Slavery in Canada West. Report to the Freedmen's Inquiry Commission* (Boston, 1864), pp. 21–22.

[19] Richard Hildreth, *Archy Moore: The White Slave* (1st ed.; 1836. New York, 1856), p. 264.

[20] As reported in Henry B. Stanton to Joshua Leavitt, Mar. 10, 1834, in *American Anti-Slavery Reporter*, I (Apr. 1834), 54.

[21] James Miller McKim, *The Freedmen of South Carolina . . .* (Philadelphia, 1862), p. 9. See also *Letters from Port Royal. Written at the Time of the Civil War*, ed. Elizabeth Ware Pearson (Boston, 1906), pp. 102–03, 315–16; The *Anti-Slavery Record* III (Feb. 1837), 15; *Letters of Theodore Dwight Weld, Angelina Grimké Weld and Sarah Grimké, 1822–1844*, eds. Gilbert H. Barnes and Dwight L. Dumond (2 vols.; New York, 1934), II, 524; and Leon Litwack, *North of Slavery*, p. 223.

²² In the Weston Papers one may find numerous examples of the patronizing antislavery attitude and of Negro response to it. See also Filler, *Crusade Against Slavery,* p. 143. In particular note Frederick Douglass to Maria Weston Chapman, Mar. 29, 1846, Weston Papers; and Martin Robinson Delany, *The Condition, Elevation, Emigration, and Destiny of the Colored People of the United States Politically Considered* (Philadelphia, 1852), pp. 25–29.

²³ Antislavery literature contains many illustrations of the preference for lighter-skinned Negroes. See Samuel May Jr., *The Fugitive Slave Law and Its Victims* (American Anti-Slavery Society, *Anti-Slavery Tract No. 18* [New York, 1855]); George Bourne, *Slavery Illustrated in its Effects Upon Woman and Domestic Society* (Boston, 1837); Hildreth's *Archy Moore;* and William I. Bowditch, *White Slavery in the United States* (American Anti-Slavery Society, *Anti-Slavery Tract No. 2* [New York, 1855]); see also in this connection Theodore Dwight Weld, *American Slavery as it is: Testimony of a Thousand Witnesses* (New York, 1839); and the juvenile [Jonathan Walker], *A Picture of Slavery, for Youth. By the Author of "The Branded Hand" and "Chattelized Humanity"* (Boston, n.d.).

²⁴ This is a summary given by D. T. Kimball and F. Laine to *Genius of Temperance,* Aug. 22, 1833, as reported in *Liberator,* Sept. 28, 1833. Similar demands for equality of treatment can be found in Child, *Appeal,* pp. 195–208.

²⁵ American Anti-Slavery Society, *Proceedings of the Anti-Slavery Convention, Assembled at Philadelphia,* contains the Declaration of Sentiments.

²⁶ See *Liberator,* Oct. 25, 1834, for information about the Noyes Academy.

²⁷ Charles Sumner, "Equality before the Law: Unconstitutionality of Separate Colored Schools in Massachusetts. Argument before the Supreme Court of Massachusetts, in the Case of Sarah C. Roberts *v.* The City of Boston . . . ," in *The Works of Charles Sumner* (Boston, 1872), II, 327–76.

²⁸ Samuel Joseph May, *Some Recollections of Our Anti-Slavery Conflict* (Boston, 1869), p. 29. See also Birney, *Letters,* II, 945; and Garrison, *Garrison,* I, 148.

²⁹ Executive Committee of the American Anti-Slavery Society to Mayor Cornelius Lawrence of New York, July 16, 1834, included in the microfilm printing of *Liberator,* between 1833 and 1834, reel 1.

³⁰ This entire argument appeared in a series of articles, signed "S. T. U.," which appeared in *Liberator,* Feb. 11, 18, 25, and Mar. 3, 1832. The quotations are from the first and last issues, respectively.

³¹ Executive Committee of the American Anti-Slavery Society to its agents, n.d. [1834–5?], included in the microfilm printing of *Liberator,* between 1833 and 1834, reel 1.

³² See, for example, the *Anti-Slavery Record,* I (June 1835), 68, urging that Negroes be apprenticed at good trades. And see also the commentary reprinted by *Liberator,* Mar. 31, 1837, from the Bangor *Mechanic,* in which it is made quite clear that the laborer is quite aware that the middle class looks down on the working class. See also, for comparisons with the Irish, Hildreth, *Archy Moore,* p. 264; Sarah Grimké to Elizabeth Pease [May 20? 1938], in *Weld-Grimké Letters,* II, 679; William Allen Diary, Nov. 10, 1863, State Historical Society of Wisconsin.

³³ The *Anti-Slavery Almanac* (1837 and 1839). The quotation is from the earlier volume, p. 44. The self-interest showed in other ways as well. Defending what later became Radical Republican Doctrine, Maria Weston Chapman wrote to Lizzy (Chapman) Laugel (Sept. 24, 1862) that "black *soldiers* would save our Armies, & Black *citizens* our *republican institutions*" (Weston Papers). And Wendell Phillips also unconsciously suggested the same prior self-concern when he spoke at the *Liberator's* 20th anniversary celebration: "My friends, if we never free a slave, we have at least freed ourselves in the effort to emancipate our brother man." (Quoted in Garrison, *Garrison,* III, 320.)

³⁴ Burleigh, *Slavery and the North,* pp. 8–9.

³⁵ See Birney, *Letters,* I, 397; Garrison, *Garrison,* II, 356; *Anti-Slavery Record,* I (June 1835), 71; and Gilbert H. Barnes, *The Antislavery Impulse, 1830–1844* (New York, 1933), p.

274, note 20. See also Louis Ruchames, "Race, Marriage and Abolition in Massachusetts," *Journal of Negro History,* XL (1955), 250–73, on the fight for repeal of discriminatory marriage laws.

[36] *Liberator,* Aug. 13, 1831.

[37] [Elizur Wright Jr.], "Caste in the United States: A Review," *Quarterly Anti-Slavery Magazine,* II (Jan. 1837), 177.

[38] Lydia Maria Child, *Anti-Slavery Catechism* (Newburyport, 1836), pp. 31–32.

[39] Howe, *Refugees from Slavery,* p. 33.

[40] Quoted in *The Legion of Liberty and Force of Truth, Containing the Thoughts, Words, and Deeds, of Some Prominent Apostles, Champions and Martyrs* (New York, 1843), np.

[41] Sumner, "Equality before the Law," II, 376.

[42] In Angelina and Sarah Grimké to Sarah Douglass, Feb. 22, 1837, *Weld-Grimké Letters,* I, 364–65. Gerda Lerner contends that the Grimké sisters were almost if not totally above prejudice in "The Grimké Sisters and the Struggle against Race Prejudice," *Journal of Negro History,* XLVIII (1936), 277–91.

[43] Letter from a New York woman, May 18, 1838, in *Liberator,* May 25, 1838.

[44] From a story in the Juvenile Department, signed "H. Sabbath School Treasury," *Liberator,* Jan. 14, 1832. The Juvenile column was a regular feature in the early years of the *Liberator.* Henry C. Wright was designated American Anti-Slavery Society agent to children.

[45] Garrison, *Garrison,* I, 427.

[46] Weld to Sarah and Angelina Grimké, Dec. 15 [1837], in *Weld-Grimké Letters,* I, 496. A similar viewpoint turns up in Unitarian observations quite frequently as a rejection of emotional-evangelical enthusiasms.

[47] In a letter to Lewis Tappan, Weld, for example, wrote concerning a slave case in Connecticut that "not one of the Abolitionists here [in Hartford] was willing to appear *openly* in the matter as the friend of the compla[i]nant. Brother Tyler and myself who are the only persons known publickly in the case as friends of the compla[i]nant, have been and are still plentifully threatened with mob vengeance." June 8, 1837, *Weld-Grimké Letters,* I, 399.

[48] *Liberator,* Jan. 10, 1835.

[49] From Litwack, *North of Slavery,* p. 218.

[50] Birney to Weld, July 26, 1834, *Weld-Grimké Letters,* I, 163.

[51] *Liberator,* July 19, 1834.

[52] Arthur Tappan to A. F. Stoddard, Aug. 27, 1863, in Tappan, *Tappan,* pp. 201–2.

[53] Sarah Forten to Angelina Grimké, Apr. 15, 1837, *Weld-Grimké Letters,* I, 380.

The Role of Blacks in the Abolitionist Movement

August Meier
Elliott Rudwick

. . . Actually, interest in colonization was much less common among blacks than among white antislavery advocates. The antislavery movement had flourished in the Border States after the passage of emancipation laws in the North. Colonization was espoused both by humanitarians who thought that free blacks would fare better in a land of their own and by Southern slaveholders who considered the free Negroes a dangerous element. In December, 1816, a group of prominent Americans, including Henry Clay, then speaker of the House of Representatives, established the American Colonization Society. While claiming to be motivated by humanitarianism, the colonizationists not only refused to oppose racist laws and customs, but many actually supported and justified such barriers in order to make the condition of the free blacks so humiliating and debasing that, by comparison, the prospect of being transported to Africa would seem inviting. Although colonizationists stated that the establishment of an African "homeland" would ultimately encourage slaveholders to liberate their slaves in the United States, actually some founders of the Society suggested that the exodus of free Negroes would strengthen the institution of slavery. Nevertheless, until after 1830 most of the white antislavery advocates coupled their interest in the slave with support for colonization as a solution of the American race problem. . . .

In the main, free blacks were suspicious of the motives of the American Colonization Society and strongly opposed it. Within a few weeks after the formation of the organization, black leaders in Philadelphia — among them Bishop Richard Allen, the Rev. Absolom Jones, and James Forten — drew a large crowd to the Bethel Church for a vigorous protest against the colonizationists. The Philadelphia Negroes reminded America that in past wars, black people had "ceased to remember their wrongs and rallied around the standard of their country. . . . Whereas our ancestors (not of choice) were the first successful cultivators of the wilds of America, we their descendants feel ourselves entitled to participate in the blessings of her

From August Meier and Elliott Rudwick, *From Plantation to Ghetto*, rev. ed., New York: Hill and Wang, 1970.

luxuriant soil, which their blood and sweat manured; and that any measure or system of measures, having a tendency to banish us from her bosom, would not only be cruel, but in direct violation of these principles, which have been the boast of this republic. . . ." They declared that their cause could not be divorced from their brothers in bondage — with whom there were ties not only of color but "of suffering and of wrong," making it impossible to "separate ourselves voluntarily from the slave population in this country . . . and we feel that there is more virtue in suffering privations with them . . ."

During the following years, free Negroes in Northern cities sponsored numerous protests against the American Colonization Society. In 1827 a group of New Yorkers founded the first black newspaper, *Freedom's Journal,* edited by Samuel Cornish and John Russwurm. The paper attacked the Colonization Society, declaring that the organization's true motives were not to end slavery but to rid the nation of its free black population. Cornish soon resigned, and in 1829, after Russwurm joined the colonizationists, *Freedom's Journal* folded. The Boston agent for the paper had been David Walker, a clothing dealer who in 1829 published an incendiary pamphlet, *Walker's Appeal, in Four Articles.* His hatred of slavery and the American Colonization Society brought him to the conclusion that if whites refused to grant emancipation voluntarily, blacks should break the "infernal chains" by an armed rebellion.

The influence of the Colonization Society and its local branches was shown in extreme form by the Cincinnati riot of 1829. Cincinnati's black population had increased substantially since the early 1820's, causing special concern among the unskilled whites, who demanded that the new arrivals be expelled. This anti-black hostility acquired respectability through the activities of the Cincinnati Colonization Society, which, since its founding in 1826, had attracted the city's most prominent citizens. These influential leaders encouraged local newspapers and ministers to agitate against the community's free Negroes, and the Society's propaganda provided justification for the campaign to drive black people from the city. During the summer of 1829, Cincinnati's officials attempted to enforce the Ohio Black Laws, which required Negroes to post $500 bonds guaranteeing "good behavior." While ghetto leaders petitioned for a legislative reprieve, white mobs attacked. More than half the black population fled to Canada and other parts of the United States.

The Cincinnati riot dramatized, as had no previous single event, the exposed and defenseless position of the free black in American society. Fearing that it was the precursor of similar outbursts elsewhere, black leaders called a conference for September, 1830, in Philadelphia, the first effort within the race to effect unified action on a national scale. Bishop Allen presided over this convention of black leaders, which was attended by representatives from Rhode Island, Connecticut, New York, Pennsylvania, Delaware, Maryland, and Virginia. Repudiating the principles of the American Colonization Society, they urged those blacks unable to endure further oppression in the United States to consider settlement only in Canada.

To the black delegates at the Philadelphia conclave, it was a source of frustration that many sincere whites in the antislavery movement supported the Colonization Society. Among these men were Gerrit Smith, one of New York State's wealthiest landowners; Arthur and Lewis Tappan, prominent New York merchants; and Benjamin Lundy, a coeditor of the *Genius of Universal Emancipation.* This antislavery newspaper had recently suspended publication because of the outspokenness of its other editor, William Lloyd Garrison. The year before the 1830 Negro convention several Baltimore Negroes had been instrumental in converting Garrison from his former sympathy with colonization. Among them was William Watkins, "A Colored Baltimorean," who had ridiculed the organization in a letter published in the *Genius* in 1828. He and the other Negroes failed to modify Lundy's attitude toward colonization projects, but in 1829 when Garrison arrived in Baltimore they held extended talks with him and brought him around to their point of view. In a biography of Garrison his children recalled: "Garrison was slow to discover [the society's] real animus. . . . Some of his colored friends in Baltimore were the first to point out to him its dangerous character and tendency, and its purpose to strengthen slavery by expelling the free people of color."

Garrison also read *Walker's Appeal* with its condemnation of colonizationists, and although considering the call for a slave rebellion "injudicious," he found the pamphlet "warranted by the creed of an independent people." Impressed by the abilities of men like Walker and Watkins, Garrison became furious with the Colonization Society for seeking to convince the nation that blacks were too degenerate to profit from American civilization. Subsequently, black antislavery men in Philadelphia, such as James Forten and his son-in-law, Robert Purvis, impressed him with their refinement, their fervent belief in emancipation, and their hatred of colonization. He addressed the second national Negro convention (1831) in Philadelphia, and the following year published *Thoughts on African Colonization,* containing a copious selection of "Resolutions, Addresses and Remonstrances of the Free People of Color," demonstrating all too clearly the long-time opposition to the Society from the race it was ostensibly aiding.

Before long, other influential whites such as the Tappans and Gerrit Smith also renounced the organization. For helping to enlist these white allies, the black leaders gratefully acknowledged their debt to Garrison, but on occasion they reminded whites that, as the Rev. Charles Gardner, a Philadelphia Presbyterian minister, said at the 1837 convention of the American Anti-Slavery Society, free people of color had held numerous meetings opposing the American Colonization Society when Garrison was still a schoolboy. . . .

The American Anti-Slavery Society, founded in 1833, merged two rather distinct antislavery traditions. One was the Garrisonian wing, with its supporters largely in Puritan New England and Quaker Philadelphia. The other was centered mainly in New York State and the Old Northwest; its roots lay in the evangelical revivalism, led by the Presbyterian Charles Grandison Finney, which had swept western New York and the Old Northwest in the 1820's. Its leading apostle was the dynamic antislavery agitator Theodore Dwight Weld; its key financial supporters were the brothers Lewis and Arthur Tappan. In contrast to earlier antislavery advocates, both groups demanded "immediate abolition" of slavery, both were anticolonizationist, and both gave at least rhetorical support to the ideology of racial equality. The two groups, however, split in 1839–40. In part due to the irascible nature of Garrison's personality, the schism also involved important tactical and ideological issues. Garrison insisted on relying only on "moral suasion," and opposed political action because slavery was recognized in the Constitution, which he denounced as a "covenant with death and an agreement with Hell." Garrison also insisted on militantly championing other reform issues, including women's rights. The Weld-Tappan faction was also interested in women's rights but felt that the slavery issue was of such transcendent importance that it should take precedence over everything else. They maintained that if antislavery societies advocated other reforms, they would alienate many potential supporters. They also concluded that propaganda or moral suasion would not of itself overthrow slavery, that political action was necessary. In the split of 1839–40 most black leaders went with the Weld-Tappan group into the American and Foreign Anti-Slavery Society. A minority, chiefly in Boston and Philadelphia, remained loyal Garrisonians.

Exactly what role did the black abolitionists play in the organized antislavery movement, and what was the nature of their relationship with the white abolitionists? Historians of the black Americans have generally stressed the importance of the black abolitionists' role, while the historians of the antislavery movement and the biographers of its leaders have usually written as if blacks played only a minor and incidental part. Some recent scholars, quoting from speeches and letters of antislavery leaders, have engaged in a spirited debate as to whether or not the white abolitionists were genuine racial egalitarians. It would appear to us that the fundamental question to be raised is: How did Negroes actually function in the abolitionist movement?

Garrison's attack on the American Colonization Society stemmed from his contacts with black leaders. Negroes were especially appreciative of the support given their cause by the new immediatist antislavery newspapers established in Boston and New York. Garrison's *Liberator,* founded in 1831, might have died without the financial help of Negroes, who constituted nearly 90 per cent of the subscribers during its first year and held meetings in several cities urging support for the publication. James Forten purchased thirty-seven subscriptions before the *Liberator* was a month old. The paper's financial crises were recurrent and three years later blacks then constituting about 75 per cent of the subscribers, helped save "our paper." In its pages Garrison published their articles, essays, letters, and reports of their meetings. They passed the paper from hand to hand and showed it to sympathetic whites. In Carlisle, Pennsylvania, a Negro barber shared his copies of the *Liberator* with J. Miller McKim, who later became a prominent abolitionist leader. Another newspaper which attracted substantial black support was the *Emancipator,* founded in 1833 by a committee of New York abolitionists. The

Underground Railroad leader David Ruggles and other black agents enthusiastically built up the paper's circulation.

Although black churches and mutual-benefit societies as well as the National Negro Convention Movement had engaged in antislavery agitation over the years, it was the white leaders who seized the initiative in creating a national network of abolition societies. It was in a Boston black church that Garrison and a small group of white friends met to organize the New England Anti-Slavery Society in 1832. Only after the plans had been formulated were Negroes invited to participate. When the Society's constitution was approved, about one fourth of the seventy-two signers were blacks. Among the local auxiliaries was the Massachusetts General Colored Association, a fraternal and antislavery organization founded in 1826, which affiliated with the New England Anti-Slavery Society in 1833. Some Negroes always attended annual conventions of the New England Society, and ordinarily a few shared the platform with the white speakers.

Only three blacks were listed on the official roll of the Philadelphia conference that created the American Anti-Slavery Society in December, 1833. The three men, James G. Barbadoes of Boston, and Robert Purvis and the dentist James McCrummell of Philadelphia, were also among the sixty-two signers of the Society's Declaration of Sentiments — a document which Garrison drafted at McCrummell's home. Published accounts of the Convention suggest that black participation in debates and motions was minimal. On one symbolic occasion Negroes had a prominent role. On a motion to praise antislavery editors, the convention resolved itself into a committee of the whole with McCrummell in the chair, and Robert Purvis was among those lauding Garrison. Yet when Purvis made a forceful speech, "impassioned, full of invective, bristling with epithets," criticizing the cautious and equivocal passage on colonization which the conferees had substituted for Garrison's indictment, the convention failed to heed him. Six Negroes were appointed to the seventy-two man Board of Managers, including the three named above. One of the others was the Episcopal minister Peter Williams of New York, who resigned before serving on it because of pressure from Bishop Onderdonk. Purvis was named to the nominating committee. Nevertheless, when it came to policy-making positions, blacks were conspicuous by their absence. There were no black officers, not even among the twenty-six vice-presidents, and none among the original nine-man Executive Committee.

In additon to its interest in abolition, the American Anti-Slavery Society publicly opposed race prejudice and undertook to advance the status of free Negroes in the North. The delegates asserted that since all men were "of one blood," blacks and whites should share equally in "civil and religious privileges." To help Northern blacks achieve their potentialities, the conference recommended a program of moral elevation similar to that adopted by the Negro Convention Movement. In 1834, the first annual report of the Society declared that the way to bear witness against race prejudice was to invite more of "our colored brethren" into active affiliation with the organization. Two New York Presbyterian ministers, Samuel E. Cornish and

Theodore S. Wright, received places on the twelve-man Executive Committee, and James Forten and William Watkins were among the fifty-eight vice-presidents. Nine blacks were named to the Board of Managers, constituting about 10 per cent of its membership. Although Cornish and Wright remained on the Executive Committee, after 1834 no blacks were named as vice-presidents of the Society for several years, and beginning in 1837 there was a sharp reduction of Negroes on the Board of Managers to half a dozen or less a year.[1] Throughout the decade, only a handful of blacks attended the Society's annual meetings.

The American and Foreign Anti-Slavery Society, with an Executive Committee twice as large as that of the American Anti-Slavery Society, appointed a somewhat larger number of Negroes, usually four, but sometimes only two, to that body. They included Cornish and Wright, Bishop Christopher Rush, Dr. James McCune Smith, who had been educated at the University of Glasgow, the Congregationalist minister J. W. C. Pennington, and Charles B. Ray, Presbyterian minister, noted Underground Railroad leader, and sometime editor of the New York *Colored American*. During the 1850's Ray and Smith each served as recording secretary, though the more powerful position of corresponding secretary always remained in the hands of a white man. After the loss of Cornish and Wright, black participation at the top levels of the American Anti-Slavery Society declined. Robert Purvis was a perennial vice-president, however; Charles Lenox Remond served on the Executive Committee of twelve for five or six years beginning in 1843; and between 1849 and 1852 Remond and Frederick Douglass were among the three dozen men who sat on the Board of Managers. From time to time men like Purvis, Remond, Douglass, and William Wells Brown sat on convention committees and occasionally addressed or presided over a convention session. A similar pattern prevailed during the 1860's. No blacks appear to have had important positions in the American Anti-Slavery Society during the Civil War, and only three, including Robert Purvis, held any but honorary posts in the same organization during the period 1865–70.

Negroes occupied prominent positions in some of the state and local auxiliaries. Among the Garrisonians, Margaretta Forten was secretary of the Philadelphia Female Anti-Slavery Society and Purvis for years presided over the Pennsylvania Anti-Slavery Society. A handful of black men worked as paid agents and lecturers for the national societies. Negroes also participated as speakers at annual meetings, black delegates contributed to the discussions on the convention floor, and Purvis, Wright, and others presided over business sessions and public meetings. Yet the evidence indicates that their role in the affairs of the antislavery societies was mainly symbolic. This conclusion receives further support from the paucity of letters to and from blacks in the papers of white abolitionist leaders; only Gerrit Smith seems to have corresponded extensively with them. As Douglass said in 1855:

Our oppressed people are wholly ignored, in one sense, in the generalship of the movement to effect our redemption. We are a poor, pitiful, dependent, and servile class of Negroes, *"unable to keep pace" with the movement* . . . not even capable

of *"perceiving what are its demands, or understanding the philosophy of its opera-*
tions!" Of course . . . we cannot expect to receive from those who indulge in this
opinion practical recognition of our Equality. This is what we . . . must receive to
inspire us with confidence in the self-appointed generals of the Anti-Slavery host,
the Euclids who are *theoretically* working out the almost insoluble problems of our
future destiny.

In view of the attitudes of some white abolitionists it might be deemed surprising that blacks received any positions at all in the affairs of the antislavery societies.
In the early years, certain auxiliaries excluded black people entirely. Shortly after
the Junior Anti-Slavery Society of Philadelphia was founded in 1836, a motion to
accept members without regard to color was passed by only two votes. In the same
year the New York women's antislavery society adamantly refused to admit blacks.
When the Fall River, Massachusetts, Female Anti-Slavery Society urged Negro
women to affiliate, the organization was nearly torn apart. In 1837 the Convention
of the Anti-Slavery Women of the United States took cognizance of the matter, and
declared, "Those Societies that reject colored members, or seek to avoid them, have
never been active or efficient," but took no steps to expel such auxiliaries. Because
of these attitudes, Negroes in places like Albany, Rochester, New York, Nantucket,
and Lexington, Ohio, formed segregated local auxiliaries. In the published lists of
auxiliaries, the American Anti-Slavery Society often designated these by the word
"colored."

Although men like Weld, Garrison, and the Tappans discountenanced such
exclusionist policies on the part of white auxiliaries, and the practice certainly was
not typical, blacks were concerned that the white antislavery workers were not
completely unprejudiced. Even the most prominent white abolitionists were criticized. For one thing, blacks were disappointed that, in spite of the rhetoric of the
1833 Declaration of Sentiments and of the many addresses by white abolitionists,
few of them actively participated in the fight against the discriminaton faced by free
people of color in the North. On the floor of annual conventions Negroes repeatedly
tried to make the white abolitionists more conscious of this discrimination. For
example, at the 1849 meeting of the American and Foreign Anti-Slavery Society,
the famous abolitionist orator and Congregationalist clergyman, the Rev. Samuel
Ringgold Ward, who was known as the "Black Daniel Webster," told of racial
exclusion in a medical college and in churches. The following year Ray complained
of discrimination in the churches, and of how blacks, "compelled by self-respect
to rent or purchase churches for themselves," had encountered obstacles to making
even this type of accommodation. Theodore Wright, speaking before the New York
Anti-Slavery Society in 1837, expressed alarm over the "constitutions of abolition
societies, where nothing was said about the improvement of the man of color! They
have overlooked the giant sin of prejudice. They have passed by this foul monster,
which is at once the parent and offspring of slavery."

The dissatisfaction ran deeper than this. Militant blacks made numerous references to the insincerity of "professed abolitionists." They reported that many white abolitionists refused to admit Negro children to their schools or to employ black men in their businesses other than in menial capacities. Wright, in his speech before the New York Anti-Slavery Society, denounced the sort of abolitionist who would invite a Negro clergyman to his home but serve him dinner in the kitchen and fail to introduce him to his family. "Our white friends are deceived," the New York *Colored American* declared in 1837, "when they imagine they are free from prejudice against color, and yet are content with a lower standard of attainments for colored youth, and inferior exhibitions of talent on the part of colored men." Eighteen years later Douglass charged that abolitionist businessmen "might employ a colored boy as a porter or packer, but would as soon put a hod-carrier to the clerk's desk as a colored boy, ever so well educated though he might be." At the 1853 convention of the American and Foreign Anti-Slavery Society white abolitionists were openly attacked for failing to employ blacks in the antislavery offices or in their places of business, and Arthur Tappan himself was criticized for using blacks only as menials in his department store.

The Negroes were right about the prejudice within the white antislavery groups. It should be emphasized that the abolitionists were a distinct improvement over their colonizationist predecessors, and far in advance of the public opinion of their age. Yet at the same time they were, in fact, ambivalent in their relationships with blacks. One must therefore distinguish carefully between their egalitarian rhetoric and their paternalistic and prejudiced actions. They spoke feelingly of the "sins of caste," but they were highly sensitive to charges that they advocated social equality and intermingling. They spoke of the importance of opposing discrimination against free blacks, but even where they fought for civil rights they often did so under prodding from their black colleagues. Much of the activity on behalf of free Negroes consisted of exhorting them to assume the responsibility for their own elevation by acquiring wealth and education and exhibiting good moral character. Due to black pressure, in 1838 the Executive Committee of the American Anti-Slavery Society praised Negroes for seeking advancement beyond unskilled jobs and urged abolitionists to offer employment to black people — but employers affiliated with the Society were unmoved by this appeal.

The Anti-Slavery Society itself had at first bypassed Negroes when hiring lecturers. The so-called "Seventy," recruited by Weld for antislavery speaking, were all whites. Not until 1839 did Weld suggest the names of several blacks as lecturers, saying, "They would do more in three months to kill prejudice . . . than all our operations up to now." At the outset of his antislavery career Weld had helped establish schools for Cincinnati's Negroes and frequently visited their homes and churches. He believed that "persons are to be treated according to their intrinsic worth irrespective of *color*" but felt that this principle sometimes required "modifications"; a sincere abolitionist must ask himself if mingling with Negroes in public would be "a *blessing* or a *curse*" to them. He regarded public association with Negroes as "an ostentatious display of superiority to prejudice," which could hurt the antislavery movement as well as create mob violence against blacks. Weld even justified his own exclusion of a black delegate from an antislavery convention in Ohio on the ground that if the man sat in the convention, mobs would make renewed attacks on Ohio blacks.

The Tappan brothers displayed a comparable attitude. As in Weld's case, it is difficult to ascertain to what degree their ambivalence and paternalism were blended with tactical considerations. Lewis Tappan, for example, was disturbed at the failure of the arrangements committee to invite Theodore Wright to speak at the 1835 convention. The committee did allow Wright's church choir to participate, but some members of the Society complained about "race amalgamation" because a white chorus sang from the same platform. They charged that the "choir mingling" had later helped to incite mob rioting. Tappan believed that this accusation was merely a mask to cover race prejudice. All the same, he himself did not want to be regarded as advocating socializing with blacks; to Weld he confided that aside from the "choir mingling" incident, the only time he had ever attempted to "mix up the two colors" involved occasional dinners with a few Negro gentlemen in the course of business conferences. Like his brother, Arthur Tappan also condemned "caste usages," but yielded to social pressures. On one occasion he was severely criticized for inviting Samuel Cornish to share his pew at church. Tappan called that action the only effort at "amalgamation that I remember," and he vowed not to associate publicly with black people until white citizens became more enlightened. The influential abolitionist James G. Birney, candidate for President on the Liberty Party ticket in 1840 and 1844, argued that granting "social privileges" to blacks should be postponed until they had attained "civil privileges." In his judgment the failure to establish clearly such a system of priorities jeopardized the entire antislavery movement, since the enemies of the Negroes used the social equality issue to defeat the cause of abolition.

The complexity of the attitudes of abolitionist leaders toward blacks was most evident in the case of William Lloyd Garrison. Actually Garrison could not work with anyone except on his own terms, but he portrayed himself as unselfishly seeking to encourage blacks to become independent, self-assertive citizens. As the founder and editor of the earliest and the most celebrated of the abolitionist newspapers, financed at least in the beginning almost entirely by Negro subscriptions, Garrison's chief personality difficulties with blacks quite naturally involved black editors. Although in the early 1830's he had urged the development of a black press to vindicate the rights of the race, when Negroes decided to become editors, Garrison discouraged them. In 1837 when Samuel Cornish sought support for his proposed *Colored American,* one of the earliest black newspapers, Garrisonians opposed the venture. After Cornish went ahead, Garrison sometimes criticized the *Colored American's* policies and at other times acted as if the paper did not exist. The editors of the *Colored American* were not intimidated. In a pointed blast at Garrison, the paper criticized those white abolitionists who "outwardly treat us as men, while in their hearts they still hold us as slaves." Years later when Cornish died, the *Liberator* carried no obituary.

More celebrated is the experience of Frederick Douglass. Garrison discovered Douglass' oratorical abilities at an antislavery meeting at Nantucket in 1841, when the fugitive slave rose from the audience to tell about the world from which he had escaped and what freedom meant to him. On the platform Garrison was so moved that he asked the crowd, "Shall such a man ever be sent back to slavery from the soil of old Massachusetts?" The spectators arose shouting, "No, No!" Afterward the Massachusetts Anti-Slavery Society engaged Douglass to lecture on his experiences as a slave. During the passing months he was intellectually "growing and needed room," and wanted to share with audiences the ideas of his "reading and thinking," rather than simply mechanically perform his stage role as a slave. Officials of the antislavery society, however, discouraged his striving toward manhood and independence. Instead of applauding his intellectual progress as an illustration of Negro potentiality, they preferred to exhibit him publicly in his frozen status of fugitive slave. Garrison told him, "Tell your story, Frederick." Others admonished, "We will take care of the philosophy. . . . Let us have the facts." As Douglass continued to acquire self-confidence and literary skill, members of the Society complained that he seemed "too learned": "People won't believe you ever were a slave, Frederick, if you keep on this way. . . . Better have a *little* of the plantation manner of speech than not."

Douglass went his own way. Within the next four years, he published his autobiography and lectured in England. He returned to the United States, grateful for the help of abolitionists but ambitious for greater independence and the opportunity to edit his own newspaper. Over the objections of Garrison and his friends, Douglass moved to Rochester and founded the *North Star.* At the time he was still a Garrisonian in his ideology, but after coming into contact with the political abolitionists of western New York, he was gradually converted to their way of thinking. In 1851 he frankly told a meeting of the American Anti-Slavery Society of his new views, whereupon Garrison declared, "There is roguery somewhere." Later Garrison denounced Douglass as "destitute of every principle of honor, ungrateful to the last degree and malevolent in spirit."

Probably nothing could better illustrate the essentially peripheral role in which whites sought to cast blacks than the two anniversary celebrations of the American Anti-Slavery Society in 1853 and 1863. While the published proceedings of the twentieth anniversary reported in infinite detail the speeches of many white delegates, the comments of the blacks received perfunctory attention. In two instances the original remarks themselves were evidently short, but in the only other case so distinguished a person as the noted antislavery and feminist orator Sojourner Truth rated only one sentence: "Previous to the calling to order, Sojourner Truth (formerly a slave in the State of New York) sang a plaintive song, touching the wrongs of the slave, and afterwards spoke of the wrong Slavery had done to herself and others." Ten years later the American Anti-Slavery Society held its thirtieth anniversary meeting. By then the Emancipation Proclamation had been issued, Negroes were accepted in the Union Army, and the abolitionists felt a pardonable pride in their accomplishments. Delegates like Garrison, McKim, and Lucretia Mott, who had attended the founding convention, reminisced about the early days. Several of the surviving signers of the historic Declaration of Sentiments were present, among them Robert Purvis and James McCrummell. Yet neither was invited to speak, and in fact the only black man addressing the convention was Frederick Douglass, who pointedly told the abolitionists that their task was unfinished until blacks were accepted in American society. If, as one participant said, an abolitionist aim was to "vindicate the ability" of blacks, the fact that neither Purvis nor McCrummell was asked to speak does seem strange. Purvis especially had made significant contributions to the cause during the three decades.

Judging from these important anniversary celebrations, Negroes, in the abolitionist cast of characters, were regarded as bit players or even as extras shunted off in the background where they would not detract from the stellar performance of the whites spotlighted downstage center. The evidence suggests that this limited participation was due to the ambivalence of white abolitionists in their relationships with Negroes. The whites appeared not to have encouraged blacks to seek other than a few symbolic roles in the antislavery societies. While blacks received token representation in the offices of the American and the American and Foreign Anti-Slavery societies, there is no indication that they were influential in shaping the strategy and tactics of the organizations. Despite their reiterated declaration that improvement of the black man's status in the North was "a most effectual means of promoting the abolition of slavery," the white abolitionists concentrated on the single issue of converting other whites to antislavery. Since Negroes recognized the reservations among the white leadership, they organized much of their protest activities outside of the antislavery societies. It was no wonder that in the later 1850's J. Mercer Langston felt it advisable to form a separate, black antislavery society in Ohio. And it was also no wonder that the only Negro to achieve a position of real influence in antislavery councils was Frederick Douglass, a man so Olympian in stature that he compelled recognition. To be of influence even he had to establish himself as essentially an independent force outside either of the two major antislavery organizations.

Yet Negroes did play a vital role in antislavery activities. To them must be given the chief credit for running the Underground Railroad. And from among the fugitives the antislavery societies found some of their most effective lecturers and propagandists.

Contrary to popular impression, and Southern fears, the Underground Railroad was not a well-organized institution and white abolitionists did not play a commanding role in it. The work of the white abolitionists of course should not be minimized — some, like Levi Coffin of Newport, Indiana, and later Cincinnati, were of great assistance to the runaways — but the most arduous and dangerous part of the fugitive's journey was in the South, where there was seldom anyone to help him. And once the fugitive did reach the North, it was usually the free Negroes who took the initiative in aiding him. Individual blacks opened their homes to runaways. Even more important was the work of the organized Vigilance Committees in several Northern cities, which elicited support from sympathetic whites but were founded and essentially run by black men.

Slaveholders charged that whites on the Underground Railroad were invading the South to lure away their bondsmen. Their view was distorted. John Fairfield's activities in bringing slaves out of Alabama and Kentucky and John Brown's abduction of slaves from Missouri were exceptional exploits that sprang from the urges of daring personalities. More often than not such "conductors" were blacks who had escaped from the South and returned to take others North. Harriet Tubman, called the Moses of the race because of the large number of trips she made to bring "passengers" to the promised land, was the most celebrated of them. Her journeys from the South usually began on Saturday night, giving the fugitives more than a day before their owners discovered their departure and sounded the alarm for their return. She is reported to have thus helped 300 slaves to their freedom. Less famous was Josiah Henson. Henson escaped from Kentucky "after a youth full of good deeds to his master." Making his way to Canada, he later returned South to help the family of another fugitive to escape, and thereafter made other trips, carrying away scores of bondsmen.

Only a small percentage of the slaves who attempted to escape actually were able to reach the North. Armed with courage and ingenuity, guided by the North Star, some began their tortuous journey by stealing supplies from their masters, "borrowing" canoes or skiffs along the way, and finding lodging with other slaves or free Negroes. William Wells Brown, later an agent for the American Anti-Slavery Society and the first American black novelist (*Clotel; or the President's Daughter,* 1853), escaped in 1834. He later recalled that his constant fear of recapture forced him to travel only at night, and to choose between stealing food or going hungry. Although determined "not to trust myself in the hands of any man, white or colored," he did receive assistance from Ohio abolitionists and an Indiana Quaker. Finding employment as a steamboat workman in Cleveland, he aided other fugitives en route to Canada, and upon moving to Buffalo opened his home to runaway slaves. On occasion Brown helped rescue runaways in danger of being recaptured by slave traders. Brown thus had received only minimal help from white abolitionists, extended after the major risks were taken. Frederick Douglass, like Brown, later became a leading agent in the Underground Railroad, an active participant in the Rochester depot. Unlike Brown, in the course of his own escape from Baltimore in 1838, Douglass received no help at all from whites. Using a method frequently employed by slaves escaping from Southern seaports, he borrowed a free seaman's "protection" papers. When he was unable to find a job in New York City, he finally revealed his plight to a sailor who notified David Ruggles, a black printer-bookseller and secretary of the New York Vigilance Committee. Ruggles supplied temporary lodging, later sending Douglass to New Bedford, where he stayed with a black family and started a new life "as a free man."

The Vigilance Committees arose in the middle 1830's. The New York Vigilance Committee — under the direction first of Ruggles and later of Charles Ray, who was also secretary of the New York State Vigilance Committee — collected pennies and nickels, mainly from Negroes, to feed, clothe, and shelter fugitives arriving from the South. Some were helped to settle in New York, while others like Frederick Douglass were sent to other cities. Even runaways who had lived in the North for years were always in danger of arrest. Because the fugitive slave laws were designed to help masters, it was even possible for free blacks to be kidnapped and taken South. The Vigilance Committees attempted to prevent these kidnappings and made numerous propaganda appeals to protest them. In New York Ruggles was always on guard against slave agents, and even compiled a Slaveholders Directory listing the names and addresses of lawyers, law enforcement officers, and others who "lend themselves to kidnapping."

In other communities, such as Boston or Philadelphia, although whites collaborated with blacks on the Vigilance Committees, most of the work was actually performed by Negroes. In Philadelphia Robert Purvis was president of the Vigilance Committee, while William Still, the corresponding secretary, was the one who co-ordinated the rescue work. In Syracuse, New York, the Committee depended on the AME Zion minister J. W. Loguen to shelter many runaways. In Rochester Frederick Douglass and many other black men in the community assisted fugitives. Douglass, "superintendent" of the Underground Railroad station there, used his home as its headquarters and equipped his office with a trap door and secret stairway for hiding fugitives. He spent many hours raising money to transport them to safety in Canada.

That the work of aiding the fugitives was largely done by blacks rather than whites was attested to by abolitionists of both races. James Birney, writing in 1837, described how slave escapes were facilitated by other Negroes: "Six weeks ago, a young married woman escaped from N. Orleans by steamboat and was successfully concealed here [Cincinnati] by her colored friends. Yesterday, her husband arrived, and at 5 o'clock in the afternoon they were both in the Stage on their way from this place to Canada. Such matters are almost uniformly managed by the colored people. I know nothing of them generally till they are passed." In the 1830's Theodore Wright complained that members of antislavery societies had not taken sufficient interest in helping fugitive slaves or protecting blacks from kidnappers. Wright, among the founders of the New York Vigilance Committee, appealed to whites to make the work of the Committee a basic objective of the American Anti-Slavery Society. While limited aid was ultimately given by such leaders as the Tappans, Weld, and Gerrit Smith, fugitive rescue work did not receive the kind of support that Wright and his colleagues sought. The New York Vigilance Committee had emphasized that the institution of slavery could not be destroyed unless large-scale efforts were undertaken to alleviate the plight of its victims in the North, but the antislavery societies did not allow fugitive aid to detract from the basic goal of abolition.

After the passage of the Fugitive Slave Law of 1850, however, more whites became sufficiently aroused to help the Vigilance Committees, or at least to give tacit support. In 1851 two publicized cases demonstrated how Negroes aided brethren whose liberty was threatened and how white juries were sympathetic toward such activities. In Christiana, a southern Pennsylvania town not far from the Maryland line, a slaveholder searching for runaways died in a gun battle waged against a group of free blacks who had armed to protect the home of one of their fellows. Thirty-eight were charged with treason and confined in jail to await a court trial. A jury deliberated only a few minutes before finding the first "traitor" not guilty, and the government's case collapsed completely. In Boston a black crowd entered the courthouse where a fugitive from Virginia named Shadrach was held in the custody of a United States marshal during proceedings preparatory to a return to slavery. On signal the Negroes seized Shadrach, spiriting him away to Canada. Several alleged conspirators were prosecuted, but a divided jury failed to find them guilty and the case was dismissed.

An important contribution of black people who had escaped was their work as abolitionist propagandists. It is true that during the first years of the American Anti-Slavery Society the leadership failed to make much use of black lecturers. In the 1830's the first Negroes to speak before local antislavery groups were Theodore Wright, James Forten, Robert Purvis, and Charles Lenox Remond, but all of these men were free Negroes who had never been slaves, and although they eloquently discussed the peculiar institution, their presentations lacked dramatic impact. Former slaves, many of whom were fugitives, were eventually asked to lecture. By the 1840's Frederick Douglass, William Wells Brown, Samuel R. Ward, Henry Bibb, Lunsford Lane, Harriet Tubman, Sojourner Truth, and many others spoke to antislavery audiences all over the North. Their activities probably constituted the Negroes' most important contribution to the abolitionist movement. In their speeches, and also in autobiographical narratives, Negroes provided the most compelling propaganda against the institution of slavery, the fugitives serving as a constant reminder of the millions of slaves who had not been able to run away. Audiences flocked to hear these speakers describe the whippings administered by overseers, the separation from loved ones sold down the river, and the often hectic efforts to get beyond the reach of slave catchers and bloodhounds. In the most personal terms they told exactly what slavery meant to them, and, speaking of what they had seen and experienced, they were deeply convincing.

Henry Bibb moved audiences to tears with a recital of how his wife, naked and bound, had been brutally whipped by an intoxicated slaveholder. Bibb's listeners would burst into cheers, laughter, and applause a few moments later as he described ways in which slaves outwitted their masters. Another crowd pleaser was Henry "Box" Brown, who recounted his escape from Richmond in a shipping box, which he later used as a prop on antislavery tours. Though white audiences felt entertained, they usually also came away impressed by the resourcefulness and indomitable will to freedom which these lecturers demonstrated. The sense of momentary aloneness and apprehension many runaways felt when they "crossed the line" to freedom was vividly portrayed by Harriet Tubman: "I was free, but there was no one to welcome me to the land of freedom. I was a stranger in a strange land. . . ." Recounting the tale of her escapes, she affected listeners with a profound faith in God and in herself.

For the many thousands of whites at these antislavery meetings who identified themselves with the sufferings of these speakers, there was often an opportunity to purchase their personal narratives, which were widely circulated. For example, the autobiography of Frederick Douglass received extensive distribution and the narratives of William Wells Brown and Josiah Henson sold thousands of copies. This body of literature became an important propaganda force in the struggle to win converts to the antislavery position and was supplemented by biographical and autobiographical sketches of thousands of slaves published by abolitionists. The printing presses kept turning as more fugitives arrived in the North and more whites joined the antislavery ranks.

Abolitionist writers heavily edited the bulk of these sketches, but there is no doubt that Douglass, Brown, Bibb, and others did their own writing. From the printed pages emerged a black hero whose aspirations for freedom and self-fulfillment represented a variation of the American dream, and in this sense a lesson in racial equality which aroused the interest and respect of many white Northerners. A contemporary reviewer of Douglass' *My Bondage and My Freedom* commented: "The mere fact that the member of an outcast and enslaved race should accomplish his freedom, and educate himself up to an equality of intellectual and moral vigor with the leaders of the race by which he was held in bondage, is, in itself, so remarkable that the story of the change cannot be otherwise than exciting."

Note

---

[1] The Board of Managers was an unwieldy and honorific group; for example, it numbered 131 in 1839 and 63 in 1841.

National Negro Conventions of the Middle 1840's: Moral Suasion vs. Political Action

Howard H. Bell

By 1840 militant abolitionism was a way of life widely accepted by many people in the North. To that date those championing moral persuasion as the best means of abolishing slavery had been the dominant group. But with the advent of the Liberty Party many turned to political action as more effective in accomplishing that end. By 1843 many Negro leaders, especially in the areas outside of New England, were ardent admirers of the new party since it offered an opportunity for a type of action which had previously been denied them. It was therefore to be expected that national conventions meeting in upstate New York during the middle 'forties would be influenced by Liberty Party ideals.

The annual national conventions which had been carried on for six consecutive years during the early 'thirties had died out when New York and Philadelphia began championing different ways of meeting the problems facing the Negro in the United States. By the end of that decade, however, there was a demand for a revival of the national conventions.[1] In the autumn of 1841 a number of men from Philadelphia set their names to a call for such an assembly. Among the items on the agenda were issues such as temperance, education, economy, agricultural and mechanical trades, and the development of a manual labor school. A new and previously unpopular feature was the consideration of petitioning for a grant of land from Congress for agricultural and other purposes for the use of the Negro.[2] Not content with petitioning for a grant of land, the subject of emigration was also listed for discussion.[3] To say the least the proposed assembly was set to deal with an ambitious schedule and one that might be expected to draw the fire of some abolitionists, especially those opposed to separate Negro organizations and to emigration.

One of the leading abolitionist journals asked God's blessing upon the new enterprise;[4] another was open in its criticism of the proposed convention and carried

Howard H. Bell, "National Negro Conventions of the Middle 1840's; Moral Suasion vs. Political Action," *Journal of Negro History*, XLII, October 1957, pp. 247–260. Reprinted by permission of the Association for the Study of Negro Life and History.

also in its columns the disapproval of at least two Negro newspapers.[5] As it turned out, both encouragement and criticism were wasted. Shortly before the proposed gathering, a Negro procession celebrating temperance and British West Indian emancipation was broken up by white boys in the streets of Philadelphia, and a protracted riot ensued. Some attempt was made to show that the proposal for the assembly was responsible for the riot,[6] but there were many other factors contributing to the outbreak. Due to the unsettled conditions following this unfortunate but not unusual affair, it was considered ill-advised to hold the convention, and the plans were dropped.[7]

One might speculate endlessly on what turn history would have taken if the convention had been held. Its agenda was broad enough that, if intelligently handled, it could have resulted in much good. And the men who called the convention were not of the same convictions as were those responsible for the revived national convention in 1843. The call for a national convention in 1843[8] was the signal for opposition from certain Boston Negroes who distrusted the politics of the New Yorkers responsible for the invitation.[9] The Bostonians decided, however, to participate in the convention "as a medium through which we may deliberately devise means to operate and cooperate with our white friends, against TWO of the greatest evils ever inflicted upon an innocent and inoffensive people — slavery and prejudice."[10] Negroes of New Bedford, Massachusetts, were not so tractable; they branded the backers of the convention as deserters of the Garrisonian tradition [which they were] and held that a good dose of real anti-slavery teaching of the old tradition was the only cure for the world's evils.[11]

Despite opposition, the convention assembled on August 15, 1843, at Buffalo, New York. Thirty of the delegates were from the Mohawk River area, five from Michigan, three from the New York metropolitan section, two from Massachusetts, two from Connecticut, and eight from Ohio. In addition, several states were represented by one person each.[12] The tone of the convention was set by a speech from the president *pro tem,* Samuel H. Davis, of Buffalo. He hailed the Constitution of the United States as a document guaranteeing freedom and equality to all citizens.[13] But Davis was not fully supported on this issue,[14] perhaps because those dictating policy were willing to let the constitutional question lie quiescent in the interest of pushing the matter of alignment with the Liberty Party.[15] Nor was Davis himself interested in putting all his faith in the Constitution. Before he had finished, he had hinted at military action by an oppressed people. His speech was aggressive enough to pave the way for any radical action the delegates might choose to take.

Like most of the others of the period the convention was interested in encouragement of accepted patterns of self-improvement — temperance, moral reform, support of mechanical trades and of antislavery.[16] The members spent some time on plans for the establishment of a national Negro press[17] and stressed the development of a frontier agricultural community. But education was neglected "until it was too late for a committee to report upon it, and do the subject justice, as was intended."[18] All of these subjects could be handled with a reasonable degree of unanimity and equanimity, but the more controversial problems were hotly debated.

It was a foregone conclusion that some attempt would be made to pay homage to the new religion of political affiliation (chiefly the Liberty Party); but when such a resolution was proposed, Frederick Douglass and Charles L. Remond, both moral suasionists at the time, leaped to spearhead the opposition. Of the two men, Remond had already attained a certain degree of prominence as an antislavery speaker in the Garrisonian tradition, while Douglass, later to become the greatest Negro orator and leader of the antebellum era, was but a few years removed from slavery. Chief supporters of the resolution were listed as Henry H. Garnet, William C. Munro, J. N. Gloucester, Theodore S. Wright, David Lewis, and Charles B. Ray. These men, with the possible exception of Lewis, were ministers, and all lived in the area of the Hudson River or west as far as Ohio and Michigan. They were, therefore, more inclined to the beliefs of western abolitionists than to those of the Garrisonians. Party affiliation, to the Garrisonians, meant affiliation with corruption; they contended, moreover, that it was unwise to tie the abolitionists to any one party. But few at the convention were of like belief, and the Liberty Party received the sanction of the assembly with but seven dissenting votes.[19] Not content with this victory, Liberty Party adherents revived the subject later in the convention and pronounced a second blessing upon the political party which stood for allowing the vote to all free men, regardless of color.[20]

As is evident, a large majority of the delegates at the Buffalo National Convention stood for radical political action, if measured by the Garrisonian standard. The scales, however, were more evenly balanced when it came to the consideration of endorsement of physical violence in the overthrow of slavery. Resort to such means had been much in the minds of the more aggressive Negroes for several years. Samuel E. Cornish had felt called upon in 1838 to criticize an ardent young man who had considered the matter favorably in a public speech.[21] Somewhat later a convention of Maine and New Hampshire Negroes had refused to condemn those who resorted to bloodshed for the sake of freedom.[22] It is not surprising, then, that Samuel H. Davis, when opening the Buffalo National Convention in 1843, should have hinted at using other than peaceful means to obtain rights long overdue, or that Henry Highland Garnet — spectacular, persuasive, and appealing — should have prepared an address to the slaves which he sought to have the convention sanction.

The speech was so effectively presented that he had his audience laughing or crying, almost at will.[23] In fact, one enthusiastic reporter went so far as to contend that Garnet had so swayed the audience that "for one hour of his life his [the reporter's] mind had not been his own, but wholly at the control of the eloquent negro."[24] This address, suppressed by the narrow margin of one vote, was not printed until five years later, and then, admittedly, with some modifications, "retaining, however, all of its original doctrine."[25] Much of the address, as printed, is plain antislavery argument. But directed to the slaves as it was, it might have been expected to attract more attention than it otherwise would. Add to this the championship of physical violence in securing freedom,[26] and it is easy to understand why the address could set off such a furor as it did on the convention floor.

Having worked up slowly to the subject of violence, Garnet suggested that the slaves go to their masters and demand their freedom, then refuse to work if that freedom were denied.

If they then commence the work of death, they and not you, will be responsible for the consequences. You had better all die, *die immediately,* than live slaves, and entail your wretchedness upon your posterity. . . . However much you and all of us may desire it there is not much hope of Redemption without the shedding of blood. If you must bleed, let it all come at once — rather *die freemen than live to be slaves.*[27]

Although the printed version has some moderating passages at the close, indicating that the speaker did not advocate an insurrection, the slaves were, even there, reminded that they were three million in number, and that resistance should be the motto.[28]

Despite the growing radicalism of the age, the preponderance of Liberty Party sympathizers in the assembly, and the eloquence of the speaker, the convention was not ready to assume the responsibility for such a message. It was turned over to a revision committee consisting of Garnet, Douglass, A. M. Sumner, S. N. [probably S. H.] Davis, and R. Banks.[29] With the exception of Douglass, these men were all from the area west of the Hudson River, and it is probable that not too much revision was made in the text. When the document was once more before the assembly, it was rejected but with the bare majority of one vote.[30] The episode was enlivened by the sardonic remark of Charles L. Remond to Charles B. Ray "not to try to sit on two stools," when Ray asked that his vote be added in support of the address after he had withheld his ballot on the first round.[31] It was not until public opinion had come around to a more aggressive attitude in 1848 that the address received the support of the free Negro community.

The Garrisonian press was bitterly opposed both to the Liberty Party tendencies of the convention and to Garnet's speech. Maria Weston Chapman, ardent Anti-Slavery Society worker, and sometimes relief editor for Garrison on *The Liberator,* was glad to see that the convention had had the good sense to reject the address. She felt that Garnet must have fallen under evil advisers, and she hoped the speech was for effect, rather than in demonstration of Garnet's real attitude. In commenting upon the current tendency to resort to ballots, she held that such action might easily lead to an exchange of bullets.[32] And at least one Negro newspaper was reported to be in accord with Mrs. Chapman's views concerning the Liberty Party.[33] But Garnet showed his readiness to defend himself against all comers when he wrote, "If it has come to this, that I must think and act as you do, because you are an abolitionist, or be exterminated by your thunder, then I do not hesitate to say that your abolitionism is abject slavery."[34] There was little in 1843 which would identify the national convention with those of the early 'thirties. Instead of serious consideration of emigration to Canada, this convention came within a trifle of advocating an insurrection of slaves. Instead of spending extensive time on a plan for a Negro college, it demanded emphatically that Negroes refrain from worshipping in churches where absolute equality was not allowed. Instead of timidly asserting that the Negro should have equality in the suffrage but admitting that there was not much to be done about it, the convention listened respectfully to a proposition for violence if equality were not forthcoming.

Here for the first time the moral suasionists, representing the old order, met in national convention with men who championed the newer confidence in political action as the means by which the salvation of all the people was to be accomplished. Though seriously outnumbered, the moral suasionists were not without modifying influence. The presence of Frederick Douglass and Charles L. Remond, along with a few others, was probably responsible for the rejection of Garnet's address to the slaves. Moreover, the two groups found that they had something in common in hatred of prejudice within the churches. And if Douglass and Remond in 1843 could not stem the tide of the Liberty Party in the West, they could at least hold up the avalanche long enough to make their opponents argue their cause and thus work for the enlightenment of the public.

As the delegates parted to go to their homes, some of them carried with them plans for state conventions which, it was expected, would advance the cause of the Negro. In other cases state conventions had been proposed before the national assembly had gathered. Indiana Negroes issued a call for a state assembly to convene at Indianapolis on September 4, 1843,[35] while to the east in Ohio plans had been set on foot as early as March for such a convention at Columbus.[36] Michigan[37] and New York[38] both held state gatherings shortly after the Buffalo National Convention, and it seems more than probable that Connecticut, and the coalition of Maine and New Hampshire were doing the same.

In 1847 upstate New York leaders once more urged the necessity of a national convention. Scheduled at first for mid-August,[39] the time of meeting was later extended to October. An examination of the list of delegates who gathered at Troy, New York, on October 6, 1847, reveals a surprising number from the state of New York (forty-six of a total of sixty-six). Of the rest, Massachusetts sent fourteen and Connecticut two, while single delegates were present from scattered states.[40] Connecticut was represented by two able ministers, Amos G. Beman, who had encouraged Negro state convention activities in his state for a decade, and J. W. C. Pennington, who had helped in getting the national convention organized in the early 'thirties. Massachusetts sent Frederick Douglass, Leonard Grimes, Boston minister, and William Wells Brown who was soon to attain some prominence as the first Negro novelist and historian. New York City commanded the services of James McCune Smith; Thomas Van Rensselaer, editor of The Ram's Horn, a new Negro newspaper; and Alexander Crummell, known chiefly for his interest in, and affiliation with, Liberia.[41] The brilliant and showy but somewhat erratic Henry

Highland Garnet was, as usual, the chief spokesman for the upstate third party men.

The idea of a national press which had been considered favorably in 1843 was revived and debated at length[42] and eventually decided in the affirmative. A separate manual labor college for the Negro was also considered favorably by the majority of those present.[43] But the subject of temperance, assigned to two ministers and an editor for recommendations, was side-stepped by the suggestion from these gentlemen that the matter be turned over to the temperance convention to meet at Great Barrington, Massachusetts, almost a year hence.[44]

The committee appointed to express the sentiments of the convention on matters of freedom and slavery was headed by Frederick Douglass. Other members included Thomas Van Rensselaer, John Lyle, R. D. Kenny, and Alexander Crummell. Their report was moral suasionist in tone and incurred the criticism of Garnet who took exception to such terms as "sanctity of religion," when used in the sense of protecting slavery. As a minister, he felt that religion was being blamed too much when it was represented as supporting slavery. It was for this reason that he urged the qualifying phrase, "falsely so called," to identify the brand of religion meant. He also took exception to sole reliance on moral suasion as a means of securing freedom for the slave. He contended that political action should be added as a legitimate means of securing the end in view.

It seems that the attack by Garnet and others was successful, and the report was canceled. Later it was reconsidered and placed in the hands of a new committee, of which Douglass and Garnet were both members.[45] When the report once more appeared, there was no reference to the term "moral suasion"; it was, nevertheless, a decidedly moral suasionist document. It abounded with such declarations as "the best means of abolishing slavery is the proclamation of the truth, and the best means of destroying caste is the mental, moral and industrial improvement of our people." And again,

Liberty is always sufficient to grapple with tyranny. Free speech — free discussion — peaceful agitation — the foolishness of preaching — these, under God, will subvert this giant crime, and send it reeling to its grave, as if smitten by a voice from the throne of God.[46]

This victory for moral suasionist doctrines at the Troy National Convention — a convention with a strong bent toward radical action — showed Frederick Douglass at his best as a champion of Garrisonian doctrines before he had come under the influence of the western abolitionists of the Gerrit Smith school of thought. Douglass was only then preparing to leave the East and to establish himself at some point in the area of the Great Lakes. It was Douglass who headed the first committee which brought in a report highly moral suasionist in tone. It was Douglass who defended it and when the report had been rejected, Douglass was appointed as one of the members of the new committee. Garnet, as chief spokesman for the opposition group, and thereby a representative of the majority of the delegates attending the convention, was unable to command more than the hollow appearance of victory in the elimination of such specific terms as "moral suasion," and in the softening of the attack on the church — an attack which had become a favorite sport of the Garrisonians.

There remains Garnet's triumph — the renewed address to the slaves, first delivered in 1843 at the Buffalo National Convention, and suppressed by that body. In describing Garnet's speech, William C. Nell, strong and loyal Garrisonian and opponent of physical force, incorporated much into the statement: "To those acquainted with his talent and eloquence, it will be unnecessary to mention that the address produced much sensation."[47] Reaction was not so intense as it had been four years earlier, partly because public opinion had moved rapidly toward accepting a more aggressive attitude in the intervening years. Moreover, Douglass's encouragement of the use of education and propaganda had its influence in softening the effect of Garnet's militancy.[48]

In the field of agriculture, various communal experiments on the American frontier were common, and some were to be found in the older settled communities. Emphasis was placed upon going to the farm as a kind of panacea for the ills of society. It was to be expected, then, that this attitude would be reflected in the Negro conventions of the period. In 1843 an able committee headed by Charles B. Ray presented a convincing address on the merits of an agricultural life. Possession of the soil was represented as giving an independence not easily attainable elsewhere. This committee was well informed. They had a report from a group in Mercer County, Ohio, who had refused to come to the convention but who were happy and reasonably prosperous on the farms which they had taken up only six years earlier.

In keeping with the communal experimentation of the times, it was recommended that agricultural communities be built up by banding together in units of about twenty family groups. These families were to settle on adjacent land, cooperate on matters of common interest such as schools, churches, roads, flour and saw mills, and share in any profits from such ventures — according to the amount of individual investment. A gesture toward erasure of the color line, or at least toward avoiding the accusation of planning a segregated community, was made by the provision that a few carefully selected white families might be accepted in the organization.[49]

When the convention met at Troy four years later the subject of agriculture was handled in much the same manner except that Gerrit Smith, philanthropist, humanitarian, and dabbler in practically every phase of the reform movement, had meantime made land in New York available for the asking. His generosity had placed 140,000 acres of land at the disposal of some 3,000 Negroes, and in so doing had made many of them eligible for the suffrage for the first time.[50] This was enough to divert the interest of the New Yorkers from such a communal frontier settlement as had been proposed in 1843. The new landholders were anxious to do something to show their appreciation to their benefactor, but Douglass and Garnet agreed that they could best accomplish that end by moving onto the land and improving it.[51]

The matter of a national press received favorable attention in the middle 'forties. Negroes had long been aware of the urgency for an organ which would be devoted entirely to the uplift of the race. *Freedom's Journal* and *The Rights of All* had attempted in the late 'twenties to fulfill such a need. *The Liberator* had served in that capacity in the early 'thirties. But as Garrison began to embrace other reforms or fads, the Negro once more sought an organ which he could call his own. To this end Philip A. Bell of New York started an ephemeral newspaper called *The Struggler,* to be followed in January, 1837, by *The Weekly Advocate.* This paper, after some reorganization, became *The Colored American,* and for several years was the chief organ of the colored people. With the opening of the decade of the 'forties, however, there were several struggling papers, and not one was receiving adequate support. It needed no prophet to foretell that all were likely to fail and that the cause of the Negro would suffer accordingly. This was one of the problems which faced the Buffalo National Convention in 1843.[52]

A committee appointed to deal with the subject held that a press could be used to build up or to tear down; that it could, if properly used, act as an agency for enlightenment and for getting acquainted; and that it could be utilized as an aid in the building of character. They recommended that a national press be established, either by the creation of a new weekly newspaper or by the support of one already set up.[53] This recommendation was followed by official action in the appointment of able men — Philip A. Bell, Samuel E. Cornish, Charles B. Ray, Amos G. Beman, Theodore S. Wright, and others — to look into the possibilities for establishing such an organ.[54] Most, if not all, of this group were experienced in the editorial field, but if they were successful in organizing a national publication it has not come to light.

Four years later at Troy the subject was again up for discussion. Again there were several Negro publications, and more in the planning stage.[55] Again a committee reported in favor of a national press. This time it was James McCune Smith, once associated with Samuel E. Cornish in editing *The Colored American,* who led the drive for such a publication.[56] Thomas Van Rensselaer had recently set up *The Ram's Horn,* and Frederick Douglass was soon to establish *The North Star;* both men were opposed to the national press. It was Douglass's opinion that such an arrangement would soon result in its being the press of a clique, rather than that of the Negro public.[57]

Opponents of the scheme, including Douglass and Van Rensselaer, came in for some of Garnet's witty sarcasm when that gentleman pointed out that those indisposed were chiefly in the newspaper business, or about to go into it. "Of course," he opined, "there was nothing of selfishness in all this."[58] But self-interest, it seems, may have colored Garnet's own reaction in favor of the press. Douglass, writing three months later, implied that there had been some thought of appointing a foreign agent to go to England to raise funds for the project.[59] But Garnet, if he was angling for such an appointment from the convention, was unsuccessful. He was awarded the place of home agent.[60]

When the vote was finally taken, less than one-fourth of those casting their ballots were opposed to the press.[61] Of the twenty from New York who voted, sixteen were in favor; of the four opposed, at least one, if not two, was involved in a current newspaper project. The total New York vote, however, was less than half of those recorded as delegates, and among those not voting were such men as William H. Topp, Albany businessman, Charles B. Ray, and Stephen Myers, Albany editor. Nine of the fourteen delegates from Massachusetts voted for the national press. Of the three who refrained from voting, Douglass was about ready to establish his own publication; Nathan Johnson was in the chair; and William Wells Brown was a loyal Garrisonian and therefore opposed to "complexional projects" of any kind. Only two from Massachusetts, William C. Nell and Charles Weeden, voted against the proposition.[62] With the vote of Massachusetts running so favorably for a Negro press, it might appear that the Garrisonian hold was not so strong as it might have been, even in the home state.

When the Cleveland National Convention met in the following year (September 6, 1848) there seem to have been but few present who had been at Troy. In the meantime, Frederick Douglass had established his *The North Star* at Rochester, New York, and it had surged rapidly to front rank among Negro publications. Furthermore, Douglass was present at the convention. And finally, the interest of the assembly was geared to the coming elections. Under these circumstances the press was dealt with effectively but perfunctorily by declaring that Douglass's publication was serving the need of a national press.[63] Thus at last, by official action but without assuming control, the Negro in convention had an official national press.

The conventions of the middle 'forties represent a definite gain for independent Negro leadership. By 1847 the break in the ranks of Negro abolitionists had been partially healed. By that time two national conventions had been held in which Garrisonian moral suasionists and ballot-minded Liberty Party adherents had worked on the problems facing the Negro and had found that they had much in common. Powerful moral suasionists of the Douglass-Nell variety had done business with the strident Garnet and the impatient Charles B. Ray of Liberty Party sympathies. This encounter demonstrated beyond a reasonable doubt that although the greatest of the giants still lived in the house of Garrison, the sheer force of numbers was slowly winning the argument for greater militancy and more dependence upon the ballot. By 1847 even the scoffers were forced to admit that the National Negro Convention was once more the most powerful voice in Negro affairs — a voice that had a militant ring which was absent from the deliberations of the 'thirties, a voice commanding the confidence of the Negro masses and the respect of all men of good will.

Notes

[1] *The Colored American,* September 23, 1837; December 30, 1837; April 12, 1838; April 19, 1838; May 3, 1838.

[2] *The Liberator*, November 5, 1841.

[3] *The Pennsylvania Freeman*, December 8, 1841.

[4] *The Liberator*, November 5, 1841.

[5] *National Anti-Slavery Standard*, July 28, 1842. The Negro newspapers involved were *The Northern Star and Freemen's Advocate* and the *Journal and Messenger*, two of those short-lived publications so characteristic of the era.

[6] *Ibid.*, August 11, 1842.

[7] *The Liberator*, August 19, 1842.

[8] *The Liberator*, July 28, 1843; *National Anti-Slavery Standard*, July 27, 1843.

[9] *The Liberator*, July 28, 1843.

[10] *Ibid.*, August 4, 1843.

[11] *National Anti-Slavery Standard*, September 7, 1843.

[12] National Negro Convention, 1843, *Minutes of the National Convention of Colored Citizens: Held at Buffalo, on the 15th, 16th, 17th, 18th and 19th of August, 1843, For the Purpose of Considering Their Moral and Political Condition as American Citizens* (New York: Piercy and Reed, printers, 1843), p. 10.

[13] *Ibid.*, p. 4.

[14] *Ibid.*, pp. 16–17, 24.

[15] The Liberty Party was founded in 1840 by abolitionists who believed in political action. Its concentration on antislavery, however, was not conducive to attracting a large following. During the years that the party remained active (1840–1848) it usually played into the hands of its worst enemies, the slaveholders. Nevertheless, it attracted many idealists and was especially appealing to Negroes because of its antislavery ideals.

[16] *National Negro Convention, 1843*, pp. 15–16.

[17] *Ibid.*, pp. 27–30.

[18] *Ibid.*, p. 21, footnote.

[19] *Ibid.*, pp. 15–16.

[20] *Ibid.*, pp. 21–22.

[21] *The Colored American*, March 3, 1838.

[22] Negro State Convention, Maine and New Hampshire, 1841, *Minutes of the First Colored Convention, Held in the City of Portland, October 6–[9], 1841* (Portland, [Maine]: 1842), p. 7.

[23] *Buffalo Commercial Advertiser*, August 23, 1843. Title varies.

[24] *Emancipator*, October 12, 1843. Title varies, as do the organizations sponsoring the paper.

[25] Henry Highland Garnet, *An Address to the Slaves of the United States of America* (*Rejected by the National Convention of 1843*), as printed in David Walker's *Walker's Appeal, in Four Articles, Together with a Preamble, to the Colored Citizens of the World, but in Particular, and Very Expressly to Those of the United States of America. Written in Boston, in the State of Massachusetts, Sept[ember] 28, 1829* (2nd ed., with corrections, etc.; [n.p.], 1830), p. 89. In this case Garnet's *Address* was merely added to Walker's *Appeal*, using consecutive pagination, or both articles were printed together in 1848, using the 1830 edition of the *Appeal*.

[26] *Ibid.*, p. 93.

[27] *Ibid.*, p. 94.

[28] *Ibid.*, p. 96.

[29] *National Negro Convention, 1843*, pp. 12–14.

[30] *Ibid.*, pp. 17–19.

[31] *The Liberator*, September 8, 1843.

[32] *Ibid.*, September 22, 1843.

[33] *Ibid.*, September 29, 1843.

[34] *Ibid.*, December 8, 1843.

[35] *The Philanthropist*, August 16, 1843. No record of this convention found.

[36] *Ibid.*, March 29, 1843. No record of this convention found.

[37] Negro State convention, Michigan, 1843, *Minutes of the State Convention of the Colored Citizens of the State of Michigan, Held in the City of Detroit, on the 26th & 27th of October, 1843, for the Purpose of Considering Their Moral & Political Condition as Citizens of the State* (Detroit: Printed by William Harsha, 1843), p. 4.

[38] *National Anti-Slavery Standard*, October 17, 1844.

[39] *The Liberator*, July 23, 1847.

[40] National Negro Convention, 1847, *Proceedings of the National Convention of Colored People, and Their Friends, held in Troy, N[ew] Y[ork] on 6th, 7th, 8th, and 9th October, 1847* (Troy, N[ew] Y[ork]: J. C. Kneeland & C[ompany], 1847), p. 3.

[41] *Ibid.*, pp. 8–9.

[42] *Ibid.*, pp. 6–9; *The North Star*, January 14, 1848. (This paper was founded and edited by Frederick Douglass; the name was later changed to *Frederick Douglass' Paper*); *The Liberator*, November 19, 1847.

[43] *The North Star*, December 3, 1847; *National Negro Convention*, 1847, pp. 9–11; *The Liberator*, November 19, 1847.

[44] *National Negro Convention, 1847*, p. 11.

[45] *Ibid.*, pp. 13–15.

[46] *Ibid.*, pp. 31–32.

[47] *The North Star*, December 3, 1847.

[48] *The Liberator*, November 19, 1847.

[49] *National Negro Convention, 1843*, pp. 30–36.

[50] *National Negro Convention, 1847*, pp. 25–30.

[51] *Ibid.*, p. 13.

[52] *The Liberator*, July 28, 1843; *National Anti-Slavery Standard*, July 27, 1843.

[53] *National Negro Convention, 1843*, pp. 27–30.

[54] *Ibid.*, p. 25.

[55] *National Negro Convention, 1847*, pp. 6–7.

[56] *The North Star*, January 14, 1848.

[57] *National Negro Convention, 1847*, pp. 6–8.

[58] *Ibid.*, p. 6.

[59] *The North Star*, January 14, 1848.

[60] *National Negro Convention, 1847*, p. 9.

[61] *The Liberator*, November 19, 1847.

[62] *National Negro Convention, 1847*, pp. 8–9.

[63] *The North Star*, September 29, 1848.

The Blacks
and John Brown

3

The Black Phalanx

W. E. B. Du Bois

. . . Of all this development [of black community institutions and social movements] John Brown knew far more than most white men and it was on this great knowledge that his great faith was based. To most Americans the inner striving of the Negro was a veiled and an unknown tale: they had heard of Douglass, they knew of fugitive slaves, but of the living, organized, struggling group that made both these phenomena possible they had no conception.

From his earliest interest in Negroes, John Brown sought to know individuals among them intimately and personally. He invited them to his home and he went to theirs. He talked to them, and listened to the history of their trials, advised them and took advice from them. His dream was to enlist the boldest and most daring spirits among them in his great plan.

When, therefore, John Brown came East in January, 1858, his object was not simply to further his campaign for funds, but more especially definitely to organize the Negroes for his work. Already he had disclosed his intentions to Thomas Thomas of Springfield and to Frederick Douglass. He now determined to enlist a larger number and he particularly had in mind the Negroes of New York and Philadelphia, and those in Canada. At no time, however, did John Brown plan to begin his foray with many Negroes. He knew that he must gain the confidence of black men first by a successful stroke, and that after initial success he could count on large numbers. His object then was to interest a few leaders like Douglass, organize societies with wide ramifications, and after the first raid to depend on these societies for aid and recruits.

During his stay with Douglass in February, 1858, he wrote to many colored leaders: Henry Highland Garnet and James N. Gloucester in New York; John Jones in Chicago, and J. W. Loguen of the Zion Church. The addresses of Downing of Rhode Island, and Martin R. Delaney were also noted. On February 23d, after he had been in Boston and Peterboro he notes writing to Loguen, one of the closest of his Negro friends: "Think I shall be ready to go with him [to Canada] by the first of March or about that time."[1]

On March 10th, John Brown and his eldest son, Henry Highland Garnet, William Still and others met at the house of Stephen Smith, the rich Negro lumber merchant, of 921 Lombard Street, Philadelphia. Brown seems to have stayed nearly

From W. E. B. Du Bois, *John Brown,* Philadelphia: Geroge Jacobs & Co., 1909, pp. 247–272.

a week in that city, and probably had long conferences with all the chief Philadelphia Negro leaders. On March 18th, he was in New Haven where he wrote Frederick Douglass and J. W. Loguen, saying: "I expect to be on the way by the 28th or 30th inst." After a flying visit home, involving a long walk to save expense, he appeared again at Douglass's in April. Gloucester collected a little money for him in New York and he probably received some in Philadelphia; at last he turned his face toward Canada.

He had long wished to see Canada, and had planned a visit as far back as 1846. Hither he had sent one of the earliest of his North Elba refugees, Walter Hawkins, who became Bishop of the British African Church. On April 8th, John Brown writes his son:

I came on here direct with J. W. Loguen the day after you left Rochester. I am succeeding, to all appearance, beyond my expectations. Harriet Tubman hooked on his whole team at once. He (Harriet) is the most of a man, naturally, that I ever met with. There is the most abundant material, and of the right quality, in this quarter, beyond all doubt. Do not forget to write Mr. Case (near Rochester) at once about hunting up every person and family of the reliable kind about, at, or near Bedford, Chambersburg, Gettysburg, and Carlisle, in Pennsylvania, and also Hagerstown and vicinity, Maryland, and Harper's Ferry, Va.[2]

He stayed at St. Catherines until the 14th or 15th, chiefly in consultation with that wonderful woman, Harriet Tubman, and sheltered in her home. Harriet Tubman was a full-blooded African, born a slave on the eastern shore of Maryland in 1820. When a girl she was injured by having an iron weight thrown on her head by an overseer, an injury that gave her wild, half-mystic ways with dreams, rhapsodies and trances. In her early womanhood she did the rudest and hardest man's work, driving, carting and plowing. Finally the slave family was broken up in 1849, when she ran away. Then began her wonderful career as a rescuer of fugitive slaves. Back and forth she traveled like some dark ghost until she had personally led over three hundred blacks to freedom, no one of whom was ever lost while in her charge. A reward of $10,000 for her, alive or dead, was offered, but she was never taken. A dreamer of dreams as she was, she ever

laid great stress on a dream which she had had just before she met Captain Brown in Canada. She thought she was in "a wilderness sort of place, all full of rocks, and bushes," when she saw a serpent raise its head among the rocks, and as it did so, it became the head of an old man with a long white beard, gazing at her, "wishful like, jes as ef he war gwine to speak to me," and then two other heads rose up beside him, younger than he, — and as she stood looking at them, and wondering what they could want with her, a great crowd of men rushed in and struck down the younger heads, and then the head of the old man, still looking at her so "wishful!" This dream she had again and again, and could not interpret it; but when she met Captain Brown, shortly after, behold he was the very image of the head she had seen. But still she could not make out what her dream signified, till the news came to her of the tragedy of Harper's Ferry, and then she knew the two other heads were his two sons.[3]

In this woman John Brown placed the utmost confidence. Wendell Phillips says: "The last time I ever saw John Brown was under my own roof, as he brought Harriet Tubman to me, saying: 'Mr. Phillips, I bring you one of the best and bravest persons on this continent — General Tubman, as we call her.' He then went on to recount her labors and sacrifices in behalf of her race."[4]

Only sickness, brought on by her toil and exposure, prevented Harriet Tubman from being present at Harper's Ferry.

From St. Catherines John Brown went to Ingersoll, Hamilton and Chatham. He also visited Toronto, holding meetings with Negroes in Temperance Hall, and at the house of the "late Mr. Holland, a colored man, on Queen Street West. On one occasion Captain Brown remained as a guest with his friend, Dr. A. M. Ross, who is distinguished as a naturalist, as well as an intrepid Abolitionist, who risked his life on several occasions in excursions into the South to enable slaves to flee to Canada."[5]

Having finally perfected plans for a convention, Brown hurried back to Iowa for his men. During his three months' absence they had been working and drilling in the Quaker settlement of Springdale, Ia., as most persons supposed, for future troubles in "bleeding Kansas." On John Brown's arrival they all hurriedly packed up — Owen Brown, Realf, Kagi, Cook, Stevens, Tidd, Leeman, Moffett, Parsons, and the colored man Richardson, together with their recruits, Gill and Taylor. The Coppocs were to come later. "The leave-taking between them and the people of Springdale was one of tears. Ties which had been knitting through many weeks were sundered, and not only so, but the natural sorrow at parting was intensified by the consciousness of all that the future was full of hazard for Brown and his followers. Before quitting the house and home of Mr. Maxon, where they had spent so long a time, each of Brown's band wrote his name in pencil on the wall of the parlor, where the writing still can be seen by the interested traveler." They all immediately started for Canada by way of Chicago and Detroit. At Chicago they had to wait twelve hours, and the first hotel refused to accommodate Richardson at the breakfast table. John Brown immediately sought another place. The company arrived shortly in Chatham and stopped at a hotel kept by Mr. Barber, a colored man. While at Chatham, John Brown, as Anderson relates,

made a profound impression upon those who saw or became acquainted with him. Some supposed him to be a staid but modernized "Quaker"; others a solid business man, from "Somewhere," and without question a philanthropist. His long white beard, thoughtful and reverent brow and physiognomy, his sturdy, measured tread, as he circulated about with hands, portrayed in the best lithograph, under the pendant coat-skirt of plain brown tweed, with other garments to match, revived to those honored with his acquaintance and knowing his history the memory of a Puritan of the most exalted type.[6]

John Brown's choice of Canada as a centre of Negro culture, was wise. There were nearly 50,000 Negroes there, and the number included many energetic, intelligent and brave men, with some wealth. Settlements had grown up, farms had been bought, schools established and an intricate social organization begun. Negroes like Henson had been loyally assisted by white men like King, and fugitives were welcomed and succored. Near Buxton, where King and the Elgin Association were working, was Chatham, the chief town of the county of Kent, with a large Negro population of farmers, merchants and mechanics; they had a graded school, Wilberforce Institute, several churches, a newspaper, a fire-engine company and several organizations for social intercourse and uplift. One of the inhabitants said:

Mr. Brown did not overestimate the state of education of the colored people. He knew that they would need leaders, and require training. His great hope was that the struggle would be supported by volunteers from Canada, educated and accustomed to self-government. He looked on our fugitives as picked men of sufficient intelligence, which, combined with a hatred for the South, would make them willing abettors of any enterprise destined to free their race.

There were many white Abolitionists near by, but they distrusted Brown and in this way he gained less influence among the Negroes than he otherwise might have had. Martin R. Delaney, who was a fervid African emigrationist, was just about to start to Africa, bearing the mandate of the last Negro convention, when John Brown appeared. "On returning home from a professional visit in the country, Mrs. Delaney informed him that an old gentleman had called to see him during his absence. She described him as having a long, white beard, very gray hair, a sad but placid countenance. In speech he was peculiarly solemn. She added, 'He looked like one of the old prophets. He would neither come in nor leave his name, but promised to be back in two weeks' time.' "

Finally Delaney met John Brown who said: " 'I come to Chatham expressly to see you, this being my third visit on the errand. I must see you at once, sir,' he continued, with emphasis, 'and that, too, in private, as I have much to do and but little time before me. If I am to do nothing here, I want to know it at once.' "

Delaney continues:

Going directly to the private parlor of a hotel near by, he at once revealed to me that he desired to carry out a great project in his scheme of Kansas emigration, which, to be successful, must be aided and countenanced by the influence of a general convention or council. That he was unable to effect in the United States, but had been advised by distinguished friends of his and mine, that, if he could but see me, his object could be attained at once. On my expressing astonishment at the conclusion to which my friends and himself had arrived, with a nervous impatience, he exclaimed, "Why should you be surprised? Sir, the people of the Northern states are cowards; slavery has made cowards of them all. The whites are afraid of each other, and the blacks are afraid of the whites. You can effect nothing among such people," he added, with decided emphasis. On assuring him if a council was all that was desired, he could readily obtain it, he replied, "That is all; but that is a great deal to me. It is men I want, and not money; money I can get plentiful enough, but no men. Money can come without being seen, but men are afraid of identification with me, though they favor my measures. They are cowards, sir! Cowards!" he reiterated. He then fully revealed his designs. With these I found no fault, but fully favored and aided in getting up the convention.[7]

Meantime John Brown proceeded carefully to sound public opinion, got the views of others, and, while revealing few of his own plans, set about getting together a body who were willing to ratify his general aims. He consulted the leading Negroes in private, and called a series of small conferences to thresh out preliminary difficulties. In these meetings and in the personal visits, many points arose and were settled. A member of the convention says:

One evening the question came up as to what flag should be used; our English colored subjects, who had been naturalized, said they would never think of fighting under the hated 'Stars and Stripes.' Too many of them thought they carried their emblem on their backs. But Brown said the old flag was good enough for him; under it freedom had been won from the tyrants of the Old World, for white men; now he intended to make it do duty for the black men. He declared emphatically that he would not give up the Stars and Stripes. That settled the question.

Some one proposed admitting women as members, but Brown strenuously opposed this, and warned the members not to intimate, even to their wives, what was done.

One day in my shop I told him how utterly hopeless his plans would be if he persisted in making an attack with the few at his command, and that we could not afford to spare white men of his stamp, ready to sacrifice their lives for the salvation of black men. While I was speaking, Mr. Brown walked to and fro, with his hands behind his back, as was his custom when thinking on his favorite subject. He stopped suddenly and bringing down his right hand with great force, exclaimed: "Did not my Master Jesus Christ come down from Heaven and sacrifice Himself upon the altar for the salvation of the race, and should I, a worm, not worthy to crawl under His feet, refuse to sacrifice myself?" With a look of determination, he resumed his walk. In all the conversations I had with him during his stay in Chatham of nearly a month, I never once saw a smile light upon his countenance. He seemed to be always in deep and earnest thought.[8]

The preliminary meeting was held in a frame cottage on Princess Street, south of King Street, then known as the "King Street High School." Some meetings were also held in the First Baptist Church on King Street. In order to mislead the inquisitive, it was pretended that the persons assembling were organizing a Masonic Lodge of colored people. The important proceedings took place in "No. 3 Engine House," a wooden building near McGregor's Creek, erected by Mr. Holden and other colored men.

The regular invitations were issued on the fifth:

Chatham, Canada, May 5, 1858

My Dear Friend:

I have called a quiet convention in this place of true friends of freedom. Your attendance is earnestly requested. . . .

Your friend,
John Brown

The convention was called together at 10 A.M., Saturday, May 8th, and opened without ceremony. There were present the following Negroes: William Charles Monroe, a Baptist clergyman, formerly president of the emigration convention and elected president of this assembly; Martin R. Delaney, afterward major in the United States Army in the Civil War; Alfred Whipper, of Pennsylvania; William Lambert and I. D. Shadd, of Detroit, Mich.; James H. Harris, of Cleveland, O., after the war a representative in Congress for two terms from North Carolina; G. J. Reynolds, an active Underground Railroad leader of Sandusky City; J. C. Grant, A. J. Smith, James M. Jones, a gunsmith and engraver, graduate of Oberlin College, 1849; M. F. Bailey, S. Hunton, John J. Jackson, Jeremiah Anderson, James M. Bell, Alfred Ellisworth, James W. Purnell, George Aiken, Stephen Dettin, Thomas Hickerson, John Cannel, Robinson Alexander, Thomas F. Cary, Thomas M. Kinnard, Robert Van Vauken, Thomas Stringer, John A. Thomas, believed by some to be John Brown's earlier confidant and employee at Springfield, Mass., afterward employed by Abraham Lincoln in his Illinois home and at the White House also; Robert Newman, Charles Smith, Simon Fislin, Isaac Holden, a merchant and surveyor and John Brown's host; James Smith, and Richard Richardson.

Hinton says: "There is no evidence to show that Douglass, Loguen, Garnet, Stephen Smith, Gloucester, Langston, or others of the prominent men of color in the states who knew John Brown, were invited to the Chatham meeting. It is doubtful if their appearance would have been wise, as it would assuredly have been commented on and aroused suspicion."⁹

The white men present were: John and Owen Brown, father and son; John Henri Kagi, Aaron Dwight Stevens, still known as Charles Whipple; John Edwin Cook, Richard Realf, George B. Gill, Charles Plummer Tidd, William Henry Leeman, Charles W. Moffett, Luke F. Parsons, all of Kansas; and Steward Taylor of Canada, twelve in all. It has been usually assumed that Jeremiah Anderson was white but the evidence makes it possible that he was a mulatto. John J. Jackson called the meeting to order and Monroe was chosen president. Delaney then asked for John Brown, and Brown spoke at length, followed by Delaney and others.

The constitution was brought forward and, after a solemn parole of honor, was read. It proved to be a frame of government based on the national Constitution, but much simplified and adapted to a moving band of guerrillas. The first forty-five articles were accepted without debate. The next article was: "The foregoing articles shall not be so as in any way to encourage the overthrow of any state government, or the general government of the United States, and look to no dissolution of the Union, but simply to amendment and repeal, and our flag shall be the same that our fathers fought for under the Revolution."

To this Reynolds, the "coppersmith," one of the strongest men in the convention, objected. He felt no allegiance to the nation that had robbed and humiliated him. Brown, Delaney, Kagi and others, however, earnestly advocated the article and it passed. Saturday afternoon the constitution was finally adopted and signed. Brown induced James M. Jones, who had not attended all the sittings, to come to this one, as the constitution must be signed, and he wished his name to be on the roll of honor. As the paper was presented for signature, Brown said, "Now, friend Jones, give us John Hancock bold and strong."

The account continues:

During one of the sittings, Mr. Jones had the floor, and discussed the chances of the success or failure of the slaves rising to support the plan proposed. Mr. Brown's scheme was to fortify some place in the mountains, and call the slaves to rally under his colors. Jones expressed fear that he would be disappointed, because the slaves did not know enough to rally to his support. The American slaves, Jones argued, were different from those of the West India Island of San Domingo, whose successful uprising is a matter of history, as they had there imbibed some of the impetuous character of their French masters, and were not so overawed by white men. "Mr. Brown, no doubt thought," says Mr. Jones, "that I was making an impression on some of the members, if not on him, for he arose suddenly and remarked, 'Friend Jones, you will please say no more on that side. There will be a plenty to defend that side of the question.' A general laugh took place."

A question as to the time for making the attack came up in the convention. Some advocated that we should wait until the United States became involved in war with some first-class power; that it would be next to madness to plunge into a strife for the abolition of slavery while the government was at peace with other nations. Mr. Brown listened to the argument for some time, then slowly arose to his full height, and said: "I would be the last one to take advantage of my country in the face of a foreign foe." He seemed to regard it as a great insult. That settled the matter in my mind that John Brown was not insane.[10]

At 6 P.M. the election of officers under the constitution took place, and was finished Monday, the tenth. John Brown was elected commander-in-chief; Kagi, secretary of war; Realf, secretary of state; Owen Brown, treasurer; and George B. Gill, secretary of the treasury. Members of congress chosen were Alfred Ellisworth and Osborne P. Anderson, colored.

After appointing a committee to fill other offices, the convention adjourned. Another and a larger body was also organized, as Delaney says: "This organization was an extensive body, holding the same relation to his movements as a state or national executive committee holds to its party principles, directing their adherence to fundamental principles."[11]

This committee still existed at the time of the Harper's Ferry raid. With characteristic reticence Brown revealed his whole plan to no one, and many of those close to him received quite different impressions, or rather read their own ideas into Brown's careful speech. One of his Kansas band says:

I am sure that Brown did not communicate the details of his plans to the members of the convention, more than in a very general way. Indeed, I do not now remember that he gave them any more than the impressions which they could gather from the methods of organization. From those who were directly connected with his movements he solicited plans and methods — including localities — of operations in writing. Of course, we had almost precise knowledge of his methods, but all of us perhaps did not know just the locality selected by him, or, if knowing, did not comprehend the resources and surroundings.[12]

"John Brown, never, I think," said Mr. Jones, "communicated his whole plan, even to his immediate followers. In his conversations with me he led me to think that he intended to sacrifice himself and a few of his followers for the purpose of arousing the people of the North from the stupor they were in on this subject. He seemed to think such sacrifice necessary to awaken the people from the deep sleep that had settled upon the minds of the whites of the North. He well knew that the sacrifice of any number of Negroes would have no effect. What he intended to do, so far as I could gather from his conversation, from time to time, was to emulate Arnold Winkelried, the Swiss chieftain, when he threw himself upon the Austrian spearmen, crying, 'Make way for Liberty.' "[13] Delaney in his own bold, original way assumed that Brown intended another Underground Railway terminating in Kansas. Delaney himself was on his way to Africa and could take no active part in the movement.

The constitution adopted by the convention was an instrument designed for the government of a band of isolated people fighting for liberty. The preamble said:

Whereas slavery, throughout its entire existence in the United States, is none other than a most barbarous, unprovoked and unjustifiable war of one portion of its citizens upon another portion — the only conditions of which are perpetual imprisonment and hopeless servitude or absolute extermination — in utter disregard and violation of those eternal and self-evident truths set forth in our Declaration of Independence: Therefore, we, citizens of the United States, and the oppressed people who, by a recent decision of the Supreme Court, are declared to have no rights which the white man is bound to respect, together with all other people degraded by the laws thereof, do, for the time being, ordain and establish ourselves the following provisional constitution and ordinances, the better to protect our persons, property, lives, and liberties, and to govern our actions.[14]

The Declaration of Independence referred to was probably designed to be adopted July 4, 1858, when, as originally planned, the blow was to be actually struck. It was a paraphrase of the original declaration and ended by saying:

Declaring that we will serve them no longer as slaves, knowing that the "Laborer is worthy of his hire," We therefore, the Representatives of the circumscribed citizens of the United States of America, in General Congress assembled, appealing to the supreme Judge of the World, for the rectitude of our intentions, Do in the name, & by authority of the oppressed Citizens of the Slave States, Solemnly publish and Declare: that the Slaves are, & of right ought to be as free & as independent as the unchangeable Law of God requires that All Men Shall be. That they are absolved from all allegiance to those Tyrants, who still persist in forcibly subjecting them to perpetual "Bondage," and that all friendly connection between them and such Tyrants, is & ought to be totally desolved, And that as free and independent citizens of these states, they have a perfect right, a sufficient and just cause, to defend themselves against the Tyrany of their oppressors, To solicit aid from & ask the protection of all true friends of humanity and reform, of whatever nation, & wherever found; A right to contract all Alliances, & to do all other acts and things which free independent Citizens may of right do. And for the support of the Declaration, with a firm reliance on the protection of divine Providence: We mutually pledge to each other, Our Lives, and Our sacred Honor.[15]

The constitution consisted of forty-eight articles. All persons of mature age were admitted to membership and there was established a congress with one house of five to ten members, a president and vice-president and a court of five members, each one of whom held circuit courts. All these officials were to unite in selecting a commander-in-chief, treasurer, secretaries, and other officials. All property was to be in common and no salaries were to be paid. All persons were to labor. All indecent behavior was forbidden: "The marriage relation shall be at all times respected, and families kept together, as far as possible; and broken families encouraged to reunite, and intelligence offices established for that purpose. Schools and churches established, as soon as may be, for the purpose of religious and other instructions; and the first day of the week regarded as a day of rest, and appropriated to moral and religious instruction and improvement, relief of the suffering, instruction of the young and ignorant, and the encouragement of personal cleanliness; nor shall any person be required on that day to perform ordinary manual labor, unless in extremely urgent cases."[16] All persons were to carry arms but not concealed. There were special provisions for the capture of prisoners, and protection of their persons and property.

John Brown was well pleased with his work and wrote home: "Had a good

Abolition convention here, from different parts, on the 8th and 10th inst. Constitution slightly amended and adopted, and society organized."[17]

Just now as everything seemed well started, came disquieting news from the East. Forbes had been there since November; growing more and more poverty-stricken and angry, and his threats, hints and visits were becoming frequent and annoying. He complained to Senator Wilson, to Charles Sumner, to Hale, Seward and Horace Greeley, and to the Boston coterie. He could not understand why these leaders of the movement against slavery, as he supposed, should leave the real power in the hands of John Brown, and neglect an experienced soldier like himself after raising false expectations. John Brown had dealt with Forbes gently but firmly, and had sought to conciliate him, but in vain. Brown was apparently determined to outwit him by haste; he had written his Massachusetts friends to join him at the Chatham Convention, but Sanborn and Howe had already received threatening letters from Forbes which alarmed them. He evidently had careful information of Brown's movements and was bent on making trouble. He probably was at this time in the confidence of McCune Smith and the able Negro group of New York who had developed a not unnatural distrust of whites, and a desire to foster race pride. Using information thus obtained, Forbes sought to put pressure on Republican leaders to organize more effective warfare on slavery, and to discredit John Brown. Sanborn wrote hastily: "It looks as if the project must, for the present, be deferred, for I find by reading Forbes's epistles to the doctor that he knows the details of the plan, and even knows (what very few do) that the doctor, Mr. Stearns, and myself are informed of it. How he got this knowledge is a mystery. He demands that Hawkins [John Brown] be dismissed as agent, and himself or some other be put in his place, threatening otherwise to make the business public."[18] Gerrit Smith concluded, "Brown must go no further." But Higginson wisely demurred. "I regard any postponement," he said, "as simply abandoning the project; for if we give it up now, at the command or threat of H. F., it will be the same next year. The only way is to circumvent the man somehow (if he cannot be restrained in his malice). When the thing is well started, who cares what he says?"[19]

Further efforts were made to conciliate Forbes but he wrote wildly:

I have been grossly defrauded in the name of humanity and anti-slavery. . . . I have for years labored in the anti-slavery cause, without wanting or thinking of a recompense. Though I have made the least possible parade of my work, it has nevertheless not been entirely without fruit. . . . Patience and mild measures having failed, I reluctantly have recourse to harshness. Let them not flatter themselves that I shall eventually become weary and shall drop the subject; it is as yet quite at its beginning.[20]

"To go on in face of this is madness," wrote Sanborn, and John Brown was urged to come to New York to meet Stearns and Howe. Brown had already been delayed nearly a month at Chatham by this trouble, but he obeyed the summons. Sanborn says:

When, about May 20th, Mr. Stearns met Brown in New York, it was arranged that hereafter the custody of the Kansas rifles should be in Brown's hands as the agent, not of this committee, but of Mr. Stearns alone. It so happened that Gerrit Smith, who seldom visited Boston, was coming there late in May. . . . He arrived and took rooms at the Revere House, where, on the 24th of May, 1858, the secret committee (organized in March, and consisting of Smith, Parker, Howe, Higginson, Stearns, and Sanborn) held a meeting to consider the situation. It had already been decided to postpone the attack, and the arms had been placed under a temporary interdict, so that they could only be used, for the present, in Kansas. The questions remaining were whether Brown should be required to go to Kansas at once, and what amount of money should be raised for him in the future. Of the six members of the committee only one (Higginson) was absent. . . . It was unanimously resolved that Brown ought to go to Kansas at once.

As soon as possible after this, on May 21st, Brown visited Boston, and while there held a conversation with Higginson, who made a record of it at the time. He states that Brown was full of regret at the decision of the Revere House council to postpone the attack till the winter or spring of 1859, when the secret committee would raise for Brown two or three thousand dollars; he meantime was to blind Forbes by going to Kansas, and to transfer the property so as to relieve the Kansas committee of responsibility, they in future not to know his plans.

"On probing Brown," Higginson goes on,

I found that he . . . considered delay very discouraging to his thirteen men, and to those in Canada. Impossible to begin in autumn; and he would not lose a day (he finally said) if he had three hundred dollars; it would not cost twenty-five dollars apiece to get his men from Ohio, and that was all he needed. The knowledge that Forbes could give of his plan would be injurious, for he wished his opponents to underrate him; but still . . . the increased terror produced would perhaps counterbalance this, and it would not make much difference. If he had the means he would not lose a day. He complained that some of his Eastern friends were not men of action; that they were intimidated by Wilson's letter, and magnified the obstacles. Still, it was essential that they should not think him reckless, he said; and as they held the purse, he was powerless without them, having spent nearly everything received this campaign, on account of delay, — a month at Chatham, etc.[21]

There was nothing now for Brown but to conceal his arms, scatter his men and hide a year in Kansas. It was a bitter necessity and it undoubtedly helped ruin the success of the foray. The Negroes in Canada fell away from the plan when it did not materialize and doubted Brown's determination and wisdom. His son hid the arms in northern Ohio in a haymow.

Meantime, a part of the company — Stevens, Cook, Tidd, Gill, Taylor and Owen Brown — immediately after the adjournment of the convention, had gone to Cleveland, O., and had found work in the surrounding country. Brown wrote from Canada at the time:

It seems that all but three have managed to stop their board bills, and I do hope the balance will follow the manlike and noble example of patience and perseverance set them by the others, instead of being either discouraged or out of humor. The weather is so wet here that no work can be obtained. I have only received $15 from the East, and such has been the effect of the course taken by F. [Col. Forbes], on our Eastern friends, that I have some fears that we shall be compelled to delay further action for the present. They [his Eastern friends] urge us to do so, promising us liberal assistance after a while. I am in hourly expectation of help sufficient to pay off our bills here, and to take us on to Cleveland, to see and advise with you, which we shall do at once when we shall get the means. Suppose we do have to defer our direct efforts; shall great and noble minds either indulge in useless complaint, or fold their arms in discouragement, or sit in idleness, when we may at least avoid losing ground? It is in times of difficulty that men show what they are; it is in such times that men mark themselves. Are our difficulties such as to make us give up one of the noblest enterprises in which men ever were engaged?[22]

Two weeks later the rest of the party, except Kagi, followed to Cleveland, John Brown going East to meet Stearns. Kagi, who was an expert printer, went to Hamilton, Canada, where he set up and printed the constitution, arriving in Cleveland about the middle of June when Brown returned from the East. Realf says that Brown did not have much money, but sent him to New York and Washington to watch Forbes and possibly regain his confidence. Realf, however, had become timid and lukewarm in the cause and sailed away to England. The rest of the men scattered. Owen Brown went to Akron, O. Cook left Cleveland for the neighborhood of Harper's Ferry; Gill secured work in a Shaker settlement, probably Lebanon, O., where Tidd was already employed; Steward Taylor went to Illinois; Stevens awaited Brown at Cleveland; while Leeman got some work in Ashtabula County. John Brown left Boston, on the 3rd of June, proceeding to the North Elba home for a short visit. Then he, Kagi, Stevens, Leeman, Gill, Parsons, Moffett, and Owen were gathered together and the party went to Kansas, arriving late in June.

Thus suddenly ended John Brown's attempt to organize the Black Phalanx. His intimate friends understood that the great plan was only postponed, but the postponement had, as Higginson predicted, a dampening effect, and Brown's chances of enlisting a large Canadian contingent were materially lessened. Nevertheless, seed had been sown. And there were millions of human beings to whom the last word of the Chatham Declaration of Independence was more than mere rhetoric: "Nature is mourning for its murdered and afflicted children. Hung be the Heavens in scarlet!"

Notes

[1] Manuscript Diary of John Brown, Boston Public Library, Vol. 2, p. 35.
[2] Letter to John Brown, Jr., 1858, in Sanborn, p. 452.

[3] Bradford, *Harriet, the Moses of Her People*, pp. 118–119.

[4] Letter of Wendell Phillips, printed in Bradford, *Harriet, the Moses of Her People*, pp. 155–156.

[5] Hamilton, *John Brown in Canada*, p. 10.

[6] Anderson, *A Voice from Harper's Ferry*, p. 9.

[7] Rollins, *Life and Public Services of Martin R. Delaney*, pp. 85–90.

[8] Reminiscences of J. M. Jones, in Hamilton, *John Brown in Canada*, pp. 14–15.

[9] Hinton, p. 178.

[10] Reminiscences of J. M. Jones, in Hamilton, *John Brown in Canada*, pp. 14 and 16.

[11] Rollins, *Life and Public Services of Martin R. Delaney*, pp. 85–90.

[12] Reminiscences of George B. Gill, in Hinton, p. 185.

[13] Reminiscences of J. M. Jones, in Hamilton, *John Brown in Canada*, p. 16.

[14] Hinton, pp. 619–633.

[15] Hinton, pp. 642–643.

[16] Provisional Constitution, Art. 42.

[17] Letter to his family, 1858, in Sanborn, pp. 455–456.

[18] Letter from Sanborn to Higginson, 1858, in Sanborn, p. 458.

[19] Letter from Higginson to Theodore Parker, in Sanborn, p. 459.

[20] Letter from Forbes to Higginson, 1858, in Sanborn, pp. 460–461.

[21] Sanborn, pp. 463–464.

[22] Letter to Owen Brown, 1858, in Richman, *John Brown Among the Quakers*, pp. 40–41.

John Brown and the Paradox of Leadership among American Negroes

David Potter

One of the anomalies in the history of American Negroes is that, as a group, they have had only very limited opportunity to choose their own leadership. Historians agree, more or less, on a selected list of men who have been Negro leaders — Frederick Douglass, Booker T. Washington, W. E. B. Du Bois, Marcus Garvey, Martin Luther King. Of course, there have also been other very distinguished figures — Thurgood Marshall, Ralph Ellison, James Baldwin, Walter White, Roy Wilkins, *et al.*, but they have not commanded large mass followings; and there have been still others like Elijah Muhammad, Malcolm X, and Stokeley Carmichael whose role is or was controversial even within the Negro community. But none of these men was ever chosen to leadership by an election in which the body of American Negroes voted for what might be called "the Negroes' choice." Despite the widespread growth of organized groups of Negro activists in recent years, there has never been an organization which we can designate with assurance as expressing the attitudes of the rank and file of American Negroes, unless it was Marcus Garvey's Universal Negro Improvement Association. Most of the others have appealed either to the middle class, as the NAACP has done, or to ideological radicals, and not to the run-of-the-mill American Negro.

This absence of an organizational basis for the selection of leaders has meant that the positions of leadership were gained in special ways, sometimes in arbitrary or, as it were, fictitious ways. For instance, Frederick Douglass received his license as spokesman for four million slaves from a small coterie of abolitionists who later quarrelled with him. True, he was an excellent choice and he proved a very able leader indeed — perhaps as able as any American Negro — but the choice was nevertheless a historical accident, as the choice of many excellent leaders has been. Booker T. Washington, also an able man, did not owe his eminence to the recognition that Negroes gave him, but was appointed to the political leadership of American Negroes by Theodore Roosevelt, and to the economic leadership by Andrew Carnegie. W. E. B. Du Bois received his investiture in an especially ironical way —

From David Potter, *The South and the Sectional Conflict,* Baton Rouge: Louisiana State University Press, 1968, pp. 201–218. Reprinted by permission of the publisher.

the anomaly of which he felt as keenly as anyone else. He was made the key figure in the NAACP by a wealthy, highly respectable, and I think one can say smug, self-appointed committee of upper-class white moderate reformers; later, he owed his more or less posthumous canonization to academic Marxist intellectuals whom most Negroes had never heard of. Today some of the militant types whose names flash like meteors across the headlines — Carmichael, Rap Brown, LeRoi Jones — have been fobbed off on American Negroes partly by social revolutionaries who care nothing for civil rights or Negro welfare within our existing society, and partly by the mass media which need sensational and extravagant material to galvanize the attention of a jaded public. If one looks for Negroes who owed their positions of leadership primarily to the support accorded them by other Negroes, the most authentic names are those of Marcus Garvey and Martin Luther King, and perhaps Roy Wilkins, despite the attacks which he has sustained from the left. At a more limited level, I think one should add Elijah Muhammad and Malcolm X.

These comments may seem extraneous indeed to a consideration of the career of John Brown, but indirectly they may have a certain pertinence because though Brown was not a Negro, he probably went farther in plans for launching a Negro revolution in the United States than anyone in history. He intended to become the commander-in-chief of an army of Negroes. Yet he had no Negro lieutenants; he took almost no advice from Negroes and acted in defiance of such advice as he did take; and most paradoxical of all, he completely concealed his intended insurrection from the Negroes who were expected to support it. His was the classic case of a man who acted in the name of American Negroes and relied upon them to follow him, but never really sought to represent them or to find out what they wanted their leader to do.

Historians of the antislavery movement have already complained, with considerable justice I think, that the Negro was neglected even by the abolitionists. Many abolitionists could not see the Negroes, as it were, for the slaves. Thus even the underground railroad became, historiographically, the first Jim Crow transportation in America. Traditional accounts pictured the railroad as an operation in which heroic white conductors braved dangers unspeakable in transporting fugitives from one hideout to the next, while the helpless and passive Negroes lay inert in the bottom of the wagon bed, concealed under a layer of hay. We now know that a good many respectable Yankee families who had never worked on the railroad later decided that they had intended to, or they would have if there had been a fugitive handy, and gradually translated this sentimental ex post facto intention into the legend of a fearless deed. But that is beside the point. What is relevant to the theme of this paper is that historically there was an anomalous relationship between the Negro slaves and their white sympathizers, and the paradox of this relationship shows up in its most striking form in the story of John Brown and Harpers Ferry. The paradox lay in the fact that the white abolitionists believed that the Negroes were all on the brink of a massive insurrection, yet they seldom consulted any Negro for corroboration and they conducted their own abolitionist activities — even John

Brown's insurrectionary activities — as if Negroes could be regarded abstractly, like some sort of chemical element which at a certain heat would fuse into a new compound, and not concretely as a plurality of diverse men and women, each one with a temperament and aspirations of his own.

What were John Brown's specific relations with Negroes? It cannot be said that Negroes were entirely an abstraction to him, as they have been to some civil rights enthusiasts, for he knew Negroes, worked with them, and included them, on terms of seeming familiarity, in the intimacy of his little band of followers. But let us examine the record in more detail.

John Brown was apparently reared from an early age to hate slavery. The details may have been overdramatized, as they have been in the story of the early life of Lincoln, but the fact appears clear. As early as the 1830's he assisted in the escape of at least one fugitive; he made plans to rear a Negro child with his own children in his home; and he also thought of conducting a school for Negroes. His systematic activity in behalf of Negroes and his actual association with Negroes, however, began in the late 1840's when he agreed to move to North Elba, New York, where Gerrit Smith proposed to make him responsible for a colony of Negroes for which Smith was prepared to give 120,000 acres. At North Elba, Brown tried to help the Negro settlers, including at least one known fugitive. He gave them advice about farming and took some into his home, where they worked and shared the Spartan life of his family. But the North Elba project failed, primarily because the region never has been good farm country; it was frigid and rigorous in a way that made adaptation by Southern Negroes especially difficult. Moreover, Brown's own financial difficulties in the wool business made it impossible for him to stay at North Elba on a regular basis, and compelled him to spend much of his time at Springfield, Massachusetts, instead. At Springfield in 1847, he invited Frederick Douglass to visit him, and there he revealed to Douglass the first version of the plan which ultimately took him to Harpers Ferry. This was a scheme to organize a band of about twenty-five men, who would operate from hideouts in the Southern Appalachians. These men would induce slaves to run away and would assist them in their escape. Douglass had been a fugitive slave himself, had lived among slaves, had known the South at first hand; but there is no evidence that Brown asked him for his opinion about the practicability of the plan or about any aspect of the operations. Douglass probably knew a great deal that might have been useful to Brown, but Brown took no advantage of this potential information. This was characteristic of him throughout his life.

By the time of the enactment of the Fugitive Slave Act in 1850, Brown was in Springfield most of the time. In response to the act, he organized a League of Gileadites, as he called it, to offer physical resistance to the enforcement of the act. He drew up an "Agreement" and nine resolutions for the League, with an emphasis upon encouraging Negroes to be brave and not to resort to halfway measures: "When engaged, do not do your work by halves, but make clean work with your enemies and be sure you meddle not with any others. . . . All traitors must die, whenever caught and proven to be guilty." Brown wrote to his wife in November, 1850: "I, of course, keep encouraging my colored friends to 'trust in God and keep their powder dry.' I did so today at a Thanksgiving meeting, publicly." Forty-four black men and women of Springfield signed Brown's agreement, but their commitment was never put to the test, for no efforts were made by Federal officials to arrest fugitives in the Springfield area. Still, the League is of great interest, for it was the only case in which this man — who gave so much of his energy while living and finally his life itself to the Negro cause — relied primarily upon Negroes in his work.

As the focus of the slavery controversy shifted to Kansas, Brown shifted his activities to that arena, and the plans which he had revealed to Douglass fell into abeyance. But ultimately it was the Kansas diversion which led him back to the Virginia project. Kansas fed his impulse toward violence, his appetite for leadership, and his hatred of slavery. It also unfitted him for his former prosaic pursuits in the wool trade. If Kansas had continued as a scene of violence, he might have ended his career as a Jayhawker on the Kansas prairies, but by 1857 Kansas was becoming pacified. Robert J. Walker had replaced Geary as governor and was giving the Free-Soilers fair treatment; the Free-Soilers had won control of the legislature when Walker threw out fraudulent proslavery votes. The antislavery party had nothing whatever to gain by a resumption of the border wars. They remembered, unpleasantly, the murders committed by Brown along Pottawatomie Creek (something which Easterners did not know about), and they regarded Brown as a troublemaker — trigger-happy and too much of a lone wolf. Brown began to perceive that his career as a Kansas guerrilla was played out, and though he still talked about organizing a crack military unit for Kansas, his thoughts were turning increasingly toward the old idea of some kind of operation in the Southern Appalachians.

Brown left Kansas twice, first in October, 1856, with a divided mind as to whether he ought to return and continue active in the border wars; and again in November, 1857, knowing that his path would lead to Virginia. It is significant that, on both occasions, he stopped off at Rochester to see Douglass (in December, 1856, and in January, 1858). What meaning the visit in 1856 may have had, no one now can tell; at least it showed, as Douglass testifies, that the relationship formed nine years previously had been kept very much alive. But the visit in 1858 lasted for three weeks, and during this time Brown unfolded in full, perhaps for the first time, his second version of a plan for operation in Virginia. Douglass did not, at that time, disassociate himself from the plan, and indeed he later helped Brown to raise funds among well-to-do Negroes. But having been both a slave and a fugitive, Douglass perceived defects in the realism of Brown's plan, and he warned Brown of the pitfalls which were involved. John Brown did with this advice what he always did with all advice — he ignored it.

An interval of twenty months was to elapse between these conferences with Douglass and the final action at Harpers Ferry. This represented a delay of over a year in Brown's original plans. The delay resulted from two things: first, lack of money; and second, the fact that a soldier of fortune named Hugh Forbes, whom Brown had taken on as a military adviser, became disaffected because he did not receive the pay which he thought he had been promised, broke confidence, and revealed much of the plot to Senators Henry Wilson and William H. Seward. This breakdown in security greatly alarmed Brown's financial supporters, who virtually ordered him to suspend his plans.

Thus, during most of 1858 and 1859, Brown, who wanted only to smite the slaveholders, discovered that he had to be a salesman and a fund-raiser first. So long as he was soliciting for funds for aid to Free-Soilers in Kansas, he was able to make public appeals. But as his insurrectionary scheme developed, it required the utmost secrecy, and he could appeal only to trusted sympathizers including principally the Secret Six — Gerrit Smith in Peterboro, New York, and five backers in Boston: George L. Stearns, Franklin B. Sanborn, Thomas Wentworth Higginson, Theodore Parker, and Samuel Gridley Howe. These men had been moderately generous since 1857, but they tended to want more action before they gave additional money, and Brown wanted additional money as a preliminary to the action. Often he was actually reduced to asking for handouts, and he never did obtain anything approaching the financial support which was needed for an operation on the scale which he projected.

Somehow, nevertheless, he weathered all these difficulties. Meanwhile, he had been looking to a means of formalizing his plans and raising recruits; and to this end he had made a curious pilgrimage with twelve of his followers, all of them white men except Richard Richardson, to Chatham, Ontario, in May, 1858. Ontario at that time had a population of upwards of thirty thousand Negroes, a vast proportion of whom were former slaves who might be expected to support a campaign against slavery in the South. Among these people, Brown had determined to make his appeal, to relax secrecy, and to seek the sanction and support of the Negro community for his daring plan. He had invited Gerrit Smith, Wendell Phillips, "and others of like kin" to be on hand.

Accordingly, on May 8, 1858, Brown presented to a secret "convention" at Chatham, consisting of twelve of his own followers and thirty-four resident Negroes, a plan of organization entitled "A Provisional Constitution and Ordinances for the people of the United States." This document condemned slavery, defined slavery as war, thus asserting for the slaves a legal status as belligerents, and provided for a provisional government, with a commander-in-chief of the army, an executive, a legislature, and a judiciary. This government was to act against slavery — indeed, to make war against it — and in explaining it Brown stated where the army would get its troops. "Upon the first intimation of a plan formed for the liberation of the slaves," he said, "they would immediately rise all over the Southern states." By "flocking to his standard" they would enable him to extend his operations outward and southward from the mountain country in which he would begin, until he could operate upon the plantations of the lower South. They could defeat any militia, or even Federal troops sent against them, and "then organize the freed blacks under this provisional Constitution." What John Brown was planning was not a raid but a revolution.

The convention politely voted for the proposed Constitution, and on the next day it elected John Brown commander-in-chief and members of his party Secretaries of State, of the Treasury, and of War. Two men were elected as members of Congress, and one of these, Osborn P. Anderson, was an Ontario Negro. All the others were whites.

But Gerrit Smith was not there; Frederick Douglass was not there; and Wendell Phillips was not there. And when John Brown left Ontario, only two new Negro recruits went with him, one of whom, fearing arrest, soon returned to Canada. This was the only real effort Brown ever made to organize Negro support, and it had failed completely. It indicated clearly that the most famous project for a Negro insurrection in the history of the United States did not have the full support of even a corporal's guard of Negroes. There must have been hundreds of Negroes in Ontario who heard all about Brown's "secret" plan, but they had learned in a realistic school, and far more shrewdly than Emerson and Thoreau, and the litterateurs of Boston, they recognized that there was something unrealistic about this man. What was wrong was that he was recruiting members of a supporting cast for a theatrical melodrama in which the protagonist and principal actor was to be John Brown.

Only a month after the Chatham "convention" Brown sent one of his very earliest recruits, John E. Cook, to Harpers Ferry, Virginia, to live as a spy and to reconnoiter the environs. Cook found employment as a lock-tender on the canal and maintained his mission for over a year, but Brown was very apprehensive that he would talk too much, and this apprehension must have increased greatly when Cook married a local Harpers Ferry girl.

Fourteen months after the Chatham convention, Brown and a small band of followers began to converge on a farmhouse in Maryland which was to be their rendezvous. At first there were twenty of them, including sixteen whites and four Negroes — two of whom were born free and two of whom had run away from slavery. After they had gathered, Frederick Douglass came down to Chambersburg, Maryland, with a friend of his, Shields Green, who was, like himself, an escaped slave. Brown and Douglass had a final conference, which must have been a strained affair on both sides. Brown now revealed a new and even more alarming design — his purpose to seize the arsenal at Harpers Ferry. To this Douglass instantly took exception. He warned Brown that the position would be a trap from which escape would be impossible, and also that an attack on Federal property would turn the whole country against Brown's plans. He said that this was such a complete change of purpose that he would no longer participate. Brown urged him not to withdraw, saying, "I want you for a special purpose. When I strike, the bees will begin to swarm, and I shall want you to help me hive ʰem." But Douglass still refused, and turning to his friend he asked what Green intended to do. Green's reply was, "I b'lieve I'll go wid de ole man."

Green was later accused of lack of courage, but there was in fact something supremely heroic about his action. His remark showed little confidence in Brown's plan but much loyalty to Brown personally; and he later died on the gallows because he had subordinated his judgment to his sense of personal devotion.

On the evening of October 16, 1859, after waiting three months for additional men, money, and munitions, most of which never arrived, John Brown marched with nineteen of his band, now grown to twenty-two, down to Harpers Ferry. There he seized the Potomac River bridge, the Shenandoah River bridge, and the Federal armory and rifle works. He also sent out a detail to bring in two of the slaveholders of the neighborhood with their slaves. This mission was accomplished. Then he settled into the arsenal and waited, while first the local militia and later a small Federal force gathered to besiege him. Within thirty-six hours, his hopes were blasted and his force was destroyed — five men had escaped, but ten were dead or dying, and seven were in prison, all to die at the end of a rope.

Technically, Brown's operation had been such an unmitigated disaster that it has lent color to the belief that he was insane. Certain aspects were indeed incongruous. After making melodramatic gestures in the direction of secrecy, he had left behind him on the Maryland farm a large accumulation of letters which revealed all his plans and exposed all his secret supporters among the elite of Boston. As Hugh Forbes wrote, "the most terrible engine of destruction which he [Brown] would carry with him in his campaign would be a carpet-bag loaded with 400 letters, to be turned against his friends, of whom the journals assert that more than forty-seven are already compromised." After three and a half months of preparation, he marched at last without taking with him food for his soldiers' next meal, so that, the following morning, the Commander-in-Chief of the Provisional Army of the North, in default of commissary, was obliged to order forty-five breakfasts sent over from the Wagner House. For the remaining twenty-five hours, the suffering of Brown's besieged men was accentuated by the fact that they were acutely and needlessly hungry. His liaison with allies in the North was so faulty that they did not know when he would strike, and John Brown, Jr., who was supposed to forward additional recruits, later stated that the raid took him completely by surprise. If this was, as is sometimes suggested, because of the disordered condition of young Brown's mind rather than because of lack of information from his father, it still leaves a question why such a vital duty should have been entrusted to one whose mental instability had been conspicuous ever since Pottawatomie. Finally, there was the seemingly incredible folly of seizing a Federal arsenal and starting a war against the state of Virginia with an army of twenty-two men. This latter folly was probably the strongest factor in the later contention that he was insane. In layman's terms, anybody who tried to conquer a state as large as one of the nations of Western Europe with less than two dozen troops might be regarded as crazy. Was John Brown crazy in these terms?

Without trying to resolve the insanity question, to which C. Vann Woodward, Allan Nevins, and others have given extensive attention, let me just make two brief comments: first, that insanity is a clear-cut legal concept concerning a psychological condition which is seldom clear-cut; second, that the insanity concept has been invoked too much by people whose ulterior purposes were too palpable — first by people who hoped to save Brown's life by proving him irresponsible; then by Republicans who wanted to disclaim his act without condemning him morally; and finally by adverse historians who wanted to discredit his deeds by saying that only a madman would do such things. The evidence shows that Brown was very intense and aloof, that he became exclusively preoccupied with his one grand design, that he sometimes behaved in a very confused way, that he alternated between brief periods of decisive action and long intervals when it is hard to tell what he was doing, that mental instability occurred with significant frequency in his family, and that some who knew him believed he had a vindictive or even a homicidal streak with strong fantasies of superhuman greatness. Also, Pottawatomie should be borne in mind. From all this, one may clearly infer that Brown was not, as we would now term it, a well-adjusted man.

But withal, the heaviest count in the argument against Brown's sanity is the seeming irrationality of the Harpers Ferry operation. Yet Harpers Ferry, it might be argued, was irrational if, and only if, the belief in a vast, self-starting slave insurrection was a delusion. But if this was a fantasy, it was one which Brown shared with Theodore Parker, Samuel Gridley Howe, Thomas Wentworth Higginson, and a great many others who have never been called insane. It was an article of faith among the abolitionists that the slaves of the South were seething with discontent and awaited only a signal to throw off their chains. It would have been heresy for an orthodox abolitionist to doubt this, quite as disloyal as for him to entertain the idea that any slave owner might be a well-intentioned and conscientious man. Gerrit Smith believed it, and two months before Brown's attempted coup he wrote, "The feeling among the blacks that they must deliver themselves gains strength with fearful rapidity." Samuel Gridley Howe believed it, and even after Brown's failure and when war came, he wrote that twenty to forty thousand volunteers could "plough through the South and be followed by a blaze of servile war that would utterly and forever root out slaveholding and slavery." Theodore Parker believed it, and wrote in 1850, "God forgive us our cowardice, if we let it come to this, that three millions of human beings . . . degraded by us, must wade through slaughter to their inalienable rights." After Harpers Ferry, Parker said, "The Fire of Vengeance may be waked up even in an African's heart, especially when it is fanned by the wickedness of a white man; then it runs from man to man, from town to town. What shall put it out? The white man's blood." William Lloyd Garrison was apparently inhibited from making such statements by his opposition on principle to the use of violence, but his *Liberator* constantly emphasized the unrest and resentment among the slaves; and he had once declared that, but for his scruples, he would place himself "at the head of a black army at the South to scatter devastation and death on every side." As J. C. Furnas has expressed it, there was a widespread "Spartacus complex" among the abolitionists, a fascinated belief that the South stood on the brink of a vast slave uprising and a wholesale slaughter of the whites. "It is not easy, though necessary," says Furnas, "to grasp that Abolitionism could, in the same breath warn the South of arson, rape, and murder and sentimentally admire the implied Negro mob leaders brandishing axes, torches, and human heads." This complex arose from the psychological needs of the abolitionists and not from any evidence which Negroes had given to them. No one really asked the Negroes what they wanted, or just how bloodthirsty they felt. There is much evidence that they wanted freedom to be sure, but again there is not much evidence that anyone even asked them how they thought their freedom could best be gained, and how they would like to go about getting it. Certainly John Brown did not ask, when he had a really good opportunity at Chatham, Ontario. All he did was talk. He did not listen at all. In fact there is no evidence that he ever listened at anytime, and this is perhaps the most convincing proof that he lived in the "private world" of an insane man.

But Brown's idea that the South was a waiting torch, and that twenty-two men without rations were enough to put a match to it, far from being a unique aberration, was actually one of the most conventional, least original notions in his whole stock of beliefs. Thus the Boston *Post* spoke much to the point when it said, "John Brown may be a lunatic but if so, then one-fourth of the people of Massachusetts are madmen."

The *Post* certainly did not intend to shift the question from one concerning Brown's personal sanity to one concerning the mass delusions of the abolitionists. A historian may, however, regard the latter as a legitimate topic of inquiry. But if he should do so, he must recognize at once the further fact that the Spartacus delusion — if delusion it was — was not confined to the abolitionists. The Southerners, too, shared this concept, in the sense that they were ever fearful of slave insurrections and were immensely relieved to learn that the slaves had not flocked to Brown's support. Clearly they had felt no assurance that this would be the outcome.

This is no place for me to go into either the extent or the realism of Southern fears of slave insurrection. The only point to make here is that John Brown, believing in the potentiality of a slave insurrection, only believed what both abolitionist and slaveholders believed. But Brown needed to know the specifics of that potentiality as others did not. He needed to know how strong it was, how it could be cultivated, how it could be triggered. The lives of himself and his men depended upon knowing. Yet there is no evidence that he ever even asked the questions. He merely said, "When I strike, the bees will swarm." But Negroes are not bees, and when figures of speech are used in argumentation, they are usually a substitute for realistic thinking.

Brown may have been right, at a certain level and in a certain sense, in believing that the Negroes might revolt. But he was completely wrong in the literal-minded way in which he held the idea, and this indiscriminate notion about Negro reactions probably led him to what was really his supreme folly. He supposed that the Negroes of Jefferson County would instantly spring to the support of an insurrection of which they had not been notified — that they would, of their own volition, join a desperate coup to which they had not even been invited. Brown evidently thought of Negroes, as so many other people have done, as abstractions, and not as men and women.

It was not as if he had not been warned: his English soldier of fortune, Hugh Forbes, told him that even slaves ripe for revolt would not come in on an enterprise like this. "No preparatory notice having been given to the slaves," he said, "the invitation to rise might, unless they were already in a state of agitation, meet with no response, or a feeble one." But Brown brushed this aside: he was sure of a response, and calculated that on the first night of the revolt, between two hundred and five hundred slaves would rally to him at the first news of his raid. Again later, when John E. Cook was keeping his lonely and secret vigil for more than a year as Brown's advance agent at Harpers Ferry, and even after Brown had moved to the farm in Maryland, Cook pleaded to be allowed to give the slaves at least some inkling of what was afoot. But Brown sternly rejected this idea. Thus, when the "Negro insurrection" began, the Negroes were as unprepared for it, as disconcerted, and as mystified as anyone else.

Brown, in his grandiose way, boasted of having studied the slave insurrections of history — of Spartacus, of Toussaint. But one wonders what those two, or even Denmark Vesley, would have had to say about John Brown's mode of conducting an insurrection. Abraham Lincoln, with his usual talent for accuracy of statement, later said, "It was not a slave insurrection. It was an attempt by white men to get up a revolt among slaves, in which the slaves refused to participate." But in a way Lincoln understated the case. The slaves were never asked to participate. Brown's remarkable technique for securing their participation was to send out a detail in the middle of the night, kidnap them, thrust a pike into their hands, and inform them that they were soldiers in the army of emancipation. He then expected them to place their necks in a noose without asking for further particulars.

Yet he was so supremely confident of their massive support that all the strange errors of October 16 and 17 sprang from that delusion. This was why he marched without rations; it was why thirteen of his twenty-one followers carried commissions as officers in their knapsacks, though none of his five Negro followers was included in this number — thirteen officers would hardly suffice to command the Negro troops who would swarm like bees to his headquarters; it was why he wanted the weapons at Harpers Ferry although he already had several times as many weapons as were needed for the men at the Maryland farm. Finally it was why he sat down at Harpers Ferry and waited while his adversaries closed the trap on him. He was still waiting for the word to spread and for the Negroes to come trooping in.

John Brown wanted to be a leader for the Negroes of America. He dwelled upon this idea almost to the exclusion of all others. Ultimately he died with singular bravery to vindicate his role. Yet he never thought to ask the Negroes if they would accept him as a leader, and if so, what kind of policy they wanted him to pursue. Of course he could not ask them all, but he never even asked Frederick Douglass or the gathering of Negroes at Chatham. He knew what he wanted them to do and did not really care what they themselves wanted to do. John Brown occupies and deserves a heroic place in the gallery of historic leaders of American Negroes. Yet, like many other prominent and less heroic figures in that gallery, he was a self-appointed savior, who was not chosen by the Negroes, who had no Negro following of any magnitude, and whose policies in the name of the Negro were not necessarily the policies of the Negroes themselves.

Douglass and John Brown

Philip Foner

On October 17, 1859, Douglass lectured in the National Hall at Philadelphia on "Self-Made Men." A capacity audience listened to his recital of men who had risen to fame "from the depths of poverty" as a result of "patient, enduring, honest, unremitting work, into which the whole heart is put. . . ." One of them was Benjamin Banneker, a Negro slave born in Maryland, who became a learned mathematician, an outstanding surveyor, who assisted in the laying out of the city of Washington, "and compelled honorable recognition from some of the most distinguished scholars and statesmen of that early day of the Republic." Douglass quoted Jefferson's letter to Banneker of August 30, 1790, in which the author of the Declaration of Independence praised the Negro's almanac, describing it as "a document to which your whole colour had a right for their justification against the doubts which have been entertained of them."

"This was the impression," Douglass declared, "made by an intelligent Negro upon the father of American Democracy, in the earlier and better years of the Republic. I wish that it were possible to make a similar impression upon the children of the American Democracy of this generation. Jefferson was not ashamed to call the black man his brother and to address him as a gentleman."[1]

At that very moment, a man who not only regarded the Negro slave as his brother but was willing to sacrifice his life for his brother's freedom, was attempting to capture the federal arsenal at Harpers Ferry. The raid was part of a more ambitious plan conceived by John Brown whose ultimate aim was the emancipation of the slaves throughout the South.

Douglass' relations with John Brown, it will be recalled, began more than ten years before the raid on Harpers Ferry. It was at Brown's home in Springfield that Douglass first learned of the former's plan to aid the slaves, a project which embraced the setting up of an armed force which would function in the very heart of the South. At that time Brown pointed to a large map of the United States. These Allegheny mountains stretching from the borders of New York State into the South, he told Douglass, afforded an excellent "pathway for a grand stampede from the

Slave States, a grand exodus into the Free States, and, through the latter, into Canada." The mountains were full of hiding places and once the slaves were brought there and scattered among the glens, deep ravines, and rocks, it would be difficult to find them and even more difficult to overpower them if they were found. "I know these mountains well," said Brown, "and could take a body of men into them and keep them there in spite of all the efforts of Virginia to dislodge me, and drive me out. I would take at first about twenty-five picked men and begin on a small scale, supply them arms and ammunition, post them in squads of fives on a line of twenty-five miles, these squads to busy themselves for a time in gathering recruits from the surrounding farms, seeking and selecting the most restless and daring." Once he had gathered a force of a hundred hardy men and drilled them properly, they would run off slaves in large numbers, keeping the braver ones in the mountains, and sending the others north by the underground railroad. Gradually the operations would be enlarged to cover the entire South, and in due course the movement would seriously weaken slavery in two ways — first, by destroying "the money value of slave property," by making it insecure, and second, by keeping alive anti-slavery agitation and thereby compelling the adoption of measures to abolish the evil altogether.

From eight o'clock in the evening until three in the morning, Douglass and Brown discussed this plan. Douglass pointed to serious flaws in the project. Once the plan went into operation, the slaveowners would sell their slaves further South or would use bloodhounds and armed forces to track down and overpower Brown and his band. Again, it would be almost impossible to keep the group in the mountains provided with supplies. Brown brushed aside these objections. If the slaves were removed to the lower South he would follow them; even to drive them out of one county would be a victory. Regardless of difficulties he would persevere in his attempt, for some startling event was necessary to prevent the agitation over the slavery question from dying out. If he should die in the effort he would be giving his life for the cause closest to his heart.[2]

Despite his original skepticism, Douglass came to think favorably of Brown's plan. The more he examined the project, the more convinced he became that it might contribute to undermining slavery, for "men do not like to buy runaway horses, nor to invest their money in a species of property likely to take legs and walk off with itself."[3] At the very least, the plan would reawaken the slumbering conscience of the nation. His sympathy for Brown's project grew as his confidence in the efficacy of moral suasion waned.

Douglass and Brown discussed the project many times after their first meeting in 1847. On several occasions Brown stopped at Douglass' home in Rochester,[4] and spent the night outlining the project for a chain of hide-outs in the Maryland and Virginia mountains from which men could go down to the plantations and encourage the slaves to escape. What Brown did not tell his friend, however, was that in the meantime in Kansas he had added a significant detail to his original plan. He now believed that it would be possible, given a few sound men, to establish a base in the mountains, to which slaves and free Negroes would come, and where, after beating off all attacking forces, whether state or federal, a free state would be set up.

On February 1, 1858, Brown arrived at Douglass' home. He would not stay long, he assured his host, and insisted upon paying for his accommodations. He remained several weeks, spending most of the time in his own room writing to numerous friends for financial assistance for his venture, the nature of which he did not reveal. At other times Brown would talk at length of his plan for mountain strongholds, even explaining them to Douglass' children and illustrating "each detail with a set of blocks."[5] Before he left Rochester he had secured a recruit in the person of Shields Green, a runaway slave who was staying at Douglass' home. Brown had also drawn up a constitution for his projected free state. Consisting of a preamble and forty-eight articles, the document provided a framework of government, under a military commander-in-chief, which was to go into operation after his forces had gained power.

Brown and Douglass were to meet again in Philadelphia on March 5, 1858, but the latter had to postpone the meeting. Writing from Syracuse on February 27, 1858, Douglass expressed the hope that Brown "would find work enough in and about New York" until his arrival. On March 11, Brown and his son John, Jr., conferred with Douglass, Garnet, and William Still, the latter a leading agent in the Underground Railroad. His funds exhausted, Brown appealed to them for men and money. He did not, however, divulge the wide reach of his new plans. Nor did Brown add to Douglass' knowledge of the project when he and his son spent the night at the Negro leader's home early in April.[6] All Douglass knew was that Brown was still proceeding with his original plan of setting up hide-outs in the mountains.

In April, 1858, Brown wrote to Douglass: "I expect to need all the help I can get by the first of May."[7] As this letter indicates, Brown had intended to strike in 1858 instead of 1859. The year's delay was made necessary by the treachery of Hugh Forbes, an Englishman who had fought with Garibaldi and had joined Brown after they had met in Kansas. Forbes had agreed to drill Brown's men and to recruit army officers. But Forbes was primarily interested in the project in order to line his own pocket. After getting as much money as he could from Brown, he began to mulct his leader's friends. When that source of income dried up, he threatened to expose the conspiracy if further funds were not forthcoming.

Douglass had reluctantly assisted Forbes in November, 1857, with "a little money" and with letters of introduction to friends.[8] But he had reacted unfavorably to the adventurer, was unimpressed by his tale of family woes, and so was not surprised when he learned that Forbes was threatening to disclose Brown's plans. He relayed this information to Brown. At the same time a committee of Brown's backers, Samuel Gridley Howe, Gerrit Smith, Theodore Parker, George L. Stearns, and Thomas Wentworth Higginson, met in secret at the Revere House in Boston and counseled Brown to postpone his operations and leave for Kansas. Assured that he would receive additional funds in the spring, Brown eventually traveled to Kansas.[9]

Douglass met Brown soon after his return from the Kansas region. En route to Peterboro during the second week of April, 1859, Brown stopped off for a few hours in Rochester. Horace McGuire, one of the employees in Douglass' printing office, recalled that "a tall, white man, with shaggy whiskers, rather unkempt, a keen piercing eye, and a restlessness of manner" called at the shop "several months prior to October 16, 1859," and asked for Douglass. The visitor gave the appearance of one whose "interview was by appointment." When Douglass returned, "the greeting between the white man and the former slave was very cordial." The two men "talked freely."[10]

In the early summer of 1859, Brown fixed upon Harpers Ferry as the base of his operations in Virginia and rented a farm about five miles from there to collect his arms and his band of followers. By mid-summer he had recruited a little army of twenty-one men, including several Negroes, and was almost ready to strike. In August, Brown decided to reveal the full details of his plan to Douglass in the hope of enlisting him as a member of the company preparing to attack Harpers Ferry. Douglass received a letter from Brown asking him to be present at Chambersburg, Pennsylvania, and to bring Shields Green along. The meeting took place on the night of August 20, in a stone quarry near Chambersburg. Brown, his lieutenant Kagi, Douglass and Green were present. It was in the old quarry that Douglass for the first time learned of Brown's plan to seize Harpers Ferry, capture the leading citizens and hold them as hostages while his band rounded up the slaves in the surrounding areas.[11] Brown was dismayed by the emphatic disapproval registered in Douglass' reaction to this plan. Douglass assured Brown that he was still prepared to join with him in carrying out the original plan of running slaves through the Alleghenies, but the raid on Harpers Ferry was an attack on the national government and was doomed to failure. But no amount of argument could dissuade Brown. The seizure would dramatize the evils of slavery, he argued, capture the attention of the nation and arouse the people to action.[12]

Brown's eloquence and his burning enthusiasm for the cause moved Douglass tremendously, but he remained adamant to all entreaties to participate in the enterprise. As he was preparing to leave, Brown made a final appeal: "Come with me, Douglass! I will defend you with my life, I want you for a special purpose. When I strike, the bees will begin to swarm and I shall want you to help me hive them." Douglass shook his head sadly, and turning to Shields Green he asked him if he had made up his mind. The former slave indicated his decisions with the now famous reply that he would go with the "old man."[13]

Brown did not give up hope of recruiting Douglass. With sufficient pressure, he was convinced, the latter would reconsider his decision. A few weeks later, Douglass received a letter signed by a number of Negro men inviting him to represent them at a convention to be held "right away" in Chambersburg. The signers pledged themselves to see that his family would be "well provided" during his absence "or until your safe return to them." They also offered to "make you a remittance." Douglass suspected that Kagi had instigated the letter, but not without Brown's approval.[14] The appeal went unanswered.

The Chambersburg meeting between Douglass and Brown marked the last time these good friends were to see one another. On the night of October 16, Brown gave the order to march on Harpers Ferry. When the morning dawned, Brown and his men were in possession of the United States armory and the bridges leading to the Ferry. A few slaves had been persuaded to join them. The following night a company of United States marines, under the command of Colonel Robert E. Lee, arrived; at dawn the building was taken by assault. Brown fought with amazing coolness and courage, but was finally overpowered. Amid popular excitement, he was tried for treason and found guilty. On December 2, 1859, Brown was hanged at Charlestown.

Douglass received the startling news of Brown's capture while lecturing in the National Hall at Philadelphia. He was informed that letters had been found in Brown's possession implicating him, among others, of knowledge of the plot.[15] He knew at once that with the mounting hysteria his life was in extreme danger. At the advice of his friends he left Philadelphia and hastened to New York City, pausing at Hoboken to wire to B. F. Blackball, telegraph operator in Rochester: "Tell Lewis to secure all the important papers in my high desk."[16] Later Douglass learned how fortunate he had been in following the advice of friends in Philadelphia. John W. Hurn, a telegraph operator, and an admirer of Douglass, suppressed for three hours the delivery of a message to the sheriff of Philadelphia ordering him to arrest Frederick Douglass.[17]

Douglass' alarm increased as he read the New York papers. The *New York Herald* headlined a report of Brown's alleged confession to Governor Wise of Virginia: *"Gerrit Smith, Joshua Giddings, Fred Douglass and Other Abolitionists and Republicans Implicated."* "Enough it seems has been ascertained to justify a requisition from Governor Wise of Virginia, upon Governor Morgan, of New York, for the delivery over to the hands of justice of Gerrit Smith and Fred Douglass, as parties implicated in the crime of murder and as accessories before the fact." From Richmond came an announcement that one hundred Southerners were offering rewards for the heads of "Traitors" among whom Douglass' name was prominently featured.

On his arrival in Rochester, several friends warned Douglass that the New York Governor would probably surrender him to the Virginia authorities upon request. As most citizens of Rochester would resist the attempt to return Douglass to the South and bloodshed and rioting would follow, he was advised both for his own safety and for the peace of the community, to cross over the border to Canada.[18] Aware that President Buchanan would employ the full power of the federal government to achieve his arrest, Douglass took the advice of his friends and fled to Canada.

Douglass barely evaded his pursuers. He had already been charged in Virginia with "murder, robbery and inciting to servile insurrection in the State of Virginia." Moreover, Governor Wise had asked President Buchanan and the Post-Master General of the United States to grant two agents from Virginia authority to serve as detectives for the post-office department for the purpose of delivering Douglass to the Virginia courts.[19] On October 25, 1859, the Rochester *Union and Advertiser* reported:

It is understood that United States Attorney Ould of Washington, and other federal officers, were here yesterday. It is supposed they came hither for the purpose of arresting Frederick Douglass for his alleged participation in the organized scheme against the slaveholding states, of which the Harper's Ferry insurrection was one of the appointed results.[20]

Had Douglass been arrested by federal authorities at that time the chances are that in the prevailing tense atmosphere he would have followed Brown to the gallows. Despite its facetious tone, the *New York Herald* knew whereof it spoke when it commented: "The black Douglass having some experience in his early life of the pleasures of Southern society had no desire to trust himself again even on the borders of the Potomac."[21] No evidence would have been required to sentence a Negro Abolitionist to death in Virginia during the weeks following the attack on Harpers Ferry.

Douglass has been severely criticized for his refusal to join Brown's expedition and for having fled to Canada after the raid.[22] John E. Cook, one of the men captured with Brown, even blamed Douglass for the failure of the expedition, charging that the latter had been assigned to bring a large body of men to reinforce Brown. In a letter to the editor of the Rochester *Democrat* from Canada on October 31, Douglass denied the charge. It was a brilliant document, opening with the caustic observation that Cook was "now in the hands of the thing calling itself the Government of Virginia, but which in fact is but an organized conspiracy by one party of the people against the other." Douglass admitted that "tried by the Harpers Ferry insurrection test," he was "deficient in courage," but denied that he had ever at any time encouraged the taking of Harpers Ferry or promised to join the expedition. This denial was motivated more by "a respectful consideration of the opinion of the slave's friends, than from my fear of being made an accomplice in the general *conspiracy* against Slavery." He was willing to support any movement against slavery, when there was "a reasonable hope of success," and he believed that any effort to overthrow the system of human bondage was basically moral. He had not joined Brown because he did not believe that this was the way in which he could best work for the abolition of slavery. "The tools to those who can use them," was the way Douglass put it. No shame could be attached to him, he added, for keeping out of the way of the United States marshals. Would a government that recognized the validity of the Dred Scott decisions be likely "to have any very charitable feelings" toward a Negro Abolitionist?[23] The question answered itself.

There is not the slightest evidence that Douglass at any time indicated his intention of joining Brown's expedition. The very fact that he had made plans to leave for Europe in November, 1859, long before the attack on Harpers Ferry, is proof that he had made no commitments to Brown and his band.[24]

Douglass felt justified at his decision not to join Brown's company. The venture, as he had told Brown, was doomed to fail, and he believed that there was more work for him to do than to end his life at this stage of his career on the gallows in Virginia. "It is gallant to go forth singlehanded," he later observed, "but is it wise?"[25]

All this did not mean that Douglass failed to grasp the significance of John Brown's raid. Two weeks after Harpers Ferry, Douglass wrote an editorial on John Brown which cut through the hysterical outpourings of the press and predicted the course the nation would soon follow:

> Posterity will owe everlasting thanks to John Brown for lifting up once more to the gaze of a nation grown fat and flabby on the garbage of lust and oppression, a true standard of heroic philanthropy, and each coming generation will pay its installment of the debt. . . .
>
> He has attacked slavery with the weapons precisely adapted to bring it to the death. Moral considerations have long since been exhausted upon slaveholders. It is in vain to reason with them. . . . Slavery is a system of brute force. It shields itself behind *might*, rather than right. It must be met with its own weapons. Capt. Brown has initiated a new mode of carrying on the crusade of freedom, and his blow has sent dread and terror throughout the entire ranks of the piratical army of slavery. His daring deeds may cost him his life, but priceless as is the value of that life, the blow he has struck, will, in the end, prove to be worth its mighty cost. Like Samson, he has laid his hands upon the pillars of this great national temple of cruelty and blood, and when he falls, that temple will speedily crumble to its final doom, burying its denizens in its ruins.[26]

On November 12, 1859, Douglass, in line with previously laid plans, sailed from Quebec for Liverpool. In his farewell note to his "Readers and Friends" in America, he cautioned them against losing heart because, owing to the frenzy aroused by Brown's raid, slavery seemed "to have gained an advantage" for the moment, and created "a more active resistance to the cause of freedom and its advocates." But this, he assured them, was only "transient." The "moment of passion and revenge" would pass away, and "reason and righteousness" would grow stronger. "Men will soon begin to look away from the plot to the purpose — from the effect to the cause." Then would come the reaction, "and the names now covered with execration will be mentioned with honor, or, as noble martyrs to a righteous cause. . . . The benumbed conscience of the nation will be revived and become susceptible of right impressions." The ultimate victory had been made more certain than ever by the "battle of Harpers Ferry."[27]

On his return to Rochester in May, 1860, Douglass found that sentiment around John Brown and those associated with him had changed. In December, 1859, a Senate Committee, headed by James M. Mason of Virginia, had been appointed to investigate the attack on Harpers Ferry. On June 14, 1860, the committee submitted an innocuous report which stated that while Brown had planned "to commence a servile insurrection" which he hoped to extend "throughout the entire

South," he did not appear to have intrusted even his immediate followers with his plans. After much consideration, the committee announced that it was "not prepared to suggest any legislation."[28]

In a letter to a group of Abolitionists assembling at North Elba, in the Adirondacks, on July 4, 1860, to do honor to the memory of John Brown, Douglass wrote:

To have been acquainted with John Brown, shared his counsels, enjoyed his confidence, and sympathized with the great objects of his life and death, I esteem as among the highest privileges of my life. We do but honor to ourselves in doing honor to him, for it implies the possession of qualities akin to his.[29]

Notes

[1] Douglass delivered the lecture, "Self-Made Men," many times after 1859. The text quoted here is from a copy of the speech in the Rochester Public Library.

[2] *John Brown — An Address by Frederick Douglass at the Fourteenth Anniversary of Storer College, Harper's Ferry, West Virginia,* May 30, 1881; *Life and Times of Frederick Douglass,* pp. 339–41.
There is no discussion of Brown's relations with Douglass in the recent study by James C. Malin, *John Brown and the Legend of Fifty-Six,* published by the American Philosophical Society. In a letter to the writer, Feb. 6, 1947, Professor Malin writes: "You ask about Frederick Douglass. I did not find anything that struck me as particularly important which relates him to my field of investigation."

[3] *Life and Times of Frederick Douglass,* p. 341.

[4] On Nov. 15, 1856, Elizabeth Cady Stanton wrote that in December she expected to see Brown at Rochester where he would be "on a visit to Frederick Douglass." (T. Stanton and H. S. Blatch, *Elizabeth Cady Stanton,* New York, 1901, vol. II, p. 69.)

[5] J. M. Parker, "Reminiscences of Frederick Douglass," *Outlook,* vol. LI, Apr. 6, 1895, p. 553; F. B. Sanborn, *The Life and Letters of John Brown,* Boston, 1885, p. 434. Brown probably stayed a little more than two weeks at Douglass' home. There are, however, conflicting reports on this question. Richard J. Hinton says he was at Douglass' home "for three weeks," and Douglass says he "remained for about a month." (Richard J. Hinton, *John Brown and His Men,* New York, 1899, p. 165; *Life and Times of Frederick Douglass,* p. 385.)

[6] Douglass to John Brown, Feb. 27, 1858, Sanborn, *op. cit.,* pp. 443, 451–52.

[7] John Brown's diary, Apr. 14, 1858, Ralph Volney Harlow, *Gerrit Smith,* New York, 1939, p. 339.

[8] *New York Herald,* Oct. 27, 1859; Anonymous, "John Brown and His Friends," *Atlantic Monthly,* vol. XXX, July, 1872, pp. 50–61; *Life and Times of Frederick Douglass,* p. 387.

[9] Franklin B. Sanborn, *Recollections of Seventy Years,* Boston, 1909, p. 138; *Atlantic Monthly,* vol. XXX, July, 1872, pp. 55 *ff.* Douglass' daughter wrote to her father on Feb. 2, 1859, concerning Brown's exploits in running off slaves from Missouri: "Old Brown will have to keep out of sight for a little while. The Governor of Missouri has a reward of $3,000 for his capture." (Douglass *Mss.,* Frederick Douglass Memorial Home, Anacostia, D.C.)

[10] Horace McGuire, "Two Episodes of Anti-Slavery Days," *Publications of the Rochester Historical Society,* Rochester, N.Y., vol. IV, 1925, pp. 219–20.

[11] On Aug. 9, 1867, Douglass wrote to Gerrit Smith: "I wish to say distinctly that John Brown never declared nor intimated to me that he was about to embark in a grand or unqualified insurrection; that the only insurrection he proposed was the escaping of slaves and

their standing for their lives against any who should pursue them. For years before, Captain Brown's long entertained plan was to go to the mountains in the Slave States and invite the Slaves to flee there. . . . Three or four weeks previous to his invasion of Harper's Ferry Captain Brown requested me to have an interview with him at Chambersburg, Pa. I did it and in this interview he had determined upon that invasion instead of carrying out his old plan of going into the mountains. . . . I do not suppose that any of his friends at the North knew of it." (Frederick Douglass *Mss.*, Frederick Douglass Memorial Home, Anacostia, D.C.) The last sentence would seem to indicate that Douglass was the first person outside of his band to whom Brown told his plan for attacking Harper's Ferry.

[12] Sanborn, *Life and Letters of John Brown,* pp. 536–38; *Life and Times of Frederick Douglass,* p. 387. Douglass brought with him a letter to Brown containing twenty-five dollars from Mrs. J. N. Gloucester, a prosperous Negro woman in Brooklyn. (Sanborn, *Life and Letters of John Brown,* p. 538.)

[13] *Life and Times of Frederick Douglass,* p. 390. Douglass' meeting with Brown lasted for three days. (Douglass to F. B. Sanborn, Apr. 15, 1885, Sanborn, *Life and Letters of John Brown,* p. 538.)

[14] Sanborn, *Life and Letters of John Brown,* p. 541 *n.* A copy of the letter to Douglass was found among the papers of John Brown captured at the farm Brown had rented early in the summer.

[15] Sanborn, *Recollections of Seventy Years,* p. 153. Only a brief, unimportant letter from Brown to Douglass was found by Brown's captors. No other material involving Douglass was discovered among his papers at the farm.

[16] Amy Hamner-Croughton, "Anti-Slavery Days in Rochester," *Publications of the Rochester Historical Society,* Rochester, N.Y., vol. XV, 1936, p. 143. Letters from Brown and a copy of the "Provisional Constitution" Brown had drawn up while at Douglass' home were in the desk. After the message was received they were removed.

[17] Washington *Evening Star,* Feb. 21, 1895.

[18] *New York Herald,* Oct. 20, 1859; *Liberator,* Dec. 23, 1859; Hamner-Croughton, *op. cit.,* p. 144.

[19] *Life and Times of Frederick Douglass,* p. 379; *New York Herald,* Oct. 22, 1859.

[20] See also Rochester *Democrat,* Oct. 26, 1859, and Rochester *Union,* Oct. 25, 1859, reprinted in *New York Herald,* Oct. 28, 1859.

[21] *New York Herald,* Nov. 4, 1859.

[22] As late as 1919 several of the surviving members of Brown's family, Henry Thompson, Salmon Brown, Annie Brown Adams, and Sarah Brown, told Oswald Garrison Villard that they had always believed that Douglass had failed "to live up to his obligations." (Oswald Garrison Villard, *John Brown,* New York, 1943, pp. 323, 627.)

[23] Douglass to Rochester *Democrat,* reprinted in *New York Herald,* Nov. 4, 1859.

[24] ". . . It is only truth to state," Douglass wrote in the Nov., 1859, issue of his monthly, "that for more than a year past I have been making arrangements not to go to Harper's Ferry, but to England."

[25] Douglass to John C. Underwood, Nov. 14, 1866, John C. Underwood Collection, Library of Congress, Manuscript Division. Douglass to Elizabeth Keckly, Oct. 29, 1867, Elizabeth Keckley, *"Behind the Scenes or Thirty Years a Slave and Four Years in the White House,"* New York, 1886, p. 319.

[26] *Douglass' Monthly,* Nov., 1859.

[27] *Douglass' Monthly,* Dec., 1859.

[28] Henry Wilson, *History of the Rise and Fall of the Slave Power in America,* vol. II, p. 606.

[29] Douglass to James Redpath, June 29, 1860, *Liberator,* July 27, 1860.

Suggestions for Further Reading

Benjamin Quarles's recent study *Black Abolitionists* (New York: Oxford University Press, 1969) is an indispensable starting point for further reading. General studies of abolitionism with data on blacks are Louis Filler, *The Crusade against Slavery* (New York: Harper & Row, 1960); Dwight Dumond, *Antislavery: The Crusade for Freedom in America* (Ann Arbor: University of Michigan Press, 1961); and Martin Duberman (ed.), *The Antislavery Vanguard* (Princeton: Princeton University Press, 1965). Leon Litwack's *North of Slavery: The Negro in the Free States, 1790–1860* (Chicago: University of Chicago Press, 1961) and Howard Bell's *A Survey of the Negro Convention Movement, 1830–1861* (New York: Arno, 1970) are also relevant.

Frederick Douglass, the leading black figure in nineteenth-century America, can be studied in Benjamin Quarles, *Frederick Douglass* (Washington, D.C.: Associated Publishers, 1948); Philip Foner (ed.), *The Life and Writings of Frederick Douglass,* 4 vols. (New York: International Publishers, 1950–1955); and *The Life and Times of Frederick Douglass* (Boston: De Wolfe, Fiske, and Company, rev. ed., 1892), an autobiography.

Larry Gara's *The Liberty Line: The Legend of the Underground Railroad* (Lexington: University of Kentucky Press, 1961) and Wilbur Siebert's *The Underground Railroad from Slavery to Freedom* (New York: Macmillan, 1898) are contrasting studies of that institution. William Still's *The Underground Railroad* (Philadelphia: Porter & Coates, 1872; Chicago: Johnson Publishing Company, 1970), a compilation of documents and events by a participant, is still valuable.

Studies of other important figures include Earl Conrad, *Harriet Tubman* (Washington, D.C.: Associated Publishers, 1943); Arthur H. Fauset, *Sojourner Truth: God's Faithful Pilgrim* (Chapel Hill: University of North Carolina Press, 1938); and Herbert Aptheker, *One Continual Cry* (New York: Humanities Press, 1965), a study of David Walker which includes a copy of his famous *Appeal.* The interested student should also consult Dorothy Porter, "David M. Ruggles: An Apostle for Human Rights," *Journal of Negro History,* XXVIII (January 1943).

A Wadsworth Series:
Explorations in the Black Experience

General Editors

John H. Bracey, Jr.
Northern Illinois University

August Meier
Kent State University

Elliott Rudwick
Kent State University

Robert C. Weaver, "The Villain—Racial Covenants"; Robert C Weaver, "The Role of the Federal Government"; Herman H Long and Charles S. Johnson, "The Role of Real Estate Organizations"; Loren Miller, "Supreme Court Covenant Decision—An Analysis"; Herbert Hill, "Demographic Change and Racial Ghettos: The Crisis of American Cities"; Roy Reed, "Resegregation: A Problem in the Urban South"

4   The Process of Ghettoization: Internal Pressures

Arnold Rose and Caroline Rose, "The Significance of Group Identification"; W. E. B. Du Bois, "The Social Evolution of the Black South"; Allan H. Spear, "The Institutional Ghetto"; Chicago Commission on Race Relations, "The Matrix of the Black Community"; E. Franklin Frazier, "The Negro's Vested Interest in Segregation"; George A. Nesbitt, "Break Up the Black Ghetto?"; Lewis G. Watts, Howard E. Freeman, Helen M. Hughes, Robert Morris, and Thomas F. Pettigrew, "Social Attractions of the Ghetto"

5   Future Prospects

Karl E. Taeuber and Alma F. Taeuber, "Is the Negro an Immigrant Group?"; H. Paul Friesema, "Black Control of Central Cities: The Hollow Prize"

Suggestions for Further Reading

Black Matriarchy: Myth or Reality?

Introduction

1   The Frazier Thesis

E. Franklin Frazier, "The Negro Family in America"; E. Franklin Frazier, "The Matriarchate"

2   The Question of African Survivals

Melville J. Herskovits, "On West African Influences"

3   The Frazier Thesis Applied

Charles S. Johnson, "The Family in the Plantation South"; Lee Rainwater, "Crucible of Identity: The Negro Lower-Class Family"; Elliot Liebow, "Fathers without Children"

4   The Moynihan Report

Daniel P. Moynihan, "The Negro Family: The Case for National Action"; Hylan Lewis and Elizabeth Herzog, "The Family: Resources for Change"

5   New Approaches

Herbert H. Hyman and John Shelton Reed, " 'Black Matriarchy' Reconsidered: Evidence from Secondary Analysis of Sample Surveys"; Virginia Heyer Young, "Family and Childhood in a Southern Negro Community"

Suggestions for Further Reading

Black Workers and Organized Labor

Introduction

Sidney H. Kessler, "The Organization of Negroes in the Knights of Labor"; Bernard Mandel, "Samuel Gompers and the Negro Workers, 1886–1914"; Paul B. Worthman, "Black Workers and Labor Unions in Birmingham, Alabama, 1897–1904"; William M. Tuttle, Jr., "Labor Conflict and Racial Violence: The Black Worker in Chicago, 1894–1919"; Sterling D. Spero and Abram L. Harris, "The Negro Longshoreman, 1870–1930"; Sterling D. Spero and Abram L. Harris, "The Negro and the IWW"; Brailsford R. Brazeal, "The Brotherhood of Sleeping Car Porters"; Horace R. Cayton and George S. Mitchell, "Blacks and Organized Labor in the Iron and Steel Industry, 1880–1939"; Herbert R. Northrup, "Blacks in the United Automobile Workers Union"; Sumner M. Rosen, "The CIO Era, 1935–1955"; William Kornhauser, "The Negro Union Official: A Study of Sponsorship and Control"; Ray Marshall, "The Negro and the AFL-CIO"

Suggestions for Further Reading

The Black Sociologists: The First Half Century

Introduction

1 Early Pioneers

W. E. B. Du Bois, "The Study of the Negro Problems"; W. E. B. Du Bois, "The Organized Life of Negroes"; George E. Haynes, "Conditions among Negroes in the Cities"

2 In the Robert E. Park Tradition

Charles S. Johnson, "Black Housing in Chicago"; E. Franklin Frazier, "The Pathology of Race Prejudice"; E. Franklin Frazier, "La Bourgeoisie Noire"; Charles S. Johnson, "The Plantation during the Depression"; Bertram W. Doyle, "The Etiquette of Race Relations—Past, Present, and Future"; E. Franklin Frazier, "The Black Matriarchate"; Charles S. Johnson, "Patterns of Negro Segregation"; E. Franklin Frazier, "The New Negro Middle Class"

3 Black Metropolis: Sociological Masterpiece

St. Clair Drake and Horace Cayton, "The Measure of the Man"

Conflict and Competition: Studies in the Recent Black Protest Movement

Introduction

1 Nonviolent Direct Action

Joseph S. Himes, "The Functions of Racial Conflict"; August Meier, "Negro Protest Movements and Organizations"; Lewis M. Killian and Charles U. Smith, "Negro Protest Leaders in a Southern Community"; Ralph H. Hines and James E. Pierce, "Negro Leadership after the Social Crisis: An Analysis of Leadership Changes in Montgomery, Alabama"; Jack L. Walker, "The Functions of Disunity: Negro Leadership in a Southern City"; Gerald A. McWorter and Robert L. Crain, "Subcommunity Gladiatorial Competition: Civil Rights Leadership as a Competitive Process"; August Meier, "On the Role of Martin Luther King"

2 By Any Means Necessary

Inge Powell Bell, "Status Discrepancy and the Radical Rejection of Nonviolence"; Donald von Eschen, Jerome Kirk, and Maurice Pinard, "The Disintegration of the Negro Non-Violent Movement"; Allen J. Matusow, "From Civil Rights to Black Power: The Case of SNCC, 1960–1966"; Joel D. Aberbach and Jack L. Walker, "The Meanings of Black Power: A Comparison of White and Black Interpretations of a Political Slogan"; David O. Sears and T. M. Tomlinson, "Riot Ideology in Los Angeles: A Study of Negro Attitudes"; Robert Blauner, "Internal Colonialism and Ghetto Revolt"; Charles V. Hamilton, "Conflict, Race, and System-Transformation in the United States"

Suggestions for Further Reading